201 Ways to Enjoy Your Dog

201 Ways to Enjoy Your Dog

A Complete Guide to Organized U.S. and Canadian Activities for Dog Lovers

by
Ellie Milon

201 Ways to Enjoy Your Dog

Copyright © 1990 by Ellie Milon

Library of Congress Cataloging-in-Publication Data

Milon, Ellie.
   201 ways to enjoy your dog: a complete guide to organized U.S. and Canadian activities for dog lovers.
      p.   cm.
   ISBN 0-931866-33-2
      1. Dog sports—United States. 2. Dog sports—Canada. I. Title. II. Title: Two hundred one ways to enjoy your dog. III. Title: Two hundred and one ways to enjoy your dog.
   SF424.M55   1990
   636.7'0097—dc20   89-18403
                                                                        CIP

Printed in the United States of America.

Illustrations: Nan Kilgore Little
Cover: Joan Harris
Design and layout: Joan Harris
Typography: Peggy Mathiesen

Disclaimer: Addresses of organizations, rules and regulations and other information listed in this book are subject to change without notice. Check with the appropriate registries and organizations for current information. The publisher and author do not assume responsibility for changes made after publication of this work.

TO LACEY
Who Showed Us The Way

Photo by Gulie Krook

September's Lovely in Lace
April 23, 1973–January 6, 1985

CONTENTS

FOREWORD

Growing up with dogs in the 40's and 50's was a wonderful adventure. Dogs were an integral part of family life, not because of the ribbons they brought home from dog shows, but because they were useful. They knew how to coexist with people and other animals because they were exposed to the interaction of everyday life. They were multipurpose animals that led busy schedules. I spent my childhood with the old Sportsman's line of German Shorthaired Pointers. My father used them for hunting and field trials; my mother used them for protection; and my sister and I used them for everything! They delivered messages to neighborhood friends in the summer and accompanied us to steep snow-packed hills in the winter where they patiently pulled our sleds to the top, then ran beside us as we raced back down to the bottom. They slept on our beds at night and reacted with love and devotion to our daily needs, licking teary faces, walking us to school, fetching lost gloves (ours and others!), and sticking to us like glue when the "baby-sitters" arrived.

When you bought a purebred dog in those days, you expected him to be able to fulfill the duties that his breed advertised. Guard dogs were expectedly sharp; hunting dogs were birdy, lean and hard; hounds were fit and able to chase down or scent their prey; sled dogs were bought and used for winter work or sport; and, companion dogs had temperaments you could count on.

As we entered the 60's and 70's, prosperity came to America and with it the general idea that if a little bit was good, a lot must be better. Americans seemed to want changes in the extreme: music changed drastically, as did dance. Many people suddenly found themselves with both extra time and money on their hands and recreational and sporting events prospered.

Purebred dogs changed too. Unfortunately, many of the changes were not in the best interests of either dog or man. Style and exaggerated type were emphasized as appearance dictated success in the show ring. Breeders concerned with their animals' welfare adapted to the changes slowly and carefully, maintaining soundness and health. But easy sales of purebred dogs made them perfect properties for puppy farms and "backyard breeders," and inherited abnormalities in some cases became the norm. Temperaments also changed. In an attempt to reduce their sharpness, guard dogs became unpredictable. In an effort to toughen up sporting dogs for competitive field and obedience events, gentleness, reliability and steadiness gave way to aggressiveness, neuroses and insensitivity. Purebred dogs were indeed suspect and under the gun. Fortunately, the 80's witnessed a change in attitude.

As awareness of changes in our animals grew, we were forced to educate ourselves. And, as fanciers began to "use" their dogs again, they recognized the necessity of having a healthy animal. Breed clubs set up screening tests for common problems such as hip dysplasia, eye abnormalities and blood diseases. The University of Pennsylvania established a data base by breed of hereditary defects to help categorize the volume and seriousness of such problems. Information obtained from these sources helps educate both breeders and buyers and should allow the decade of the 90's to witness the restoration of the health and usefulness of man's best friend.

In this vein, *201 Ways to Enjoy Your Dog* is an extremely timely book. Armed with the knowledge to purchase a sound and reliable animal that suits your interests, this encyclopedia of events enables you to find and contact those people who support your interests. Field events for hounds; hunting tests and trials for sporting dogs; terrier tests; sighthound lure and field coursing; sled dog, herding, and schutzhund events are all covered, as are competitions for obedience and conformation dogs. The events are fully described, as are the rules and regulations governing the sport. Requirements for titles, degrees or certification are detailed. Names and addresses of supporting organizations are listed for each event.

After teaching, exhibiting in and judging competitive events for 35 years, I find this compilation of ways to enjoy your dog a needed and welcome source of information for myself and for all dog enthusiasts!

Nancy Johnson
Blue Springs 'n' Katydid Training Center

INTRODUCTION

Seventeen years ago, my husband and I were little more than aware of dog shows and obedience classes. Our first Sheltie opened the world of dog activities up to us; we have made many friends and have gone many places we would not otherwise have visited.

As we became more knowledgeable, many of our puppy customers asked about "things to do" with their new canine companions, which gave me the idea for this book. When I began my research in 1985, I wondered why no one had embarked on such a task before. By the time I realized how much work was entailed, I had come too far to give up!

I have learned that dog lovers invariably create new ways to enjoy their dogs or improve upon old established activities. Today there is a healthy, happy return to events that test different breeds' abilities to do the work for which they were bred. There is virtually an activity for every dog and owner.

One person owning one dog can take part in all of the fun and challenge embraced by this book; even in sled dog racing there are classes for one dog and handler! No one has to be lonely if he has a dog, for in showing, hunting, tracking or racing him, you find a new community of friends.

Ellie Milon, 1990

ACKNOWLEDGMENTS

For their wonderful cooperation and encouragement while I gathered material and photographs for this book, I wish to thank Gary and Sheila Cook, Linda Smith, Diana Darling, Andy Johnson, John C. Gough, Roberta Vesley, Steve Willett, Irv Lander, Linda C. Franklin, Michelle Sage, Jeanne Joy Hartnagle, Donna Bartell, Bunny Reed, Kelly Patterson, Daryl Breese, Dave Kayser, Kathy Reiland, Carol Butterworth, Barbara Kemp, Nancy Dougherty, Sharon Groves, Jane Bulman, Donna Hawley, Noel Flanders, Janet E. Larson, Nancy Bickerton Vollmer, Linda C. Rorem, Sue Morlan, Rossine Kirsh, and Mrs. Jerry West.

I also wish to thank my husband, Gene, for his excellent suggestions and supportive "You can do it!" when I faltered. Finally, thanks to all of you whom I have interviewed, called, or corresponded with during the past five years. Without your help, this book could not have been completed.

1

A MEMBER OF THE FAMILY

It is natural for human beings to have pets, and dogs have been man's friend for over 12 million years. In the United States over 85 million homes have pets of some kind: dogs, cats, hamsters, goldfish, gerbils, birds, or more exotic pets. According to *American Demographics Magazine*, more than one-third of all American households own dogs, which are divided into 49 million registered dogs and an estimated 7 million unregistered. Americans spend about $120 million dollars annually on veterinary services alone.

Of all household pets, dogs apparently have the most capacity for interaction with people, giving love and accepting it in return. With this in mind, it seems only natural that we should take the time to find out how to fully enjoy them. This process starts right at the beginning—when you are selecting your puppy.

Your dog should be compatible with *all* family members. The stray dog that follows one of the children home; that darling puppy in the pet shop window; the fuzzy, fluffy puppy at the animal shelter may or may not be good candidates for your household. The decision is up to you. But I personally feel it wiser to select a purebred dog for the following reasons. First, you will know what to expect of the breed as to temperament, size and other traits in addition to its esthetic points. Second, the initial cost of the dog is the smallest amount of money you will spend in comparison with the years of maintenance in food, medications, veterinary care, and recreational pursuits. Third, there are many activities open to the registered purebred dog whch are not available to the dog of mixed breeding. If you plan to participate in some of the more rugged sports or show the dog, the quality, inherited traits or abilities, and soundness of the animal are especially important.

1

OWNERSHIP MEANS RESPONSIBILITY

Regardless of the type of dog you select, it is important for you to know ahead of time that you will have responsibilities to him, just as you would to a baby or child that you might bring into your home. In so many ways, dogs are like small children, which is one of the things that captivates us human beings. This is attested to by the names we give them. In the past most dogs were called Rover, Spot, Towser, Topsy, Prince, Duke, Patches, Laddy, Lassie, King, and so on. More and more we give our dogs such names as Alex, Jason, Merry, Rick, Billy, Barbie, Sonny, Buddy, Sean, Casey, and so on. We give them names according to their national breed origins—Scottish, English, German, Irish—or name them after favorite family members or even after celebrities. In fact, our dogs are often surrogate children or grandchildren. But the realities are that the dog must be fed properly, housebroken, given water, exercise, play, disciplined, educated, and taught his work. He will need toys and playthings. He will need to learn to travel in the car. He will need to learn his special

Your dog should be compatible with all family members. *Photo by Richard Piliero.*

place in the family and parameters of behavior will have to be defined. He will need special treats when he has been good. In short, all the things that a child needs, a dog needs.

Recently, a woman called about our Irish Terrier puppies that we had advertised. When I asked whether they had a fenced-in yard, she answered that they planned to tie the dog out in the yard on a chain. When asked why she wanted to buy a dog, she said she wanted it for the children. I explained to her that a dog on a tie-out chain was easy victim to any other dog and that serious injury could result as an Irish Terrier would do battle. I told her we would not sell her one of our puppies. Obviously, this woman was not thinking of a dog as a member of the family. Would she tie one of her children out in the yard for the day? Of course not. Would she never give her children any attention at all? Of course not. I feel that breeders who give much loving care to their dogs and puppies have a right and responsibility to place those animals in loving homes with people who realize that responsibilities are part of owning a pet.

Many dogs are brought into the household to play with the children and teach them responsibility. Unfortunately, unless the children are old enough, the care and feeding of the dog winds up with the mother, who hopefully will have been enthusiastic about the purchase. If she had not been included in the decision to get this particular dog, life will soon be miserable for both of them.

Again, I stress the involvement of *all* family members in choosing their "companion." For if the dog is chosen by and treated as a family member with all that involves, he really will be a most wonderful companion for everyone.

For whatever reason a dog is purchased, there is a particular dog to fit in with every family or person in this country. But different living conditions require different dogs. For example, dogs in city apartments will have to be leash-broken and taught to walk (or run) with their owners on city sidewalks and in city parks. The owners will have to become familiar with the leash and sanitation laws of their particular city or community. Conversely, dogs that live in rural settings spend very little time on-leash. Their training needs will more likely involve learning about their territory (the yard around the house, corral area, etc.) However, most dogs love to go for walks, even if they have a fenced (or unfenced) yard at home. There is something about going for a walk on a leash with a family member that is special to them. They step out very proudly with their owners as if to say, "Look, I'm out for a walk with my friend."

Taking your dog for a walk is one of the many ways to give him extra attention, and dogs, like people, love attention. They like the attention given them when they are being educated (even disciplined), when they are being groomed, bathed, talked to, and of course, when they are being petted. Attention is almost everything outside of being fed and watered and given a good place to sleep. In return, they will give their attention to their family members in the forms of sympathy, consolation, and pure enjoyment of their company.

OWNING A DOG HAS MANY BENEFITS

In fact, dogs are just plain good therapy! This aspect of dog owner-ship is only recently being explored and used. It has been found that a dog can lower a person's blood pressure. He can serve as a confidante when a person can't tell his problems to anyone else. Just as a psychiatrist listens, a dog listens, but doesn't charge for his services. After a person has stroked and petted his dog and talked to him about all his problems, his blood pressure goes down and he feels comforted.

I can personally vouch that puppies and dogs are very therapeu-tic. After a tiring, frustrating day, I will sometimes take a soft, furry, cuddly puppy into my lap and stroke him and talk to him. Or I will sit on the floor inside an exercise pen full of puppies and play with them. Finally, they go to sleep in my lap or lying up against my legs and I feel less tired, more refreshed. The weight of the world has been lifted and my frustrations are forgotten; in simple ways, we have com-municated and our separate needs have been satisfied.

Just as touching is communicating, so too is vocabulary—ours *and* theirs. The wise owner develops a broad vocabulary with his dog which enables him to get more enjoyment from the relationship.

Dogs develop a vocabulary which the understanding owner can use to great advantage. They understand much of what we say to them and are able to express to us many things that they want. Their facial expressions, body language, and little noises give us aid and comfort. In the same manner, dogs tell us when they want to go out, when they want to come in, when they are hungry, when they want water, when they want to go for a walk, when they are happy, when they are sad, when they don't feel good. They tell us they are sorry that check didn't come in the mail today. They kiss us to show they care when there are tears. Above all, they tell us they love us. That is the single most important part of their vocabulary—"I love you." They love us no matter what happens. And they are forgiving. After disciplining for bad behavior, do we have a sulking dog? No! Dogs know when they have not been good, when they have transgressed,

Companionship. *Photo courtesy Missy Green.*

when they have had an accident on the rug, when they have gone too far. They expect to be disciplined, but not too harshly, and five minutes later they are ready to give us a kiss and say I love you all over again.

Aside from these positive aspects of living with a dog you should be aware that dogs are creatures of habit. Often your pet will fit easily into your routine, but if you have no particular routine to follow, you should establish one for the dog and stick to it. Somehow, routines make dogs feel more secure and a secure dog is a happy and more enjoyable companion. Dogs seem to have clocks in their heads. I can't explain it, but they know when it is time to be fed. If they are usually fed at 5 o'clock in the afternoon, when 5 o'clock comes they are restless and will let you know it is time to eat. Whenever I have been working and come home at a certain time, they know when I am due home and know the sound of my car; it has become part of their routine. This is typical of any dog. If you usually take your dog for a walk at seven in the morning and five in the evening, that is when he will start telling you, "Hey, come on, it's time for my walk, hurry up." Your dog may even go and get his leash as a broader hint and will certainly run to the door. Do not fear that you will be a slave to your dog's routine—simply establish one at the outset that is comfortable for *you*. Your dog will adjust to it.

Similarly, do not feel that you will have to entertain your dog at all times. Dogs don't have to constantly play with people to get in their playtime. Just as children learn to play by themselves and enjoy it, dogs learn to enjoy solitary activities. We keep a toy box for our dogs just inside the family room. It is a cardboard box containing empty vitamin bottles, rawhide bones, pull toys, balls, anything that they especially enjoy. Each dog knows when he is in the kitchen and family room that he can go to the toy box and pull out anything he

Communication between dog and owner is important. Dogs understand more than we think. *Photo by Gary Bennett.*

wishes to play with. Your dog doesn't need to be demanding your attention when you want to watch television or read a book. He should be trained to know when he should play by himself, just as you have trained your children to play by themselves when you need to work on something alone.

In making your decision on which dog to purchase, you should be aware that many breeds of dogs like to supervise their humans. If you are sitting down reading or writing, they lie down or play by themselves; but if you get up, *they* get up. They like to come along to supervise whatever you are doing as they have a natural curiosity about what you are doing. If your dog doesn't interfere or get in the way and if what you are doing isn't dangerous to him, let him fulfill this natural tendency.

Dogs have a truly great capacity to love. Some dogs love the whole family equally; others pick one family member in particular to love. If this happens, don't be jealous. He will love you too, just slightly less, than the one he has chosen as his particular idol. Regardless of the *way* dogs love, they can also be enjoyed by the extended family. For instance, grandparents can enjoy the dog, too, if he has been trained to be well-behaved. He should be taken on visits to their home so they too can enjoy and benefit from knowing him.

Since many dogs have a long life span, the loss of a much-loved dog can cause as much bereavement as the loss of a human family member. For any pet owner, this is a reality which must be faced. Often after the impact of the loss has abated, the instinct is to buy a dog that looks just like the one that died. This is often difficult to do. After much contact with such people and from my own experience, I feel people will be much happier in the long run if they choose a puppy they like and who likes them whether or not it looks like the one they lost. They will recover from their bereavement much more quickly and may be better off not being reminded of their lost pet.

FACTORS TO CONSIDER BEFORE YOU BUY

For some people who are considering bringing a dog into the family, price is an important factor. Even puppies in the same litter may be different in quality, hence different in price. The very best ones are held back to go to show homes or perhaps kept by the breeder for show and/or breeding stock. We grade our puppies according to quality, even the ones we sell as companion dogs. The very high quality ones are priced higher. Sometimes people who come to us had previously bought a puppy of lesser conformation quality and we now have a puppy that seems to be exactly like that other one. However, this one is of much better quality (more hair, better muzzle, better personality) and is therefore priced from fifty to a hundred dollars more than the first one. Other times, years have gone by and prices have gone up. We have had people tell us they paid $125 ten years ago for a puppy that looked just like the one that we are asking $200 for today. They want to know why. Well, ten years have gone by and although prices for dogs have increased less in proportion to almost anything else that we buy today, they *have* gone up. I still think that anyone buying a purebred dog today gets the best value for his money than in anything he could possibly buy.

Finally, consider what you will be doing with your new family member once he has become established in your home. Just as we pursue various activities and sports with the human members of our family, we also pursue many activities and sports with our dogs. There are so many sports involving dogs, that almost anyone can find one that appeals to him and his particular dog. Besides specific dog-oriented activities, dogs can be trained to enjoy many of our own sports—swimming at the beach or in a pool, boating, hunting.

Happily, the different breeds of dogs are placed together in different groups, or categories, which indicate to us in general terms the organized sports for which they are suited. These sports are usually simulations of the actual work these dogs were originally bred for, or they are tests of their skill and ability to do that work. Thus, we have the Hound Group (divided into scent- and sight-hounds), the Working Group, the Herding Group, the Sporting Group (divided into retrieving, pointing and flushing dogs to hunt birds), the Toy Group (mostly little dogs meant as companions only but who can participate well in obedience work), the Non-Sporting Group, and the Terrier Group (breeds developed to "go to ground" after vermin). In the following chapters we will explore many things you can do at home to fully enjoy your dog and many different ways that you can participate in sports with him. In that way sport with your dog becomes more fun than watching one of your children participate in his chosen sport—because you get to be in it yourself. There is another benefit of being out and about with your dog, whether it is walking on the street and in the park, traveling, or competing in a sport—you will meet people. I guarantee that no one who has a dog has to be lonely. Having a dog and getting out with him is the best way of meeting people with like interests than any other I know of in this society. Forget about singles bars, computer dating services, singles clubs, etc., if you are looking for companionship and friends—get out there with your dog and enjoy.

Your dog will be part of the family for many years. Fifteen-year-old Samoyed, "Vodka." *Photo by Richard Piliero.*

A final word about the dog as a family member is necessary. It is a discouraging statistic that one-eighth of all dogs bought each year are taken to animal shelters. Certainly, none of these dogs were ever considered members of the family and weren't trained to participate with their owners in sports and fun at home. Their owners were not responsible dog owners. Perhaps the dog was a stray that wandered into the yard and the children begged to keep it, or it was a "free" puppy. A free puppy is less likely to become a member of the family in every respect unless that puppy is a requested gift at Christmas, or for a birthday or anniversary. The higher the price of the dog, the more valuable he is to the owner, the more likely that owner is to love and cherish him and treat him as a family member. This is not to say that a puppy acquired at an animal shelter or one that followed the children home won't be loved and become a family member; it is just generally less likely to be.

Many people might want to become members of the American Dog Owners Association (ADOA). It is the first and only nationwide organization dedicated to protection of dogs and our rights as dog owners. Its objectives are to protect the breeding and exhibiting of dogs as a non-commercial venture and to engage in educational and legislative activities. It is a non-profit organization and its sole source of income is dues and donations. On the federal level, ADOA is successfully combating dog fighting, puppy mills, improper care during air transport of animals, give-away puppies for promotional purposes, etc. On the state and local level, ADOA has been victorious in furthering the rights of hobby breeders and pet owners, in prohibiting dog fighting and in assisting individuals whenever and wherever possible. As you can imagine, a major portion of the organization's expenses are legal fees.

This young Lhasa Apso puppy would charm any dog lover. Before you go shopping for a puppy, decide what role your pet will fulfill. This breed makes a great pet or show dog, but is not suited to long walks in the mountains or to the family that wants to get involved in field sports. *Photo by Robert Spanner.*

2

CHOOSING A DOG FOR SPORTS

Many of us grew up with a certain breed of dog and find it admirably suited to our own adult lifestyle. For others, choosing a dog can be difficult and mystifying because there is such a variety from which to choose. In this instance, it is important to take a lot of time reviewing some basic factors: the purpose for having the dog; what appeals to you esthetically; your lifestyle and personality; whether the dog requires much grooming or even professional grooming; and size of the dog.

Most dogs are purchased to be family companions, but certain breeds fit in better with one type of family than another. What kind of family do you have? Will the puppy be a companion for a couple or a single person? Will he be living with a senior citizen or will he be expected to deal with children?

Some dogs are purchased to be working dogs on farms and ranches, herding sheep or cattle. Others serve as hunting companions, as guard or watch dogs, for showing in conformation or competing in obedience or field trials. In short, there is a dog for every purpose; some dogs are multi-purpose dogs. Of course, if you have a particular dog sport in mind you will need to learn all you can about it *before* you start shopping for a puppy.

THE BREED

What kind of dog appeals to you—popular or unique? Among the most consistently popular breeds are poodles (all three sizes), Miniature Schnauzers, Cocker Spaniels, German Shepherd Dogs, Shetland Sheepdogs, Labrador Retrievers, Doberman Pinchers,

Match the dog's breed and personality to the activity you want. *Photo by Bobbee Christensen.*

Beagles, Golden Retrievers, Dachshunds and Lhasa Apsos. If you want a puppy from one of these breeds, you will have a much greater selection from which to choose.

For someone who wants a pet from a long-established but rarer breed, there are some unique benefits. You may have to initially pay more for your puppy, and you may have difficulty finding a local breeder with a litter of puppies, but you will get a puppy from a breed that has not been subjected to the fads and whims of the public and show-going fanciers. The original look and the traits for which the dog was bred will still be intact, since breeders through the years won't have gone off on tangents to beautify the breed for show purposes, sometimes at the expense of the basic character and temperament of the dogs.

When you and your rare breed dog step out for a walk, go to the veterinarian's office or to obedience classes, you will find yourself the center of attention as people ask you, "What kind of dog is that?" If you become a member of the parent club, you will receive regular newsletters about what's going on with the breed all over the country; you will feel a part of a rather elite brotherhood of people who are discriminating enough to choose this breed; you will feel pride in hearing of the wins of any of the other owners' dogs in any of the sports, as they will take pride in hearing of your dog's accomplishments.

Many of these rarer breeds are quite old and have been registered both in England and in the United States for over 100 years. They are purposely kept rare by the people who breed and exhibit them. These people recognize that their breeds are not for everyone, that they are unique and require a special type of person to own and appreciate them. They don't want them becoming overly popular because they want their breeds to retain all the qualities that they now have. For these reasons, they do like to place their puppies in appropriate homes.

Whatever the registry, I feel it is important to select a purebred dog as you will know what to expect of him in terms of temperament, looks, size when grown, need for grooming, and purpose for which he was bred. Many mixed-breed dogs end up at the local animal shelter because they grew into someting quite different from what was expected when they were puppies. A small bundle of fur can grow up to be a 125-pounder that doesn't fit in the one bedroom apartment. That cute little guy with the big brown eyes can turn into a bundle of nerves that barks all night and bites the mailman. Both will probably end up at the animal shelter where their fate is precarious at best. A registered dog has a pedigree that shows his ancestors were of pure breeding and he is registered as part of his litter in a recognized studbook. When you buy a purebred dog that is eligible for registration, part of the reason for the price is this eligibility. You owe it to yourself and your dog to complete his registration, for by not obtaining his certificate of registration in your name as owner, you throw away something for which you have paid. Registration means that your dog's name and number are his alone and officially on record for all time.

This may also be very important to you if you want to participate in the various organized sports. Almost all of them are open only to registered breeds. Although any dog may be trained in obedience classes (and it is desirable for all dogs to be so trained), you may find you liked the classes so much that you would like to go into competition. You cannot if you do not have a purebred registered (or registrable) dog. Perhaps you enjoy hunting with a pointer, retriever or spaniel. You may want to prove your dog and your training in tests or field trials. Your dog must be purebred and registrable.

If you plan to purchase a dog so that you can participate in one of the many sports included in this book, it is very important to select a puppy for the sport that interests you. Any dog registered with the two national kennel clubs may be shown in those clubs' licensed dog shows and may participate in the obedience trials. However, some breeds do better in the obedience ring then others. Although obedience is not a contest *between* dogs but a test of each dog, you may be a highly competitive person who wants a dog that can become High in Trial or win a *Dog World* Award for attaining his Companion Dog degree in three consecutive trials. Also, whenever several breeds are eligible for competition in certain field trials or coonhunts, you will find there are one or two breeds that are standouts in those events and do most of the winning. Read up on the sports; go to some events; see the dogs in action; then select a breed for that sport and an individual puppy that is pleasing to you.

"Beauty is in the eye of the beholder." Not every breed is beautiful to everyone and it is important that you pick one that to *you* is esthetically pleasing. Whereas one person likes a short-haired dog, another likes a long-haired one. Some people love black dogs, others love white ones. There are dogs of almost every color and shape you can imagine. Take your time and make your choice based on what you consider to be beautiful.

Be sure to also consider your lifestyle. If you travel a lot and live alone in an apartment in a large city but still want a dog as a companion, you can have that dog. But, do yourself a favor and choose one that is on the small side, likes strangers, is outgoing and happy, can travel in a small crate with you or will adjust to being left in a kennel. If you have a family with several children and have a house in the suburbs with a large fenced-in backyard, you will want an entirely different type of dog.

There are dogs of all sizes and temperaments, from the Toy Poodle or Chihuahua to the big Irish Wolfhound. Remember, though, that a large dog usually needs a lot of exercise; and if you don't have the space for that exercise, you will have to take the dog to a large exercise area regularly.

Older puppies can be the very best choice for many people, although many people think they want a puppy just as young as they can possibly get him. Breeders sometimes have older puppies that didn't quite turn out right for show. These are usually exceptionally handsome dogs but have some fault that only a judge or breeder will notice. On the other hand, he may not have grown big enough or got too large, as many breeds have size requirements. The breeder has probably spent a lot of time with that puppy: housebreaking, crate training, taking him to conformation classes, and lead-training him. Then, by the time he is six months old, the breeder decides that the puppy will never make champion and he doesn't want to spend any more time with him, as his purpose was to show the dog and finish his championship. So, he decides to sell him. This puppy will be priced as a high quality pet, but probably will cost very little more than when he was a young puppy. Whoever buys him will reap the benefits of the personal attention the pup has received plus he will have a puppy that is housebroken, lead-trained and crate-trained.

It may take just a little longer for the older puppy to adjust to the new household, but he *will* adjust. For someone who wants a dog but isn't home enough, or doesn't care to do all the training, an older puppy is ideal. Prospective owners of these older puppies might be apartment dwellers, older people, or people who don't have someone home during the day.

Who are you? A person's personality will affect his choice of a dog. A quiet, dignified, reserved person may not be happy with a Miniature Schnauzer, whereas an outgoing, talkative person will probably love the little dog. I have noticed that a lot of people tend to buy dogs that are compatible with their own national origins; so you find people of German extraction owning German Shepherds, Doberman Pinschers, Rottweilers, or Boxers; Irish people have Irish Terriers, Irish Wolfhounds, Kerry Blues, Wheaten Terriers, or Irish Setters; Scottish

When you have decided on the breed and found a reputable breeder, pick the puppy that appeals the most to you. *Photo by Jim Spencer.*

people prefer Scottish or West Highland White Terriers, Shetland Sheepdogs, or Collies; and so on.

In making your choice, don't forget that some dogs require more grooming than others, and some even need professional grooming. If you select a Poodle, a Wirehaired Fox Terrier, a Miniature Schnauzer, or any of the breeds that require professional grooming to look their best, be prepared to foot the bill for this service. The only alternative will be for you to learn how to do it yourself and *continue* doing it at home. Before you buy your dog, be honest with yourself about how much extra time or money you are willing to put into grooming.

"But mom, it was such fun!" Boston Terrier puppies. *Photo by Mrs. Pat Jackna.*

The time of year for your purchase can be a factor if you buy a puppy that has to be shipped by air to you. You and the breeder may agree on a date for shipment, but on the breeder's end, he may find the weather is too hot, too cold, or too snowy to ship a young puppy to you. You will have to leave this up to the breeder's good judgement. He will be glad to wait for a break in the weather since he cares about the health and safety of your puppy. When your puppy arrives, keep him crated until you have him at home, then let him out *in the house*, with few people around and no possibility of escape (doors and windows closed) until he becomes used to his environment.

There are many more ways of examining prospective breeds than you can imagine. Never buy on impulse. If you do your homework before you make the important decision to bring this new family member into your home, you will be repaid a thousandfold. You can begin your homework either by buying or checking out from the library one of the books which details all the different breeds. When you have narrowed your choice down to one or two breeds, you can either buy or check out a book from the library on that specific breed. You will learn in detail all about the breed standard of perfection, history, grooming, important champions and sires, etc.

Go to a bookstore and pick up a magazine, either *Dog World* (the largest) or *Dog Fancy*. You will find a wealth of material about dogs in general and many breeds in particular. There will be advertising on most breeds, both AKC and UKC registered, and purebreds that have their own studbooks.

You may decide on a breed because you know someone who has it and you like their dog, but be sure to discuss all the pros and cons of their breed. Don't buy a breed just because your folks had that kind of dog. It may have suited them admirably but be entirely unsuited for your own particular lifestyle and needs.

If you can't decide on a breed by reading books, magazines, talking to owners of various breeds, and looking at photos, then go to a dog show or match. Chapter 5 covers how to understand a dog show, where to find out about them, the judging program, the catalog, etc.

BUYING A DOG

Now that you have decided on the breed you want, where do you go to buy it? *From a breeder.* Do not buy from a pet shop as they stock popular breeds that they can quickly sell to make a large profit. They buy their puppies from commercial breeding kennels that don't give the pups the tender loving care that is required for them to make a real contribution to the adoptive family.

You want to buy a healthy pup from healthy parents, one that has been socialized and has had ample contact with human beings, one that has been in a house and knows what a vacuum cleaner sounds like, has been played with and has had loving and kissing. A caring breeder will have done all this, knows his breed and will give you a lot of information that you need to know. Also, you will get a higher quality puppy for less money than a pet shop charges.

Costs

The price you will pay for your puppy will be determined by several factors. Rare breeds usually cost more because there aren't as many of them. You may pay from $300 to $500 for a pet-quality puppy in a rare breed. On the other hand, many popular breeds are priced from $150 to $250 for pet-quality puppies. Some breeders sell all their males for one price and all their females for another. Usually, females are priced higher as they are more in demand.

If you want to buy a show-prospect puppy, you may find the price to be $500 to $800 for a 10-week or 12-week-old puppy, but most breeders give some type of guarantee when they sell show-prospect puppies. For example, if the puppy is a male, you are guaranteed a replacement puppy if both testicles do not drop. If there is a height requirement for the breed, you are guaranteed a replacement if the puppy matures at a height under or over those required. The guarantees depend upon how much you pay for the puppy, his age, and upon the individual breeder. There is room for a lot of variation in any guarantee, so the terms should be spelled out in writing to you and signed by the breeder at the time of purchase.

If you are buying a puppy from one of the breeds used for hunting or field trials, he might be a "started" puppy. This means the breeder has already begun its training, probably because the particular puppy has been evaluated for aptitude and shows promise. Such a puppy will naturally cost somewhat more.

Finding a Breeder

There are many ways to find a good breeder. *Dog World* or *Dog Fancy* magazines have many ads, and the AKC's *Pure-Bred Dogs/American Kennel Gazette* also carries advertising. To locate a

These labrador puppies could fit easily into a wide variety of active lifestyles. *Photo by Janet L. Yosay.*

breeder of sporting dogs (setters, retrievers, spaniels, coonhounds) buy a *Field and Stream, Sports Afield,* or *American Cooner* magazine, or send for a copy of *American Field.* The United Kennel Club can also refer you to a breeder of one of their registered breeds in your particular area if you write or call them. Many of the parent (national) clubs of breeds have a referral or puppy placement service. Most of these clubs advertise in *Dog World* for AKC registered breeds and other purebred breeds.

The best way to find the name of a reputable breeder is by referral. We sell almost as many puppies through referrals as we do from advertising. Ask your friends, co-workers, a local veterinarian, or a grooming shop to recommend a breeder. Sometimes pet shops have lists of breeders for breeds that they do not carry. Also, check the classified ads of your local newspaper or of a newspaper in the largest city near you. If you do call from one of these ads, be sure to ask the seller if he is a breeder or if he just has one pet that he has bred.

If you know someone who bought the breed you want from a breeder, ask that person a lot of questions. Is he happy with the breed and the particular dog? Is he typical of the breed? Was he a healthy, happy pup when he was purchased? Did the breeder know his breed and was he able to answer all the questions?

If you have chosen a rarer breed, you may have to buy it through phone calls and correspondence. If the breeder has a litter ready, a photo will probably be sent if you request it. They will also send a pedigree and possibly photos of dam and/or sire, especially if the litter is on the way. You must specify what sex, age, and color you want (if there is more than one color). You may find that the rarer breeds do not sell as quickly and the breeder may still have an older puppy (maybe four- to six-months old) waiting for a really good home. In this case, you may be able to purchase the puppy at a slight discount.

Contacting a Breeder

First of all I would like to impress on you that you, the customer, have some responsibilities to fulfill to the breeder. Most breeders have invested a lot of time and money in showing, hunting, or field trialing their dogs, in learning the breed, and in trying to improve it over a period of years. They deserve courtesy from the prospective customer. If a breeder sends you photos and pedigree copies and *asks for their return*, be courteous enough to return them in a reasonable length of time even if you decide to buy from someone else.

When writing to a breeder, be specific about your needs and desires. Tell him whether you want a companion, show prospect, or hunting or field trial prospect. Detail the sex, color, and age of the dog you wish to purchase. Also, if you write him an individual letter, you will be more certain of a response. We have received Xeroxed or carbon copies of letters saying, "I want a female puppy. I have written to other breeders and the first one who answers I'm going to buy from," or words to that effect. Well, this is the only kind of letter I don't answer. Also don't write and say, "Tell me about your dogs," without saying what you want.

If an ad says that phone calls are preferred, nine times out of ten a letter will not be answered for many weeks, if at all. "Phone calls preferred" may sound arrogant, but breeders are usually people with very little free time. If they work at a full-time job (and many do), they have all their dog chores to do before and after work each day and many are off to shows or field trials on weekends. Others also run boarding kennels or grooming shops. In other words, breeders are busy people. They all *prefer* phone calls, but most of them try to answer promptly and in detail serious letters of inquiry which state the writer's *specific* needs.

When calling a breeder, be sure to let the phone ring quite a few times, as often the breeder is out in the kennel and may even be in the process of whelping a litter. If the breeder does not have any puppies available, find out when the next ones are due. If he has none due in a reasonable length of time, ask if he can recommend someone else who may have puppies. It is always a good idea to call breeders well before you are ready to buy a puppy so you do not run into the problem of having nothing available when you are ready to buy.

If you are answering a particular ad, you will already know what sex, colors and age of puppies are available. Be sure the breeder still has what you are looking for before you go out to visit. Also be sure that your are both talking about the same thing with regard to color as this is commonly an area of misunderstanding on the part of the customer. For instance, we have tri-colored (black, white and tan) Shelties. We have had people call specifying a tri-color thinking that the dark sable (reddish brown) which has an overlay of black hairs beside the white trim, is the tri-color. We tell them we have them; then when they come out to see the puppies, they say, "Oh, these are black ones. We wanted a brown one." We have learned from such experiences and now ask questions to make sure the prospective customer knows what a tri-color actually is. If the breeder you call doesn't ask such questions, take the responsibility to do so as you are the one who will be inconvenienced if there is a misunderstanding.

If you have to buy a puppy from a breeder who is so far away that you will have to have him shipped, it is better to call first to find out whether he has what you want and then both he and you can follow up with correspondence. If you write first, you may miss out on a choice puppy because of the lag in time necessary for letters to go back and forth. Do not be afraid of buying from a distant breeder and having your puppy shipped to you. Just make sure that he has had sufficient experience in shipping. If he has, he will take care of all the details on his end and keep you informed as to when and how the puppy will be shipped. Most experienced breeders have shipped puppies fairly frequently and can handle this expeditiously.

Visiting the Breeder

After asking all the questions you have to have answered, make a definite appointment and get good directions. If you are going to a different city or town or maybe even a different state, have a map handy so you can refer to it while you are getting your directions.

Try to be on time for your appointment with the breeder. Dog breeders, as I have mentioned, are very busy people. They will most likely try to take care of all their dog chores before or after your

Consider the space, food, and time requirements of your chosen breed before purchasing. *Photo by Dolores Reinke.*

scheduled appointment and if you are two hours late, you will throw them off by those two hours. If you *know* you will be late, have the courtesy to call so they can rearrange their busy schedule.

At this point, I feel a word of advice is necessary—if you have children and those children are not going to have any input into which puppy is selected, don't take them with you. Puppies love kids and kids love puppies. I have never seen anyone so disappointed as a child who has been told he could pick out a puppy only to be overruled by the parents who decided on a different one. The *most* disappointment I have ever seen was that of a girl whose father brought her out to look at puppies and after she had picked one out told her that he was not going to buy a puppy at all. "Maybe some day," he said. Such tears, such heartbreak, such cruelty to a child's emotions I could never have imagined.

On the other hand, we have had many people come to look at our Irish Terrier puppies who have never actually seen one before. One couple wanted their children to be able to play with one and see whether they would like the breed. We told them to come ahead, not expecting them to buy a puppy; however, the children were delighted with the puppy and he adored them. Since they were on their way to a camping vacation in Florida, they put down a deposit and on their return came by to complete their purchase and take him home. What a happy reunion of puppy and people that was—a truly pleasant experience for breeder and customer alike.

When arriving on time at the breeder's home, you will find the puppies ready for your inspection. In addition to seeing them, you will probably want to ask a lot more questions of the breeder—this is your chance to find out more about the breed in case you don't already know as much as you would like. Pay attention to the breeder's answers to determine *his* qualifications as a "good" breeder. The breeder should be steeped in the history of the breed and be able to answer all of your questions. He should know about the pillars of the breed and well-known dogs across the nation, not just in his particular area.

Ask to see the dam and sire (if he is on the premises). Seeing the parents gives you a good idea of just what your puppy will look and act like when he grows up. If the breeder does not own the sire but sent his bitch off to be bred to someone else's stud dog, ask if he has a photo of the sire to show you. Don't ask to see every dog the breeder owns as this is not necessary and is quite an imposition on his time.

Look for the same things in a puppy as you look for in his parents. Is he healthy? Is he outgoing? Does he look like the breed should look? (This is more applicable to the parents as in many breeds the puppies look very little like they will look as adults; some will even change color.) Is the puppy playful? Are his eyes clear and bright? Does he have runny eyes or nose? Can the breeder give you a good idea of how large (or small) the puppy will be when grown? He should be able to. Many breeds have a disparity of size, but the breeder should be able to tell you from his past experience in raising litters and by the growth rate of his puppies just about what size the puppy will be when mature.

Does the breeder impress you as caring about the welfare of his own dogs and of the puppies he is going to sell? If so, he will probably ask you questions also, such as: do you have a fenced yard, is anyone home during the day to housebreak the pup, will you spay or neuter (if sold as a pet), will you obedience train (especially if it is a larger breed), and so on. If you are looking for a show-prospect puppy, the breeder may ask you more questions than you ask him. He will want to know if you have ever shown before, if you know how to do the show grooming, if anyone is going to help you, if you are going to show the dog yourself or hire a handler, if you plan to show extensively or just locally, if you belong to a kennel club which has a handling class, and so on. If you live close by, he will probably offer his help and expertise. By all means, take him up on it.

If you have never owned a dog, be sure to tell the breeder when you call so he can plan to spend more time with you. Most breeders will detail in writing what to feed the puppy and when, when he was wormed and for which type of worms with which medicine, whether he has had any injections (the puppy should have his first shots for distemper, parvovirus, hepatitis, leptospirosis, and kennel cough), when to go to the veterinarian for the next shot, and any other things that he considers pertinent. If he doesn't offer this, ask him to please write it down for you.

The breeder should fill out and sign the puppy's registration application paper (blue form if it is an AKC puppy), which you are responsible for sending in to get the puppy properly registered. He should explain how to do this correctly. A pedigree will usually be furnished although a breeder of AKC breeds is not required to give you a pedigree. The breeder can give you a little show-and-tell session with the pedigree and he probably still has some of the dogs or photos of dogs that are in older generations of the pedigree.

After you have bought your puppy and taken him home, that breeder is just a phone call away when you need to know something. Most breeders are very happy to give you that time, as they feel they owe it to you. Whether the dog eventually becomes a champion in show or field or titled in obedience trials or just makes his owners a loyal and loving companion, the breeder of that dog feels a deep satisfaction on hearing from the owner.

3

CARE AND CONDITIONING FOR THE ACTIVE DOG

A great deal of care goes into the physical well-being of an active dog, just as for an athletic person. If the dog is healthy and well fed, he will be more receptive to training, sports, traveling, visiting and all the things that are explored in the latter parts of his book.

FEEDING

Dog owners today are fortunate to have a wide choice of nutritional foods, as most of the readily available commercial dry and canned dog foods are of high quality. Although you will probably start your new puppy off on whatever food the breeder recommends, as your dog grows, remember that it is better to avoid bargain brands as you never know what source of protein is used in them. Also, buying cheap brands of food is not a savings as you usually have to feed more and they are not good for your dog. Better quality dog foods contain protein from meat or meat by-products. The cheaper and generic brands do not always contain digestible proteins, carbohydrates and fats.

Most dogs thrive on dry dog food. In addition, this type of food exercises the jaws through necessary chewing and helps keep teeth clean. If your dog doesn't like dry food, mixing it with a small amount of canned food will usually convince him to eat it. If this doesn't work and you are forced to feed him straight canned food or semi-moist food, you will need to provide milk bones or rawhide bones to chew to keep his teeth free of tartar and plaque.

All foods have a recommended amount to feed. On the back of the sack of dry food is a table of weights and amounts to feed. You

25

An active breed like this Doberman requires plenty of exercise. *Photo by Cindy Noland.*

should be aware of the correct weight for your dog. To weigh him, just step on the bathroom scale and weigh yourself then get on the scale with the dog and subtract your weight from the total. You also must take into consideration your dog's age, amount of exercise, and the time of year (in cold weather a dog that is outside or is kenneled in an unheated garage or dog house needs extra calories).

Since the dog food manufacturer cannot see *your* dog, you have to use common sense. On a dog that has short hair, you can tell pretty well whether he is too fat or too thin; you can either see his ribs or you can't. On a dog with long hair, you will need to feel his ribs to see if there is a sufficient layer of flesh over them. If you can't feel the ribs at all, your dog is too fat, Also, you can feel the flesh over the hip bones and over the withers (where the shoulder blades come together). If the bones are too prominent, the dog needs more to eat. If you can't feel them at all, he needs to go on a diet. Finally, feeding table scraps is okay if they're fed to him along with a balanced diet.

Before putting a dog on a weight-reduction diet, you should consult your veterinarian; but if he needs more to eat, increase his food or add cooked rice or potatoes for awhile. There are some excellent commercial foods designed for obese dogs and for older dogs as well as for growing puppies.

If your dog is on a well-balanced commercial dog food, whatever the brand, his diet should not need any supplementation. In fact it is better to avoid giving extra vitamins or calcium unless the veterinarian prescribes it for your dog. The one exception to this rule of thumb is young puppies. When we sell our puppies at eight weeks, we recommend that the new owners give them either liquid puppy vitamins or liquid baby vitamins until the puppy is about four months old. Later on, if your veterinarian recommends supplementation, you can buy regular dog vitamins which dogs love as they taste like a treat. We do give hard-boiled eggs to our dogs that we want to get into peak condition for showing as this seems to help give them a shiny coat.

I highly recommend rawhide bones no matter what the age of the dog as the chewing action cleans the teeth. In older dogs these bones keep down tartar and plaque; in puppies they aid in the process of cutting new teeth and losing the baby teeth. When the puppy begins to cut his permanent canine teeth, a rawhide bone is almost a necessity. If he doesn't lose the baby teeth and the permanent canines come in, there is a possibility you will have to have them pulled. At the very least, there is a chance that the new teeth will come in crooked.

There is a multitude of treats on the market which your puppy or dog will enjoy *and* which are good for him. There are jerky treats in different flavors, *Liva-snaps*® , dried liver treats and others. These should be used in training as rewards.

Fresh water is absolutely essential. Be sure that it is *always* available. This can be a problem in winter as water in a bucket rapidly freezes. If there is snow on the ground, the dog will eat it but this should not be his only source of liquid—he should have his fresh water as usual. One solution to this problem is the immersion-type electric heater that fits all types of buckets with 8- to 20-quart capacities. This device can be ordered from a catalog supply house. The snap-acting thermostat keeps the water temperature at about 50 degrees and cuts off automatically when the bucket runs dry. The 6-foot electric cord has a grounded plug and is encased with heavy wall aluminum tubing for protection from wear and chewing. In addition, a security chain will prevent the heater cord from being pulled inside a dog run. There is also a smaller unit for 4- to 8-quart capacity buckets. In more clement weather or climates, a permanent supply of clean, fresh drinking water can be provided with a self-waterer which fits onto the outside faucet.

Colder weather also calls for higher caloric intake for dogs that are housed in a garage or dog house. Even though they get less exercise in the winter, outside dogs need more food just to keep warm. It is a good idea to add a little corn oil to their increased food intake in winter and I have also kept suet in the refridgerator to feed to our dogs at that time of year. When warm weather comes again, they can be put back on their regular maintenance diet.

Dogs demand a schedule, but you don't have to fit yourself to their routine. Instead tailor his schedule to yours. Whether you feed him once or twice a day, feed him at approximately the same time. Occasionally you may miss his regular feeding time, but as a general rule, keep to the same time to feed him. For instance, if you feed him twice a day, feed your dog while you are having your breakfast. No need to rush to feed him before you eat. Then feed him in the evening after you get home fom work or as you are having your dinner. Don't leave the food down for him all day as this practice tends to create finicky eaters. Do measure the food so you can tell how much to decrease or increase according to whether he needs to lose or gain weight.

SANITATION

Even if there is only one dog in a household, there will be cleanup chores. I recommend that anyone with even just one dog have what is called a "pooper scooper." This is available from pet shops or catalog supply houses. Although dogs tend to go to the perimeters of a fenced-in area to do their business, if the stools are allowed to accumulate, there will be an abundance of worrisome flies besides the smell and the chance of someone walking through them. The pooper scooper makes it easy to clean up the stools, put them in the garbage, and keep the yard sanitary.

Whether you have a fenced backyard, a dog run, patio, or no fence but your dog does his business in your own yard, you will need to practice these sanitary techniques. If you live in the city and have no fence but frequently walk your dog and let him do his business while on-leash, train him to do it in your yard, not the neighbor's. Dogs that live in city apartments have to be walked and usually have no place of their own to use, unless it is a small patio.

While on your walks, you will need to take along a baggie or two to scoop up any stools deposited along the way, even if you walk your dog in a park. Deposit the container in a city receptacle or take it home with you and put it in your own garbage. Parks are for the enjoyment of everyone and people don't appreciate dog stools left around for them to walk into. The stools will also kill the grass. If we dog owners want the general public to tolerate us and our dogs (even if they don't really like us), we have to respect their rights to clean streets, sidewalks and parks. More and more nationwide anti-dog legislation is being passed because of careless owners whose dogs leave little presents on public sidewalks and in neighborhood yards.

In cases when the weather is so inclement that you just can't take your dog out for his walk, you will need to train him to use a paper in the kitchen, utility room, back porch or balcony. Dogs are such creatures of habit that it will not be difficult for you to train him "to paper."

EXERCISE

Obesity is the most common nutritional problem occurring in the dog and is associated with many other health problems. Therefore, aside from food, water, sleep and interaction with family members, exercise is one of the big factors in keeping your dog well and happy. Boredom and idleness are known to increase food intake in people and probably are the cause of obesity in many dogs. Adequate exercise not only relieves the boredom and idleness but keeps your dog physically fit and trim. If your dog gets the amount of exercise he

Resting after a run. *Photo by Janet Yosay.*

should for the type and size of dog that he is, (and you don't overfeed him) you should never have to face the worry of an obese dog that is therefore subject to many additional illnesses.

Some dogs need tremendous amounts of exercise while others need to exercise only moderately.

Dogs that need *small to moderate* amounts of exercise include all toy dogs such as the Yorkshire Terrier, Chihuahua, Pug, Shih Tzu, and Lhasa Apso. The Bulldog and the Dachshund, both standard and miniature, need small to moderate amounts of exercise.

Moderate to large amounts of exercise are required by most of the working, herding, annd terrier breeds. The Cocker Spaniel, the Keeshond, Irish Wolfhound, Norwegian Elkhound, Akita, and Beagle also fit into this exercise category.

Maximum amounts of exercise are needed by some spaniels such as the Brittany and American Water Spaniel, also the retrievers and setters, the sighthounds, the Collie, Dalmatian, Doberman Pinscher and the German Shepherd Dog.

If you live in an apartment or in a house which doesn't have a fenced-in yard, you will need to walk your dog several times a day. At one time we lived in a house with an unfenced yard in Houston and we all took turns walking our Collie. Sometimes he just about got his feet walked off as each day my husband and I would walk him separately or together and my three children also always managed to each take him for a walk. In addition, we played ball with him in our yard. He always got his exercise with a family member, sat and shook hands with every kid on the block who asked, and lived to a ripe old age always happy, well-fed and well-exercised. If you live in the city and have a dog that needs the maximum amount of exercise, I highly recommend that you look around for a park to which you can walk or a field not too far away where you can really let him run and play.

The amount of exercise needed also depends on the age and condition of your dog. Use common sense. An older dog doesn't need as much exercise as does a youngster. You can overdo on puppies, too, even if they are breeds which as adults need large amounts of exercise.

Jogging is a way of life and a popular form of exercise for many people today. Many dogs get their exercise by going jogging with their owners. However, as this is a rigorous activity (especially if you are a 5-mile-a-day jogger), only the dog that needs *lots* of exercise should join you on your runs.

Just as you got a checkup from your doctor before starting your jogging, so should your dog be checked out by your veterinarian.

Teaching your dog to retrieve a ball is a good way to give him exercise. *Photo by Ken Hesterman.*

Listen to your veterinarian's advice on a training regimen for your dog. One of the things he will probably tell you is to start your dog out gradually. His feet will need to be toughened by walks, and then slowly, you will progress to short runs. Later on, after you have become jogging partners, be alert to your dog's needs. If he gets tired or pants excessively, it's time to stop for a rest. *Never* run during the heat of the day.

HOME HEALTH CARE

Part of home health care is making sure that he has proper sleeping quarters. This means shade in the summer and protection from bad weather, winter or summer. In the winter, of course, he needs warm quarters. If you use a doghouse, it should be at least six inches off the ground. An insulated doghouse is best for both winter *and* summer. Cedar bedding provides additional insulation and keeps fleas away. It should be enclosed inside a canvas cover.

If your dog's sleeping quarters are in the garage, a magnetic pet door for access to the fenced-in backyard can be installed. These come in sizes for small dogs up to very large dogs and can be purchased fairly inexpensively from a catalog house. The dog can open it from inside or outside and it closes tightly behind him.

Even outdoor dogs should be brought inside in extremely cold weather. During some winters here in Indiana we have had temperatures dip to around 30 degrees below zero. The wind blew very hard, dropping the wind chill to 65 degrees below. The weather, literally, was not fit for man or beast. It was extremely dangerous to be outside. In weather this severe, you should fix up a place for your dog in the kitchen, laundry room, or closed-in porch where there is some kind of heat. When he does have to go outside, he should be allowed out only long enough to do his business. When he comes back in, check his pads and clean out what snow you find. If you walk your dog on city sidewalks in the winter, the salt that was put down to keep us all from falling on the icy spots is also bad news for your dog's pads. Be sure to rinse off his feet when you get home.

During the summer you have to consider the opposite extreme— heatstroke. Basically, if your dog has plenty of shade and fresh water, he should be safe from heatstroke. Some common conditions under which heatstroke can occur include leaving a dog in a closed-in car; running the dog in the heat of the day; and leaving a dog in a fenced-in yard where no shade is available. When it is 78 degrees F in the shade, the temperature of a closed car will shoot up to 90 degrees F in five minutes under the direct sun. In twenty-five minutes, the temperature will reach 110 degrees F. If you absolutely must leave your dog in the car for a short while, be sure that he has air coming in from windows that are rolled down at least a little and that the car is in the shade.

Most dogs have a normal temperature of 101.5 degrees F, some a little over and some a little under. They cannot perspire as human beings do but sweat through their noses and mouths. If your dog becomes groggy or unconscious because of the heat, it is important to get him out of the sun and immediately hose down his body or immerse him up to his head in a tub of cold water. You can apply ice packs to the head and neck, then see your veterinarian as soon as possible.

Dogs with long or double coats should *not* be clipped in the summer as their coat serves as insulation, both in winter and in summer. The breeds of dogs that usually go to a groomer, such as Poodles, Miniature Schnauzers and terriers, should have a summer clip.

Home health care of your dog is a lot easier if you take your new puppy or dog to a good veterinarian and get him put on a regular regimen. This would include periodic vaccinations, stool checks for worms and worming, and tests for heartworm. (In some areas of the country preventive medication is routinely prescribed to keep heartworm in check.) You can help your veterinarian by being observant while you are grooming your dog and when cleaning up his stools. If stools are very dark, this may indicate blood, or you may actually see bloody stools. Also, the stool may be loose and watery or mucous-filled. This condition is often a sign of worms and *could* indicate hookworm—the most deadly of all worms. If you suspect that your dog has worms, it will be necessary for your veterinarian to do a stool specimen analysis to determine the type of worm infecting your dog. The only worm that you can actually see is the tapeworm. If you see little white segments that look like grains of rice in the stool or around the anus, this is tapeworm. The flea is the host for the tapeworm so you can see the importance of keeping your dog flea-free as another aspect of his home health care.

Fleas are your dog's enemy in more ways than one. In addition to carrying the tapeworm larvae, they can cause a dog to scratch excessively. Fleas also may permeate your home and cause you and your family great discomfort. We went through a period of six years with no flea in sight anywhere, and we got very smug about it. Well, we were brought back to reality two years ago when we bought a new place and moved. The fleas were everywhere and what a battle it was to overcome them! We had to attack on all fronts. Of course, the more dogs you have the harder the battle. There are many good products on the market, both for your dog, the house and the yard, but they all must be used conscientiously and simultaneously.

You will need to give your dog a bath with a flea shampoo and then spray him with a flea spray when he is dry. You should spray him weekly until he is rid of the fleas. Sprays are available as either an aerosol or a pump. Many dogs don't like the sound of the aerosol but don't object to the pump. The yard and dog quarters will need to be treated about once a month. Caution—do not use pesticide strips or flea collars when you are spraying or bathing with insecticides.

If you are one of those who prefer the herbal method of flea control, which is becoming more popular as it is safe for you, your dog, and ecologically sound, there are products on the market made from citrus which are 100 percent organic. Shampoos, sprays, and dips are available. I started using these products two years ago and find them very effective for killing fleas but they do not have any residual action. I highly recommend the shampoo to kill the fleas and give the coat a wonderful shine and gloss. The shampoo is also soothing to the skin. I find that following up with flea spray that has residual action makes a good combination without giving the dog a double dose of toxic chemicals.

Part of home health care is just using common sense. If your dog vomits right after drinking water, he probably has drunk the water too fast or was too hot when he drank. If this is the case and it just happens once or twice, it is self-limiting. Don't rush him right over to the veterinarian unless it continues. Be alert for coughing, runny nose, red or tearing eyes. If your dog becomes lethargic or off his feed for more than a couple of days, something is wrong and you should have him checked over.

One very important telephone number to post near your telephone is 217-333-3611. This is the 24-hour Poison Hotline located at the University of Illinois. Fast action can save your dog's life when you know or even suspect that he has been poisoned. A dog may accidentally ingest any of a number of toxic substances such as: insecticides or pesticides, rat bait, antifreeze you drained from your car and left in a puddle on the driveway, toxic plants, paint, or even your own prescription medicine. As you describe your dog's symptoms over the phone, the attendant at the Hotline number will try to determine whether or not he has been poisoned and tell you what to do. Of course, if your veterinarian's office is open, you should probably call there first.

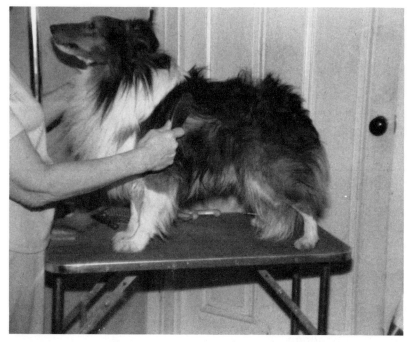

Brushing removes tangles and provides a bond of companionship with your dog.

4
HOW TO GET INVOLVED: THE KENNEL CLUBS

There are two national kennel clubs in the United States and one in Canada, plus several different registries. Individuals do not actually join national organizations but local clubs, which will be discussed later in this chapter. National clubs serve as registries and governing bodies for the local clubs which sponsor the dog sports events we will be considering.

AMERICAN KENNEL CLUB

The largest is the American Kennel Club, 51 Madison Avenue, New York, NY 10010. Founded in 1884 as a non-profit organization, the AKC is devoted to the advancement of purebred dogs. It was organized by a group of amateur sportsmen interested in establishing a uniform set of rules for running dog shows. At present, AKC recognizes 130 different breeds of dogs and maintains the studbook for each. A board of directors is responsible for its operation. The AKC registers about a million dogs each year, and is composed of almost 400 dog clubs throughout the United States. Each club elects a delegate who attends the annual meetings of the AKC. The delegates are the legislative body of the AKC, making the rules and electing directors from among their number.

More than 8,000 competitive events are licensed and held under AKC rules each year. These include dog shows, field trials, obedience trials, tracking tests, and hunting retriever tests.

The club publishes a monthly magazine, *Pure-Bred Dogs/American Kennel Gazette* (called merely "The Gazette" by dog people). This magazine contains breed columns, photos of show winners, informative and useful articles, and advertising. Another magazine is the *American Kennel Club Show, Obedience and Field Trial Awards*, which reports only show and trial results.

Litters and individual dogs are registered through the AKC, which also keeps stud books, furnishes pedigrees for a fee, and publishes rules and regulations for AKC licensed events, licenses judges, and performs other regulatory activities.

UNITED KENNEL CLUB

The United Kennel Club, founded by Chauncey Zachariah Bennett in 1898, has an entirely different orientation from that of the AKC, which concentrates on the showing of dogs. The UKC from its outset has accentuated the need for maintaining working qualities and breed standards that complement those qualities.

The UKC is this country's second largest and second oldest registry for purebred dogs; it is headquartered at 100 East Kilgore, Kalamazooo, Michigan 49001. It registers ninety breeds including six basic American coonhound breeds; Black and Tan, Redbone, English, Plott, Bluetick, and Treeing Walker. Also among the various breeds registered are the Toy Fox Terrier, the American Water Spaniel, the English and Australian Shepherd, the American Eskimo, and the American Pit Bull Terrier (which is registered with AKC as American Staffordshire Terrier.)

When you buy a puppy which is eligible for registration with the UKC, you will receive a pedigree from the kennel club when you register him rather than from the breeder or from ordering it. UKC is the sole registrar of PR Purple Ribbon bred bloodlines. Having the ''PR'' Seal in front of a dog's name is a guarantee of purebred status. It signifies that at least all the dogs of the last six generations (126 dogs) are purebred and that all fourteen of the ancestors in the last three generations are on file at UKC's office with their own UKC registration numbers.

There is a major difference between the UKC and the AKC pedigrees. Since its beginning, the UKC has maintained a policy on the practice of inbreeding and insists on no common ancestors in the pedigree for at least the first three generations back. If there is any inbreeding (mother to son, father to daughter, brother to sister) in the pedigree, UKC will stamp ''Inbred'' on the dog's UKC registration certificate. On the other hand, the AKC and breeders of AKC registered dogs do not consider ancestors three generations back as inbred, but linebred. In other words, breeders of AKC registered dogs *want* to see one or more common ancestor within the first three generations behind the puppy, and the UKC does not. The pros and cons on both sides could be endlessly debated but are merely stated here to show the differences in the two national kennel clubs.

The UKC publishes three magazines: *Coonhound Bloodlines, Bloodlines* and *Hunting Retriever.* It registers over 200,000 dogs each year in all fifty states and about a dozen foreign countries. Information about the breeds it registers can be obtained by writing to the United Kennel Club. The UKC recognizes 1200 clubs and licenses more than 5,000 purebred dog events each year in forty-four states and Canada.

OTHER REGISTRIES

Another national all-breed club, the States Kennel Club, was formed in 1987 to promote the interests of purebred dogs in conformation showing as well as working events.

The Chase, Lexington, Kentucky, publishes the *International Foxhunter's Studbook*, a registry for Foxhounds, and there are several other magazine agencies which register various breeds of hunting hounds. Among these other registries are several coonhound registries: United Coon Hunters of America, Inc., Professional Kennel Club, National Kennel Club, and World Coon Hunters Association.

The American Field Publishing Co. (*Field Dog Studbook*), is a registry for pointers and setters used in field sports and also registers other recognized breeds, mostly sporting breeds.

In addition, many miscellaneous and rare breeds have their own studbooks and registeries with their national organizations.

CANADIAN KENNEL CLUB

The Canadian Kennel Club (CKC), 89 Skyway Avenue, Etobicoke, Ontario, Canada M9W 6R4, has been in existence since September 27, 1988. It was founded in London, Ontario, with the objectives of promoting the breeding and exhibiting of purebred dogs, formulating rules governing dog shows, approving suitable judges, and opening a register for the recording of purebred dogs. The CKC was incorporated under the Livestock Pedigree Act on April 15, 1915 as a Record Association which is part of the Canadian National Livestock Record system under the Ministry of Agriculture. The CKC currently registers about 70,000 individual dogs a year and licenses about 400 dog shows. They register most of the breeds that the American Kennel Club recognizes plus a few native to Canada.

There is a difference in the types of membership between the American and Canadian Kennel Clubs. The AKC has member clubs that send their delegates to annual meetings where the delegates elect the board member and officers. The Canadian Kennel Club has individual members who control the management of the club. The types of CKC memberships are: Associate (people who have paid their fees and been elected to membership by the board but who are not entitled to vote), Ordinary (people who have been associate members for three years prior to payment of the ordinary membership fee), Non-resident (people who reside outside Canada and are elected to membership but who cannot vote or hold office), and Life (people who have been members in good standing for thirty continuous years).

The ordinary members elect the officers and board of directors. These are non-salaried positions. The administrative staff (which includes the secretary-treasurer) is salaried. There are approximately 18,000 members. With the membership fee comes a subscription to *Dogs in Canada*, a monthly magazine which contains an official section of all club business, calendar of events, show and trial results, breed articles, and advertising. In addition to dog shows, the CKC licenses field trials, working certificate tests, obedience trials, tracking tests, lure coursing trials, and dog sled trials.

The only major difference in registration between the CKC and the AKC is that the Canadian club offers a Non-Breeding Agreement so that breeders can sell puppies to be registered as "not to be bred." One copy of the agreement goes to the Canadian Kennel Club, one to the new puppy owner, and one is kept by the breeder. If the dog is later used for breeding, the owner must pay the seller a liquidation fee, which is stated in the contract. Also, any progeny of this dog cannot be registered with the CKC.

JOINING A LOCAL KENNEL CLUB

There are two kinds of kennel clubs on the local level: all-breed and specialty. All-breed clubs may be actual members of the AKC or they may operate according to the AKC regulations, holding AKC sanctioned matches and licensed point shows. All-breed clubs may be oriented specifically to conformation showing, but most also have obedience activities. There are also dog training clubs which concentrate only on obedience work for all breeds of dogs. Specialty clubs are usually regional in nature and are associated with the national clubs of a particular breed. These clubs are dedicated to the improvement and promotion of one breed only. The national specialty breed clubs are members of the American Kennel Club and are called "parent" clubs.

Canada has both all-breed and specialty clubs just as we do here in the United States. The UKC doesn't have local all-breed clubs but there are both national and regional specialty clubs for Toy Fox Terriers, American Eskimos, and American Pit Bull Terriers, plus the national associations for the different coonhound breeds and regional coon hunters associations.

There are advantages to both types of clubs. An all-breed kennel club gives you the opportunity to meet owners of different breeds of dogs and to learn more about other breeds. My husband and I have been members of an all-breed kennel club for the past ten years. I am amazed sometimes at how much we have learned about dogs by being around other breeds and learning from their owners. In a specialty club you meet people who have the same breed of dog as you. We started with a breed specialty club and years later joined an all-breed

Walking is healthy and fun for dog and owner. Afghan puppy. *Photo by Dode Avila.*

club, but I doubt that we would ever have learned as much about our breed of dog had we not first become members of the regional breed club.

All the efforts of a specialty club are centered on that one breed. You learn the standard backwards and forwards, all phases of grooming, showing, breeding and whelping, and raising puppies of your breed. If you want to gain a really thorough knowledge of the particular breed that you have chosen, there is no substitute for a specialty club.

How do you find out about these clubs? Here we go again. . .ask someone involved with dogs—veterinarian, kennel owner, dog groomer, or the breeder from whom you bought your dog. Contact the AKC (CKC in Canada). Call the local newspaper as they may have news bulletins from the clubs. Go to a dog show or match sponsored by the local club—officers and members will probably be there. You will also be able to pick up printed material with a list of officers and the phone number of the secretary. I'm sure you will find club members eager to talk to you about the club, its meetings and activities. If you are enrolled in an obedience training class, the instructor will probably give you information about the local obedience or dog training clubs.

Once you find out where and when the club meets, visit once or twice to see if you like the people and *want* to become a member. Most clubs require new members to attend two meetings after they apply for membership. The club wants to look *you* over, too. Most clubs also require that you have one or two sponsors. If you don't already know a member to sponsor you, you will meet people who will, so long as they perceive you to be a person to be really interested in dogs and in becoming active. You don't have to be a breeder or exhibitor in order to become a member of a kennel club. I have even known members of clubs who didn't have dogs anymore, but who were people who, when younger, were very active and still enjoy the old friends and the meetings.

Most kennel clubs are open for membership to any sincere person who owns a purebred dog and wants to join. However, there are some clubs which have a closed membership and are difficult to get into. Even in this day and age there are a few kennel clubs that exclude women from membership. If you run up against either of these types of clubs, at least you have been forewarned as to their existence. Don't give up! There really aren't that many exclusive clubs. Whenever I find out that a club has a "men only" membership, I stop attending their shows and encourage other women to follow suit.

One of the purposes of a kennel club is to hold matches and shows. An obedience club's purpose is to hold obedience matches and trials as well as training. The local kennel club is responsible for all the many details and planning that go into holding those matches, shows and classes. But this is not the sole purpose of a kennel club. It must also promote purebred dogs and further their advancement and it should serve as a bridge between the community and doggie people, educating the general public to better understand their goals and purposes.

You may find that your area club has not yet attained the status required to hold licensed point shows but is still working up to it by holding sanctioned matches. It is a rather long procedure to attain this status. The club has to learn how to do it just as a novice dog handler learns—by stages. The club has to prove to the national kennel club that it has the knowledge and experience. If you join a specialty club before it has attained this status, you will be helping them to gain it by working with the other members to hold successful matches. As we all know, there is a lot of satisfaction in working toward a goal and finally attaining it.

Both all-breed and specialty kennel clubs are encouraged to include obedience in their matches and their point shows, and to offer obedience training for members. Many clubs offer both obedience classes and conformation handling classes, either to the general public or exclusively to club members.

Obedience classes may include both Novice and Advanced Obedience. Fees are competitive with local obedience schools or privately taught classes, but will vary according to the section of the country in which you live.

Once you join a kennel club, get involved and participate in as many of the activities as you can. Clubs need active members, and by pitching in, you can make good friends while learning. There are committees for everything: programs for meetings, publicity, refreshments, shows, matches, obedience and conformation handling. For the actual shows there are more committees: trophies, ring stewards, hospitality, publicity, building and grounds, catalog sales, parking, booth space, and advertising.

When the club's first match show comes up, volunteer to work on one of the committees. Since a match is practice for the point show, this is the place to get your feet wet by learning the workings of a club and showing. Obedience clubs and field trial clubs have sanctioned matches as well as their licensed trials; so if you join one of these clubs, you will have the same type of opportunity to learn in a practice atmosphere before committing to the real thing.

Shorthaired Pointer and owner. *Photo by Betty Nagle.*

Shows and
Obedience Trials

5

UNDERSTANDING AND ENJOYING CONFORMATION

If you have already attended dog shows and been disappointed by them, perhaps you didn't really understand what was going on. I experienced the same thing at the first dog show I attended, which happened to be in Germany. I didn't understand much about the show and the only dog I remember was one on exhibition. He was called a Bismarck Hound and had belonged to Hermann Goering, infamous Nazi and right-hand man of Adolph Hitler. I remember the dog as a very large one, the size of a Great Dane, but more muscular and stockily built. From that day to this I have never heard of another Bismarck Hound, but that is the only feature of the show that stuck in my mind. Had I known beforehand what shows were all about, I would have enjoyed the show much more—and so will you.

With few exceptions, dog shows include both the conformation (or breed) rings and obedience rings all in one arena. No matter what the registry or sponsor, the conformation show tests how closely each dog of a breed conforms to that breed's Standard of Perfection. Obedience trials test each dog's performance against working standards of the trial. *(See Chapter 6.)* These shows and trials are open to all registered dogs of the licensing kennel club or association. Every breed participates in the all-breed conformation shows and the owners represent every occupation in the country. The handlers will include owners who want to enjoy their dogs and maybe win a few ribbons, serious breeders who want to prove the quality of their stock in competition, and professional handlers who make a living showing dogs for others. It is very easy to "get hooked" on showing your dog—to the point that it becomes many people's weekend recreation to the exclusion of all other sports or hobbies. Participation in this sport is much more fun than sitting on the sidelines or in front of a television set watching someone else engaging in a sport.

When selecting your first dog show to attend, choose one that is held at a fairground or other outside location so you can plan a picnic lunch for the entire family and perhaps find it more enjoyable to have more to do than just watch classes. Of course, the inherent disadvantages of outdoor shows may convince you to go for the indoor variety. At an outdoor show the rings are sometimes rather far apart. There might be three on one side of the exhibition buildings, four in another part of the fairgrounds and maybe a couple more inside another building. And if it rains, things can get pretty messy, but the show will not be cancelled; dog show people and their dogs are real troupers.

The advantages of attending an inside show are that it may be in a convention center, a college gymnasium, or a large exhibition center. In cold weather there is heat; in hot weather there is air-conditioning. You can be sure that you will be comfortable. Usually, the rings are all on one floor. If there are two levels, there will be rings on both levels. In gymnasiums, there is tier seating so you can have an overall view or move to another seat to get a better view of one particular ring.

Whether you will be showing or merely attending a show, to find out what shows are coming up in your area you may write to a show Superintendent (see Appendix) in your area and request premium lists for shows in whichever cities you wish to try. The premium list will have all the information about where, when, directions, cost to enter, where to send the entry, the date entries close, the actual entry forms, the judging panel, and what prizes are offered by whom. The AKC also publishes lists of upcoming shows and judging panels and the name of the superintendent or show secretary. Shows are also listed in *Dog World* Magazine, which may be bought at newsstands and bookstores.

AMERICAN KENNEL CLUB SHOWS

For over 100 years the AKC has held shows to promote purebred dogs and provide a regulated arena for breeders to prove the breeding quality of their stock against others of their breed. AKC dog shows are held throughout the year all over the country. They are usually scheduled for weekends but sometimes include Friday and Monday as well. Hardly anyone lives so far from a dog show location that he can't get to one. Shows are held in hot weather, cold weather, rain, snow, sleet, and under threat of tornadoes. The all-breed shows range in size from 800 up to 2,000 or more dogs.

Most shows these days are unbenched, which means that the dogs do not have to remain for the entire day on benches but may be taken directly from a car or van into the ring, or may sit most of the day in a crate in a gooming area until the time for judging. If you are lucky enough to attend a benched show (there are still a very few held), you can see all the breeds on their benches and learn a lot more. Very large benched shows are 2-day events where half the dogs will be benched and shown one day and the rest the next. Exhibitors' and judges' attire are more formal than at unbenched shows.

Regardless of the type of show you attend, plan to spend the whole day and take the family. Wear comfortable clothes and shoes as you will be on your feet a lot looking at dogs being groomed, maybe taking pictures of some, and walking from one ring to another. If you have small children, make sure that they don't frighten the dogs or step on their toes (a lame dog can't compete). Many families attend both inside and outside shows, sometimes backpacking babies or pushing strollers, and have a very pleasant day.

By spending the whole day, you will learn about dog shows from start to finish. Get there early (around 8 or 9 a.m.), watch as many of the rings as you can, watch the Group judging, and do stay for Best in Show. (Leaving before Best in Show is chosen is like attending a beauty pageant and leaving before the queen is crowned.) Make sure that you see the judging of your own breed (if you have one) or at least of the ones that appeal to you.

The cost of taking in a show, even with a family, won't be as much as going out for dinner or a movie. Admission averages from $1.50 to $3, although the fee may be higher depending on the area and site of the show, and you may have to pay to park the car.

Once inside, buy a catalog so you will be sure to see the classes important to you. The catalogs are organized by Group and contain alphabetical listings by breed of all dogs entered in the show with the number (which will be on the handler's armband), dog's name, class in which he is entered, name and address of owner, breeder's name, and the names of the dog's sire and dam. There is a space at the bottom of the listing of all dogs (males), and at the bottom of the listing of all bitches and lastly at the end of the breed listing (after Best of Breed Competition) for marking the number of the Winners, Reserve Winners, Best of Breed, Best of Opposite Sex, and Best of Winners. At the beginning of the catalog or in the very back, there will be a scale of points for the particular area of the country where the show is being held. (Points vary for the different breeds in different regions.) The United States is divided into nine sections for the forty-eight contiguous states; Alaska, Hawaii, and Puerto Rico have their own schedules.

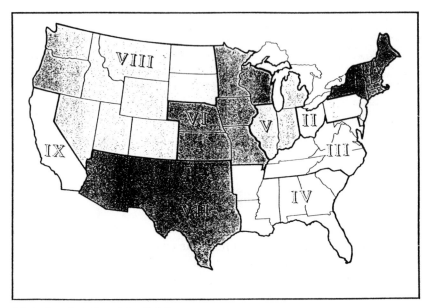

Map showing the nine divisions.

SCHEDULE OF POINTS FOR DIVISION 1 - EFFECTIVE MAY 15, 1989

Division 1 is comprised of: Maine, New Hampshire, Vermont, Massachusetts, Rhode Island, Connecticut, New York.

D = Dog B = Bitches	1 Point		2 Points		3 Points		4 Points		5 Points	
	D	B	D	B	D	B	D	B	D	B
Brittanys	2	2	4	6	6	10	8	14	12	20
Pointers	2	2	3	4	5	6	6	7	7	9
Pointers (German Shorthaired)	2	3	5	8	9	13	13	17	19	24
Pointers (German Wirehaired)	2	2	3	3	4	5	5	6	6	8
Retrievers (Chesapeake Bay)	2	2	3	4	5	6	6	7	8	9
Retrievers (Flat-Coated)	2	2	3	3	4	5	6	7	10	12
Retrievers (Golden)	5	5	12	13	19	22	26	30	40	45
Retrievers (Labrador)	4	5	10	12	16	20	20	30	28	48
Setters (English)	2	2	4	5	7	9	11	14	18	23
Setters (Gordon)	2	2	4	4	6	7	8	9	12	14
Setters (Irish)	2	2	5	8	9	14	19	23	37	39
Spaniels (Cocker), Solid Color, Black, including Black and Tan	2	2	4	7	6	12	10	17	18	26

Comparison of points for Divisions 1 and 9.

SCHEDULE OF POINTS FOR DIVISION 9 - EFFECTIVE MAY 15, 1989

State of California

D = Dog　　B = Bitches	1 Point		2 Points		3 Points		4 Points		5 Points	
	D	B	D	B	D	B	D	B	D	B
Brittanys	2	2	7	6	12	11	17	15	25	23
Pointers	2	2	3	3	4	5	5	6	7	9
Pointers (German Shorthaired)	2	2	6	6	10	10	12	15	17	24
Pointers (German Wirehaired)	2	2	3	3	5	4	7	7	10	12
Retrievers (Chesapeake Bay)	2	2	3	5	5	8	6	11	9	17
Retrievers (Curly-Coated)	2	2	3	3	4	5	8	6	14	8
Retrievers (Flat-Coated)	2	2	3	3	5	5	6	6	9	8
Retrievers (Golden)	6	6	15	16	24	26	37	39	60	64
Retrievers (Labrador)	3	3	9	11	16	19	27	32	53	62
Setters (English)	2	2	7	8	12	15	20	24	34	41
Setters (Gordon)	2	2	3	4	5	6	6	8	9	13
Setters (Irish)	2	2	6	7	11	13	19	22	33	40
Spaniels (Clumber)	2	2	3	3	4	5	5	6	6	8
Spaniels (Cocker), Solid Color, Black, including Black and Tan	2	2	6	7	11	12	15	18	21	28

Comparison of points for Divisions 1 and 9.

Since the accumulation of points is what shows are all about, the more you understand about them, the more you will enjoy attending shows. The dogs are all competing to win points toward their championships; their goal is not to win the prizes that are offered in addition to points, although those are nice too. In addition to competing for points, the owners are proving the breed quality of their dogs. Fifteen points must be accumulated to acquire a championship. The possible points range from one to five and the show schedule will tell you how many dogs or bitches have to be entered AND EXHIBITED in order for the show to offer a one, two, three, four or five points for that particular breed. When only enough dogs compete to make one or two points for a breed, it is called a "minor". Major points are three to five. To become a champion, a dog (meaning here either male or female) must accumulate the fifteen points with at least two shows being major for its breed or sex. These two majors must be under two different judges to count toward the championship. A dog may win three points twice under the same judge, but he will still need another major win (three to five points) under another judge. The balance of the points must also be under one or more different judges than the ones who gave the dog the major wins. It is conceivable that a dog could win his championship in three shows, if the entries in his breed were large enough so he could take five points at each show under three different judges. This doesn't often happen.

There are other ways that a dog can take more points than shown in the schedule of points, such as a class dog winning over a champion to take Best of Breed or Best of Opposite Sex, or winning first in Group from the classes, or taking Best of Winners and being awarded the same number of points of the opposite sex if that sex had higher points. This may seem complicated at first, but the more you attend shows, the more familiar it will become. In the meantime, let me give you one easy example.

Our Irish Terrier bitch was six months old (the youngest age a dog can be shown) the day of her first show. Since there was no competition in her class, she could not earn any points. However, a champion bitch was entered in the Best of Breed competition. A dog that was shown in the classes won Best of Breed and our bitch won Best of Opposite Sex over the champion bitch. Therefore, according to the rules, our bitch was entitled to one point, as the champion counted as the second bitch in competition—but only because she was defeated.

In addition to the show catalog, a judging program will help you to better understand what is going on. Occasionally, the judging program is printed in the front of the catalog. If not, the judging programs (which are usually free) can probably be found at the table or booth where the catalogs are being sold. If you can't locate one, ask. This program gives the time, ring number, and judge's name for each breed to be judged, and the number of entries in each breed. The total number is to the left, then comes the name of the breed and after that, three numbers. The first one is the number of dogs, the second the number of bitches, and the third is how many Specials are entered for Best of Breed competition. (Specials are the champions competing only for Best of Breed so that they can go on to the Group competition.)

Once you know what time your breed is going to be shown and in which ring, find that ring ahead of the time you will need to be there. Breeds are judged in the order listed. Your breed will not be judged until judging of all the breeds scheduled earlier has been completed. Thus, it may be later than the scheduled time before a breed enters the ring; according to AKC rules it cannot be judged earlier than the scheduled hour. This can be more difficult than you may think since they aren't always set up in numerical order and the quickest route may be to simply ask someone. Once you have located the ring, you can relax and stroll around looking at the different breeds being groomed or watch some of the dogs already being judged in the ring. You may want to locate and talk to some exhibitors of your breed where they are grooming. However, if it is getting close to show time, you can expect the handlers to be very busy and tense with little inclination to conversation. Don't be offended if you are asked to come back later. There will be time to talk after the judging is over.

Return to your ring well ahead of the time scheduled for the judging of your breed. There will be spectators' chairs alongside the ring, which has an opening for the exhibitors and dogs to enter and exit. If you get to ringside just before the end of the class that precedes yours, you will be in time to grab a chair as soon as it is vacated. If you will be attending an outdoor show, take along folding lawn chairs so you will be sure of a seat.

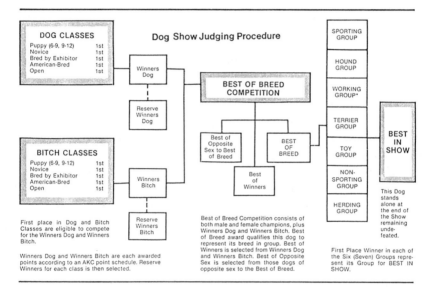

Judging procedure from classes through best in show.

The Classes

Once seated, take out your catalog—it will detail the order of events for this day, this ring, this show. The chart illustrates the progression of the judging from the classes up to Best in Show. All the breeds have the same classes. (The only exception to this would be a Specialty Club that is using its classes as a Specialty Show. In that case, there would be extra classes, such as Veterans Class, Stud Dog Class, Brood Bitch Class.) Dogs (males) always go first, then the bitches (females).

First, you will see the 6- to 9-month-old Puppy Dog Class; next will be the 9- to 12-month-old Puppy Dog Class. If a puppy is nine months old the day of the show, he must be entered in 9- to 12-month class. If he is a year old that day, he can no longer be entered in a Puppy Class and must go in one of the others. There will not necessarily be entries in every class that is offered and sometimes the Puppy Dog and Puppy Bitch classes are not divided, so all puppies from six months up to one year are shown in the same class.

After the Puppy Class will be the Novice Dog Class, which means the *dog* is a novice, not the handler; although both may be. Novice Class is for beginning dogs, so when a dog has won Novice Class three times (or has won any other class once), he may no longer compete in Novice. Next is Bred-by-Exhibitor Dog Class. The dog must be shown by the person who bred or co-bred the dog and still owns him, or by a member of the family. If the Bred-by-Exhibitor dog wins Best of Breed, he can be handled by anyone for Group competition. Next is the American-Bred Dog Class, which is for any dog born in the United States.

Next are the Open Dog Classes. These may be divided by color so that in any Open Class only dogs of the same color compete. In Collies and Shetland Sheepdogs you might have Open Sable, Open Blue, and Open Black, or you might have Open Sable and Open Any Other Allowed Color (merles, tri-colors, bi-blues or bi-blacks). In every class the dog has to be six months old on or before the day of the show, and no dog can be neutered or spayed.

In every class the judge will follow the same procedure, although this procedure will vary according to the judge's preference. A ring steward helps the judge and when it is time for judging, the ring steward gets everyone into the ring, checking off each exhibitor's armband number against the number in the catalog. So, the first class of 6- to 9-month puppy dogs are all in the ring lined up along the mat. The judge may go up and down the line looking them over, then go back to the front of the line and ask all of the handlers and their dogs to gait around the circle. When they have circled the ring once or twice, he stops them and begins to examine the first dog. Smaller breeds are judged on tables. The judge checks the dog's bite or asks the handler to show it to him. He goes over the dog, feeling his structure, checking coat texture, shoulder layback, rear angulation, length of tail, and checking males for both testicles. (If a puppy dog doesn't have both testicles down, the judge is required to dismiss him from the ring.) The judge will also pay a lot of attention to the head and ears. After he has finished his hands-on inspection, he will probably step back to get another overall look at the dog before asking the handler to gait the dog around the ring in either a triangle or L pattern. (See diagrams.)

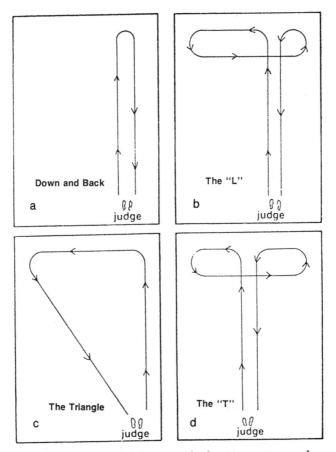

Most judges use one of these standard gaiting patterns when evaluting dogs individually.

Either pattern will give the judge a view of the complete dog— right and left, from the rear and front. Once the dog and handler are back before the judge, either the handler or the judge will "bait" the dog to get a reaction from him so the judge can see his expression. At this point the judge thanks the handler and again watches as the pair go away from him around the ring to the end of the line. When

The author receiving the Best of Opposite Sex award with her Irish Terrier, Barra Mrs. Calabash. *Booth photo.*

the judge has inspected and gaited each individual dog, he may have them all gait around the ring together again for one last look. Finally he will pick his first, second, third and fourth place winners.

This process is repeated in each and every class. When all the males (dogs) have competed and there is a first place winner for every class, these will go back into the ring to compete for Winners Dog. During this competition, since the judge has already gone over all the dogs individually, he will have them all go around the ring once or twice, may go back to one or two to check some detail, then choose his winner. It is a matter of the judge's style as to how he announces the winner—some will be quite flamboyant, others very matter-of-fact. But, rest assured, there will be a choice.

Once the Winners Dog has been selected, the judge must determine the Reserve Winners Dog. The reason for this is that if for some reason the Winners Dog is disqualified, the Reserve Winner will then get the points. The dogs remaining in the ring compete for Reserve Winners Dog, but there is also one more dog allowed to compete. Whatever class the Winners Dog is from, the dog that placed second in that class comes back into the ring to compete. A Reserve is important especially when the win is a major, because so many dogs are competing and when a dog takes a major reserve win, he is on the way to taking the points at future shows—maybe even the next one. Once the judge has selected the Reserve Dog and given him a ribbon, the dog classes are over and the bitch classes begin. They are exactly the same as for the dogs.

After the Winners Bitch and Reserve Winner have been selected, the competition progresses to Best of Breed. The two Winners and any champions in the breed that are competing for Best of Breed come into the ring. Usually the champions line up in front with the Winners Dog and Winners Bitch in the rear. The judge will have them all go around in a circle once or twice, then he will examine each of the champions individually as he has not seen them until now. He might be familiar with some of these dogs from previous shows, but he has to satisfy himself as to what condition the dog is in today. After the examinations, the judge will usually have all the dogs go around again as he points to his Best of Breed, then the Best of Winners and finally the Best of Opposite Sex. If the Best of Breed is a champion bitch, then a dog will be chosen as Best of Opposite Sex. This could be a champion dog or it could be a Winners Dog. Sometimes, the Winners Dog or Winners Bitch takes Best of Breed over the Specials. When this happens, the Winners Dog or Winners Bitch is automatically Best of Winners since only those two compete for Best of Winners. Sometimes, there are no champions competing for Best of Breed. In that case, the Winners Dog or Winners Bitch will be chosen as Best of Breed *and* Best of Winners, with the other Best of Opposite Sex.

After Breed judging is over, the Best of Breed winner in each breed stays until Group judging starts. This takes place later in the day as all the breeds in a group must be judged before the Group classes can start. American Kennel Club shows are divided into seven different groups—Group 1) Sporting Dogs; Group 2) Hounds; Group 3) Working Dogs; Group 4) Terriers; Group 5) Toy Dogs; Group 6) Non-

Sporting Dogs; and Group 7) Herding Dogs. Announcements will be made to inform exhibitors and spectators where a particular Group will be competing. Basically, the judge will follow his previous procedures to determine his Group winner, but with each level the competition gets stiffer and more exciting for the spectators.

Miscellaneous Classes

The exception to the breed classes which progress from Breed winners to Group to Best in Show is the Miscellaneous Class. Here, no points are awarded. These classes are open to new, rare or unapproved purebred dogs which the AKC designates from time to time. As of July 1989 the breeds are Australian Kelpies, Border Collies, Cavalier King Charles Spaniels, Miniature Bull Terriers, Spinoni Italiani, and the Petit Basset Griffon Vendeen. The dog's owner must obtain an Indefinite Listing Privilege showing the dog is purebred from the AKC and this ILP number is given on the entry form. The Miscellaneous breeds are exhibited together in a single class, but there may be a division by sex. First through fourth place ribbons are given, but there is no further competition and no championship points are awarded.

Best in Show Competition

When the Groups have been judged, there will be only seven Group winners left to compete for Best in Show from a thousand or more in competition that day. The ring steward calls them into the ring, and they will all gait around the ring while the spectators applaud; then the judge goes over and gaits each dog individually. He may have them go around again in a circle as he points out one and calls, "Best in Show." What excitement, what applause, especially if the winner is a favorite of the spectators and other exhibitors. What a happy handler and owner. The king or queen has been chosen, but instead of a crown receives a large red, white and blue rosette and a valuable prize. Another AKC dog show has wound to a close, and we can all go home, tired but ready to do it again.

AKC SPECIALTY SHOWS

Specialty shows licensed by the American Kennel Club are run just like all-breed shows except that only one breed is entered and, therefore, there will be no Group or Best in Show judging. A specialty show runs at a more leisurely pace than an all-breed show. The judge goes over the dogs much more carefully. You may notice the judge talking into a tape recorder after going over each dog. This is for a judge's critique which will be typed up and published in the specialty club's newsletter. Extra classes may be offered—Junior Dog and Junior Bitch for dogs and bitches a year old and up to eighteen months, Brace Class, Stud Dog Class, Brood Bitch Class, Veteran Dog and Veteran Bitch Class. Specialty shows also have a Puppy Sweepstakes for 6- to 9, 9- to 12, and 12- to 18-month old puppies, and a Best in Sweeps puppy is chosen.

There are regional and national specialties, at which a huge number of dogs of a breed are seen. Sometimes, several area specialty clubs will hold a combined specialty. If you go to a specialty show, you will see some of the well-known local and regional champions as well as some from across the country. This is a wonderful chance to learn more about your breed, see how it is groomed for show, and have an opportunity to meet a cross-section of breeders and exhibitors. National Specialty shows are a social and educational gathering as well, with seminars, educational programs, banquets, and other social activities. All specialty shows are listed in both the *Gazette* and *Dog World* with the name of the secretary to contact for a premium list.

How To Get Started at Showing Your Dog

If you are interested in showing your dog, write to the AKC for the booklet called *Rules Applying to Registration and Dog Shows*. Single copies are sent out at no charge. Read it carefully.

From personal experience I recommend that the first time you exhibit, do so close to home. I will never forget what happened to us when we entered a show with our Sheltie bitch, Lacey. In preparation for the big event, we had gone to matches. Then we entered her in two shows in New Orleans, quite a drive from Houston. The first show was a big specialty and the next day was the all-breed show. We would be spending two nights away from home. . .and I forgot our clothes! Fortunately, I had remembered the tack box with the grooming equipment. But the clothes we were to wear at the two shows and banquet were left hanging in their vinyl bag on the closet door. By the time I discovered that the clothes weren't with us, we were halfway to New Orleans. So, distressing as it was, we went through the whole weekend with the casual clothes we had on our backs.

AKC SANCTIONED MATCHES AND FUN MATCHES

If you really want to practice showing your dog or just want a chance to see more dogs up close and talk to owners and breeders in a less formal atmosphere where there are no championship points at stake, go to a match. AKC sanctioned matches are held all over the country by clubs that are either trying to qualify for having point shows or clubs which have one point show a year and one sanctioned match. These matches are the place for both handlers and dogs to learn by experience.

Matches especially are where puppies get their training in competition. Match judges are usually handlers or breeders who aspire to becoming licensed to judge point shows. So, they too are practicing. The match is informal; hardly anyone dresses up. Quite often you will find really good food at a match as the club members pitch in and contribute homemade pies, cakes, potato salad, and sandwiches to raise funds. Matches rarely make money; members just hope to break even and give everyone a good time and experience.

Classes are sometimes offered for puppies as young as 2- to 4 months, then 4- to 6, 6- to 9, and 9- to 12 months. The winners of each class may compete for Best Puppy and Best of Opposite Sex Puppy. The Best of Breed Puppy then goes on to compete in Puppy Group, and the Group winners compete for Best Puppy in Match. Showing puppies or watching them in matches can be *very* entertaining.

The classes for the adult dogs are usually just Open or Open and American-Bred. They progress as in a regular show to Group and Best in Match. There is not as much order to a match because entries don't close until shortly before the classes begin. The entry fees are considerably lower than the fees paid to enter a licensed point show.

Sometimes a local kennel club will advertise its match in the local newspaper for a couple of weeks before the match. Kennel clubs all receive notices of matches from other clubs in the general area; and a lot of individual flyers are sent out as all clubs keep mailing lists of people who have attended their shows or matches in the past. If someone tells you about a match coming up, all you really have to know is where it is being held, directions to get there, and the date and time entries close. Make your plans accordingly, have your dog clean and groomed, get there early and file your entry form. After taking care of this business, you will be able to watch others who have the same breed as you grooming their dogs and most of them will be glad to give you tips. In short, matches are a great way to get your feet wet and find out whether your dog is of good enough conforma-

A Japanese Shiba Inu competes at a rare breed show. *Photo courtesy Elaine Wishnow.*

tion to show. Besides that, you will find out if you will *like* this sport of showing dogs.

"A" matches sometimes require pre-entry with a closing date prior to the date of the show. Another type of match popular in some areas is for drop-in "practice only." Dogs are exhibited in "classes" according to puppy or adult but not divided by breed—in other words you may see puppies of six different breds in the ring at once—all learning ring procedure and experiencing the atmosphere and routine of a show, but not actually being judged. No ribbons are awarded.

UKC CONFORMATION SHOWS

The United Kennel Club licensed shows are specialties except for some all-hound bench shows held in conjunction with field trials and night hunts. The objective is the same as the AKC's—evaluation of breeding stock. The American Eskimo, American Pit Bull Terrier, and Toy Fox Terrier associations hold national and regional specialty shows, often in conjunction with obedience trials that are open to other breeds. (See Appendix for complete listing of UKC registered breeds.) The dogs entered in these shows must be registered with the United Kennel Club, be six months old by the day of the show, and unaltered.

The schedule of points to become a UKC champion is entirely different from the one used for AKC shows, but the classes are generally the same as an AKC specialty show except for a difference in designation of ages and sex. Whereas AKC uses the term ''dog'' and ''bitch,'' the UKC uses ''male'' and ''female.''

The classes are the same for males and females:

Puppy Class—6 months and under one year

Junior Class—1 year and under 2 years

Senior Class—2 years and under 3 years

Veterans Class—3 years and over

Best Male (or Female) of Show—This class is composed of first place winners of all the above classes.

Only the Best Female of Show and Best Male of Show compete for Best of Show.

The United Kennel Club has an additional competition called the ''Champion of Champions'' Class which is made up of UKC recognized male and female champions that compete against each other in the same ring at the same time. The winner is the Champion of Champions. The champions are competing for the title of Grand Champion. There may also be a class for grand champions to compete against each other for Grand Champion of Show; however, this class is usually offered only at a large national show.

A total of 100 points is required to earn the title of UKC Champion. Ten points are awarded to the winners of each sex in the Puppy, Junior, Senior and Veterans classes. The Best Male and Best Female of Show each wins fifteen points and the Best of Show winner gets another ten points. Thus the total number of UKC points possible at one show is thirty-five. It follows that it would take a minimum of three shows to make champion. In order to earn the title of Grand Champion (the highest conformation title UKC awards), a dog must win three Champion of Champions classes under three different judges. In order for a Champion of Champions class to be held, there must be an entry (pre-entered) of five champions and a minimum of three present and exhibited at the show.

In the matter of entries, UKC conformation shows differ from those of the AKC. Dogs competing in the Champion of Champions Class working toward the title of Grand Champion must be pre-entered; others can be. If there are not enough entries present to hold the class, the entry fees are refunded. All other classes can be entered the day of the show (as in an AKC sanctioned match) or can be pre-entered. Usually, registration is taken for a couple of hours in the morning and entries close anywhere from a half-hour to an hour before official showtime.

Quite often two back-to-back shows on a Saturday and Sunday are sponsored by the same club. Sometimes, two different breeds will sponsor shows at the same site. Since these are specialty shows, most of them also hold non-licensed events for fun and experience for novice handlers, young puppies, and inexperienced dogs. These events may include Junior Handling, Junior and Adult Handling, Movement, Stud Dog Class, Brood Bitch Class, Bred-by-Exhibitor, Puppy Classes 0- to 3 months and 3- to 6 months, or a Puppy Match for 2- to 4 months and 4- to 6 months. These fun classes are held before the licensed classes begin.

Just as in AKC shows, ribbons, rosettes and trophies plus championship points are awarded. However, all entries must present their UKC registration paper, three-generation pedigree, proof of rabies and DHLP-Parvo vaccination, and sometimes a fifteen-day health certificate at the registration desk.

UKC bench shows for Coonhounds have the same classes as the conformation shows for the other three breeds; however, they are held in conjunction with hunts. (See Chapter 14.) To become a champion, a Coonhound must have 100 points plus at least one Best Male or Best Female of Show and the points must be earned under two different judges. If there is a night hunt on a Saturday night, the bench show will be on Saturday afternoon. If it is a two-day event, there will be a night hunt one night, the bench show the next afternoon followed by another hunt.

The six breeds that compete in the Coonhounds competition are American Black and Tan Coonhound, Bluetick Coonhound, English Coonhound, Plott Hound, Redbone Hound, and the Treeing Walker

Hound. The hound bench shows work a little like the AKC all-breed shows in that after each breed's Best Male of Breed and Best Female of Breed are selected, they compete against the other winners of their sex for Best Male and Best Female of Show. There is usually a Champion of Champions Class and sometimes a Grand Champions Class (although this class is mostly found at the two big events of the year: Autumn Oaks and the World Show). At bench shows for these two

This German Shepherd Dog and handler are obviously professionals in the dog show game. *McKinney photo.*

events, a National Grand Show Champion is selected; grand champions only compete for this honor.

The best source of information about these shows is the UKC official magazine, *Bloodlines*. The conformation shows for UKC breeds are fully advertised. The ads serve as premium lists and detail all pertinent information. (See Appendix.) For showing or hunting any of the coonhound breeds, the magazine you will want is *Coonhound Bloodlines* at the same address. Both magazines list results of shows, names of new champions and grand champions, much useful information, and contain helpful articles.

GLOSSARY OF TERMS

AOAC	Any other allowed color, class division.
AOC	Any other color, class division.
ASCOB	Any solid color other than black, class division.
Benched and unbenched shows	Benched show requires all entered dogs to remain leashed on their show benches the day they are shown; unbenched show has no show benches; dogs may arrive at any time on show grounds and may be removed immediately after being shown.
Bitch	Female dog.
Bite	The dog's front teeth.
Conformation	The form and structure of a dog and how it conforms to its breed standard.
Dog	Male Dog.
Gait	Pattern of dogs footsteps—usually a walk or trot in the show ring.
Junior Puppy	A dog 12 months old but under 18 months the day of show.
Lead	Leash or all-in-one lead to lead the dog.
Mat	Long rubber mat on which the dog is gaited in the ring at indoor shows.
Pattern	The way the dog is gaited so the judge may see front, rear and sides of the dog.
Puppy	Dog which is 6 months old but under 12 months old.
Put down	In showing there are two meanings:
	1. The grooming, especially of terriers and poodles and
	2. In judging, not being put in the ribbons.
Put up	Placed as winner, or in the ribbons.
Ring stewards	People who run the rings for the judges.
Stack	Arrange the dog's legs and body so he is in the proper show pose. Some dogs walk into their stack.
Standard	Actually Standard of Perfection—the description of the ideal dog of each recognized breed. It serves as a word picture by which dogs are judged at shows.
Tack box	Box with snap-closed lid in which handler carries all the grooming supplies, leads, bait, etc. (or tack).

6

OBEDIENCE TRIALS

In the United States, obedience has been the fastest growing dog-related sport in this country. It is a sport which has caught on with the American public because of the challenge of training yourself and your dog to compete together as a team. The purpose of obedience trials is to demonstrate the usefulness of the purebred dog as a companion to man. In the process of the training required to do this, both owners and dogs find themselves enjoying each other more; the owner has the reward of an obedient dog that is a good canine citizen and a really pleasant member of the family. At dog shows which include obedience trials, the spectators at the obedience rings can be two and three deep. All different breeds compete, and you will hear people pulling for their own particular breed or perhaps for that awkward English Bulldog or for a tiny Chihuahua. But because obedience trials test both dog and human, a dog can turn in a good performance and have it all blown due to handler errors. The handler has to know his stuff, and the rules, just as much as the dog.

AMERICAN KENNEL CLUB OBEDIENCE TRIALS

Obedience was started in this country by Mrs. Helen Whitehouse Walker. In 1933, she proposed to the AKC that it hold obedience tests like those held in England. In October of that year, she organized the first all-breed obedience test at her estate in Mt. Kisco, New York. There were eight entries. In 1934, she introduced a tracking test. Also in that year, two AKC all-breed clubs held obedience tests. In the fall of 1935, she wrote, published, and submitted to the AKC a booklet entitled "Obedience Tests—Procedures for Judges, Handlers, and

Show Giving Clubs." In March 1936, the AKC officially recognized the sport, and obedience trials were off and running.

Not only did Mrs. Walker work hard for official recognition of obedience by the AKC, she also traveled 10,000 miles in 1937 with her poodles and trainer Blanche Saunders (who has written several books on obedience), giving exhibitions and talks to inform the general public about obedience. In that year, ninety-five dogs earned their Companion Dog titles; in 1982, more than 8,000 dogs earned that title. Mrs. Walker's contribution to the sport cannot be overestimated, for not only is obedience a marvelous sport enjoyed by thousands, but obedience classes help countless dog owners train their dogs to be good companions.

It is a fair assumption that every handler (professional or amateur) starts out in an obedience class of some kind. To go into competition all the things you and your dog have learned must be honed and perfected if your goal is to obtain a passing score. You will want to attend an obedience trial or two as a spectator to get an idea of just what you can expect when and if you decide to enter into competition. If you faithfully train yourself and your dog and learn the regulations so you won't make handler errors, you are sure to be rewarded, for obedience judging is objective as opposed to conformation showing in the breed ring where judges' decisions are subjective. In obedience, each handler and dog is scored exactly the same way; and each team has the same opportunity as every other one.

In addition, the sport of obedience allows for the handicapped handler to compete. Judges may modify the requirements of the obedience regulations to permit physically handicapped handlers just so long as they are able to move about the ring without physical assistance from another person. So people in wheelchairs can compete, and many are the cheers a handicapped person will hear when he and his dog qualify.

Obedience competition proceeds from one level to another. Each level is more difficult than the previous one. The first title to be earned is Companion Dog (CD) in the Novice classes; next is Companion Dog Excellent (CDX) in the Open classes; third is Utility Dog (UD) in the Utility classes. (The AKC obedience titles all follow the dog's registered name.)

The ultimate title is that of Obedience Trial Champion. When a dog achieves this title, it *precedes* his registered name as "OT Ch." Before a dog can compete for this title, he must attain a UD and win 100 points. Points are figured according to the number of competitors in a class at a trial and the dog's placement—first or second—in a class. The 100 points must include a first place in Utility with at least three dogs in competition; a first place in Open B with at least six dogs in competition; and another first place in either of these classes. The three wins must be under three different judges. Remember, the dog must already have attained the title of Utility Dog to compete for Obedience Trial Champion, so you can see how difficult it is to earn this title. However, every champion starts out the same way—at the bottom—and that is where you and your dog will begin.

Preparing for Competition—Novice Classes

The first step to take is to obtain the pamphlet "Obedience Regulations" from the AKC. Single copies are free. (See Appendix.) This booklet will give you all the details you will need to know. . .study it.

Your dog must be six months old and individually registered with the AKC before he can be entered in an obedience trial. He does not have to be a conformation show dog and he may be spayed or neutered. If you and your dog have attended obedience classes, you will have been exposed to all the exercises that are contained in the competitive Novice classes.

The Novice Class is divided into "A" and "B" divisions. Novice A is for dogs that have not earned a CD and handlers who have never handled a dog to a CD title. In addition the handler must own or co-own the dog or be a member of the owner's family. Novice B is for the novice dog being handled by an experienced owner or any other person, including a professional handler. In order to attain the Companion Dog title, the dog must achieve a qualifying score in three separate Novice trials (each called a leg) under three different judges.

The Novice exercises and the maximum scores are:

Heel on Leash and Figure 8	40 points
Stand for Examination	30 points
Heel Free	40 points
Recall	30 points
Long Sit	30 points
Long Down	30 points
Maximum Total Score	200 points

Perfect scores of 200 are the exception, but there are many scores as high as 198½, 199, and even 199½. A qualifying score is comprised of scores of more than fifty percent of the points in each exercise and a total score of at least 170 points. If the dog or handler scores a zero on any one of the six exercises, they cannot qualify in that trial. Examples of dog errors which will result in a zero are: lagging behind or forging ahead; not sitting straight; not standing for examination; sitting before or during the exam; or moving away from where he had been left on a stay. Also, if the handler guides the dog with the leash to correct lagging or forging, the *handler* is going to lose points.

The first four exercises are completed individually by each dog and handler. None of the exercises starts until the judge gives the command; none ends until the judge says, "Exercise finished." Only the first exercise is done on-leash; in all the others, the dog is off-leash. The last two exercises are performed with the rest of the group.

The purposes of the exercises are:

Heel on Leash and Figure Eight—to show the ability of the dog and handler to work as a team.

Stand for Examination—to show that the dog will accept examination from a stranger while staying in position and not display either shyness nor resentment.

Heel Free—same as exercise one but off-leash.

The Figure Eight exercise. *Photo by Mike Godsil.*

Recall—to show that the dog will stay where left until called and will respond promptly to his handler's command or signal to come.

Long Sit—to show that the dog will sit for one full minute and stay until his handler comes back to him and releases him.

Long Down—same as above but the dog must lie down for three minutes.

There is endless potential for something to go wrong even when the handler and dog have worked very hard together. There are numerous distractions. Maybe your dog has a very keen nose and two rings over is a bitch in season in the conformation ring. In this situation the chances are good that your dog will be too distracted to remember anything he has learned.

Many dogs blow it on the Long Sit or Long Down. Suddenly, one dog looks around and decides he doesn't want to stay and starts to wander around the ring. When this happens, until the judge instructs the handler or steward to get the dog and take him out of the ring, nothing can be done. Naturally, the handler is crushed and feels humiliated since this outcome is very discouraging for anyone. The only way to avoid this sort of disappointment is to be better prepared. Practice with more distractions present and go to more matches before the next attempt.

Open Classes

In the Open classes, you will see dogs that have attained the Companion Dog title and are competing for the title of Companion Dog Excellent (CDX). Again, there are three legs; the dog must achieve a qualifying score in three separate trials under three different judges. The exercises are much more difficult and require additional training and practice, but many dogs do go on to earn their CDX.

Open classes also are divided: Open A for owners or immediate family and Open B for owners or professional handlers. Dogs that have already earned a CDX or UD degree can continue to compete in the Open B Class to attain first place points to apply toward their Obedience Trial Championships. When you watch an Open B Class, you will probably see some UD dogs that will be skilled performers; they might even make it look easy. So, if you are contemplating going into obedience trials with your dog, watch the Open A Class, as those dogs have earned only their CD titles. By observing the Open A Class, you will be more likely to see the kinds of mistakes you and your dog want to avoid making.

Ready for the Long Sit. *Photo by Mike Godsil.*

The Open Exercises and Scores are as follows:

Heel Free and Figure 8	40 points
Drop on Recall	30 points
Retrieve on Flat	20 points
Retrieve over High Jump	30 points
Broad Jump	20 points
Long Sit	30 points
Long Down	30 points
Maximum Total Score	200 points

The first exercise is exactly like the first Novice exercise except that the dogs are off-leash. The second exercise is exactly like the Novice Recall except that the handler is also ordered to drop the dog to a down position on command or signal, and then on command call the dog in. A zero will result if the dog doesn't drop completely to the down position on a single command or signal or if he does not stay down until he is called. Also, a delay or slow response can cause a substantial deduction in his score.

The third exercise, Retrieve on the Flat, must demonstrate prompt retrieval by the dog. The handler stands with his dog sitting in the heel position. On the order from the judge "Throw it," the handler gives his dog a stay signal and throws the dumbbell at least twenty feet. When the judge says, "Send your dog," the handler gives the command or signal to retrieve. The dog must go directly to the dumbbell and pick it up, turn around, and bring it back to the handler with no delays. He must sit in front of the handler until the judge tells the handler to take the dumbbell. ("Take it.") Then on command from the judge ("Finish"), the handler, with the dog, goes to the heel position. Dog errors will result in a zero if he doesn't go out on the first command or signal, if he goes out to retrieve before the command, or if he fails to retrieve or does not return with the dumbbell close enough to the handler so that he can easily take it from the dog. The dog will be heavily penalized if he is slow, plays around, mouths the dumbbell, refuses to give it up to the handler, or is slow about it.

The fourth exercise, Retrieve over High Jump is similar to the one before except that the dog has to clear a jump. Heights have just been lowered (March, 1989). The maximum height is still thirty-six inches and the minimum is eight inches, but there are new, lower heights for most dogs. These heights are specified in the new Rules book and demonstrate a realization of the great difference in dogs' body types as well as heights. Obedience people campaigned long

The Long Sit. *Photo by Mike Godsil.*

and hard for this change. The dog has to clear the high jump twice, going and returning. The dog will be penalized or given a zero for all the errors that could be made in the Retrieve on the Flat, for failing to go over the jump, or for climbing the jump. In this exercise, we begin to see dogs as athletes, like high hurdlers in human track and field competition.

We also see them as athletes in the fifth exercise: the Broad Jump. In this test there are two- to four hurdles made of boards about eight inches wide, with the largest being about five feet long and six inches high. They are spaced evenly to cover a distance equal to twice the height of the high jump for the particular dog. So, if the high jump was thirty-six inches high, the broad jump will use four hurdles spaced for a maximum of seventy-two inches. A smaller dog will only have to clear two or three hurdles. In the broad jump the handler stands with his dog sitting at heel position in front of and eight feet from the jump. When the judge says, "Leave your dog," the handler gives his dog the command or signal to stay and goes to a position facing the right side of the jump. When the judge says, "Send your dog," the handler gives the command or signal to jump. The dog must clear the entire distance of the broad jump without touching it, and without any further command or signal, return immediately to a sitting position in front of the handler. Then the dog performs the finish. A zero score results if the dog fails to stay until he is directed to jump, refuses to jump, walks over any part of the jump, doesn't clear the jump, or doesn't return directly to the handler. In addition, there may be other deductions for dallying, not sitting straight, etc.

In the group exercises (the Long Sit and Long Down), the handlers are required to go completely out of sight of their dogs. The Long Sit lasts for three minutes and the Long Down for five minutes. These two exercises are scored exactly like the Novice group exercises.

When you watch the Open Class exercises, you will begin to realize how much work is required of the dogs and their trainers to compete for the highly prized title of Companion Dog Excellent.

Utility Classes

Utility trials truly test the degree of perfection of both handler and dog. The classes may or may not be divided into A and B. If they are, the A division is for dogs that have a CDX title and the B division is for dogs that already have won their UD titles. Again, to attain the title of Utility Dog, the dog must complete three legs by attaining a qualifying score in three different trials under three different judges.

Doberman returning over bar jump.

Only three dogs are required to compete instead of six in Novice and Open.

The Utility exercises and scores are:

Signal Exercise	40 points
Scent Discrimination Article No. 1	30 points
Scent Discrimination Article No. 2	30 points
Directed Retrieve	30 points
Moving Stand and Examination	30 points
Direct Jumping	40 points
Maximum Total Score	200 points

The first exercise demonstrates the ability of the dog and handler to work as a team while heeling, and the dog's correct responses to the signals to stand, stay, drop, sit, and come. The handler uses no verbal commands, *only* signals (hence the name, Signal Exercise). What a temptation for the handler to whisper encouragement to his dog; what a temptation to give a soft spoken command! But if the handler succumbs to the temptation, a zero will be the result. Of course there are also all the usual deductions applicable in the Heeling, Figure 8, and Recall exercises.

In the two Scent Discrimination exercises, the purpose is to demonstrate the dog's ability to select the handler's articles by scent alone and to promptly deliver the correct articles to the handler. The handler brings with him ten articles divided into two sets. One set of five articles is made of leather, such as key cases, gloves, or baby shoes. The other set of five is made of rigid metal, such as purchased metal dumbbells or metal cylinders. None is more than six inches long and each is legibly marked with a different number. The handler gives these to the judge, who selects one article from each set and makes a written note of the numbers of the two articles he has selected. These two are placed on a table in the ring until picked up by the handler. The judge or a ring steward handles each of the remaining eight articles then places them on the ground at random about six inches apart and about twenty feet from the dog handler. The dog and handler then turn around facing away from the articles, and the judge asks the handler to take the first article, handle it, and place it on the judge's book. The judge then puts it among those on the ground, without touching it with his own hands.

Labrador Retrievers on the Long Down. *Photo by Janet Yosay.*

When the judge commands "Send your dog," the handler turns and sends his dog out to retrieve. He may give his scent to the dog by touching his nose with one open hand before they turn to face the articles. The dog must go at a brisk trot directly to the articles and should not take too much time selecting the correct article (the one with the handler's scent). He then must return briskly and complete the exercise as in the Retrieve on the Flat. The dog will be scored zero if he doesn't go out to the group of articles, if he retrieves the wrong article, or if he doesn't bring the correct one back. Heavy deductions are made if he picks up a wrong article, puts it back down, and then brings the right one. The handler too can be penalized for being too rough in giving his scent to his dog or for moving excessively when turning to face the articles. A dog that works slowly in picking the right articles but does so continuously, not stopping or dallying, just making sure, will not be penalized. After the first article has been retrieved, the procedure is repeated for the second article.

The fourth exercise is the Directed Retrieve and is meant to demonstrate the dog's ability to stay until sent to retrieve, then go directly to the designated glove and retrieve it promptly. The handler brings three white cotton work gloves which must be approved by the judge. Then he and the dog stand with their backs to the other end of the ring midway in between two jumps (a bar jump and a high jump). The judge or steward drops the three gloves across the end of the ring, one in each corner and one in the center. They are designated One, Two, and Three from left to right. When the handler and dog turn to face the gloves, the judge gives the order "One," "Two," or "Three." The handler gives his dog the heel command and turns in place to face the designated glove. Then he gives the dog the direction to the proper glove with a single motion of his left hand and arm along the right side of the dog, and gives the command to retrieve. The dog must go directly to the glove at a brisk trot, retrieve it promptly, and complete the exercise as he did in the Retrieve on the Flat.

The handler can blow this one by giving any command or signal after turning to position the dog to face the glove, and the dog can blow it by not going to the designated glove or by not retrieving the glove. The handler, again, can be penalized for over-turning, touching the dog, or using excessive motions while turning to face the glove. In addition, all the penalties which apply to the Recall and the Retrieve on the Flat can be assessed.

Fifth is the Moving Stand and Examination which is intended to show that the dog will heel, stand and stay on command and accept examination without shyness or resentment. The handler must command his dog to heel, walk at a normal pace a short distance, stand the dog on judge's command, keep going another ten feet or so, then turn to face his dog and stop. The judge jwill approach the dog and go over the dog with his hands. (He doesn't check the bite or testicles.) On the judge's command, the handler commands his dog to return to heel. A dog can fail this exercise by being shy, showing resentment, moving from the place where it was left, sitting or lying down, growling, snapping, barking, whining repeatedly, or failing to heel, stand, or stay. Penalties are the same as Novice Heel Free, Stand for Examination, and Recall.

The last exercise is Directed Jumping. This exercise demonstrates the dog's ability to go away from the handler in the direction indicated, stop when commanded, jump as directed and return as in the Recall. The two jumps (bar and high jumps) are about in the middle of the ring at right angles to the sides and about twenty feet apart. They are set at the height required for the particular dog. First, the handler sends the dog out to about twenty feet beyond the jumps and in the center and gives him a sit command. Then the judge says either "High," or "Bar," and the handler directs his dog to that jump by command or signal. When the dog is in midair, the handler turns to face the dog for his return. The dog sits in front of his handler and on order of the judge does the finish. Then the judge asks the handler, "Are you ready?" and the procedure is repeated with the dog jumping the second jump.

There is ample opportunity to score a zero here as the dog can blow it by anticipating the handler's command to go out, not leaving the handler, not going out between the jumps, not stopping on command and remaining at least ten feet beyond the jumps, anticipating the handler's command to jump, not jumping as directed, knocking the bar off the uprights, or climbing or using the top of the high jump to get over. In addition, he can be penalized for slowness in going out or for touching the jumps, plus all of the penalties he can accumulate as listed under Novice Recall.

The Utility exercises are tough. It takes many months of practice and a great deal of patience and love on the part of the handler. Boredom has been known to rob a dog of his UD title, since he must successfully repeat his performance at three different trials. The reality is that there are more failures in the Utility classes than in any of the obedience exercises, but the dogs that *do* qualify have had handlers who give a lot of praise during practice and kept it interesting enough for the dog to keep having fun. The dog that is having fun during obedience exercises will be the one continually wagging his tail and seeming to sparkle the whole time he is working.

A Golden Retriever making the Retrieve Over High Jump. *McKinney photo.*

In any of the obedience classes no one knows his score until the class has ended. The judge calls in the dogs that have qualified, informs the spectators of the maximum number of points for a perfect score, announces to the handlers the score of each dog that has qualified, and awards the ribbons. Dogs that qualify but do not place first, second, third, or fourth are awarded a qualifying ribbon. In the case of a tie for a ribbon in any of the classes, there is a run-off between the dogs—the entire Novice Heel Free Exercise.

The High in Trial dog is announced at the end of the trial. If the trial is held in conjunction with a dog show, the winner is announced after the Best in Show judging and is given his award, a blue and gold rosette and a prize or trophy.

Find out about obedience trials the same way as dog shows. *Dog World* magazine lists the separate obedience trials as well as those being held in conjunction with dog shows. The information will include the place, time, date, and the name and address of the club or superintendent to contact for a premium list. The AKC *Gazette* lists similar information along with the names of the judges, closing date for entries, the fee, and the name of the superintendent.

UNITED KENNEL CLUB OBEDIENCE TRIALS

The United Kennel Club started holding obedience trials at the beginning of 1979 and had the advantage of selecting from the different types of trials in this country and abroad. Some of the UKC exercises are similar to those of the American and Canadian Kennel Clubs, but others were patterned after the European Working Dog Trials. The exercises reflect the difference in orientation and philosophy of the UKC, which always stresses the working aspects of the dog. This organization feels that dogs should be fully recognized for their working abilities as well as for conformation to breed standards. Therefore, the UKC places obedience titles *before* the registered name of the dog rather than after it.

UKC trials are held separately or in conjunction with specialty shows. The obedience trials are all-breed trials open to any dog that is registered with the UKC and at least six months old.

The first title to be attained is the U-CD (United Companion Dog); next is the U-CDX (United Companion Dog Excellent); and finally the U-UD (United Utility Dog). Class divisions are the same as for AKC (A and B), except there is no class division in the Utility Class. The total maximum scores are also the same, but the exercises are a little different. The major differences in the Novice Classes are in the Honor exercise and the Recall Over Jump.

The Honor exercise is derived from European-born Schutzhund trials and is substituted for the AKC's Long Down. The working dog goes through his exercises while the next dog in the class "honors" the working dog by being placed in a down position in the ring. The handler of the honoring dog is across the ring facing his dog. If the honoring dog breaks, he gets a zero for that exercise. The Heel On-Leash, Figure 8, Stand for Examination, Heel Off-Leash, and the Long Sit are similar to the AKC exercises.

The Recall Over Jump exercise is different in that two ring stewards are placed one on each side of the jump to serve as distractions. UKC feels that this offers a greater challenge to the dog and is a logical step in training for the higher obedience titles. Another difference in this exercise is the jump height. UKC requires a maximum height of twenty-four inches or the dog's shoulder height, whichever is less.

Qualifying scores in all classes of both the AKC and UKC are the same (170 points), and the requirements of three legs (qualifying at three different trials) are the same. But in UKC trials, the dogs may qualify under only two different judges rather than the three required by the AKC.

Scoring of the exercises in the Novice classes is roughly the same with a few minor differences. UKC gives thirty maximum points for Standing for Examination and the Long Sit; but for Honoring (Long Down) and Recall Over Jump it gives a maximum of thirty-five points instead of thirty and on Heel On- and Off-Leash gives thirty-five points each maximum, five less than AKC. The total maximum points still amount to 200.

The U-CDX exercises also differ somewhat from those of the AKC. The Honoring exercise is done with the owner out of sight of his dog while the working dog is performing the Heel Off-Leash and the Figure 8. During the Heel Off-Leash a ring steward walks to meet the dog and handler twice during the exercise, once nearest the dog and once nearest the handler. The Figure 8, Retrieve on Flat, and the Group Sit Stay are the same as AKC. The Retrieve Over Jump is also the same except for the difference in the height of the jump.

The Drop on Recall exercise is done with the distraction of a ring steward. The steward is in the ring beside the handler, and once the handler drops the dog, the steward leaves the handler's side and walks toward the dog, continuing past him. The dog must not bolt or rise from the down position.

The number of points available in each of the U-CDX exercises is exactly the same as the AKC, with the total number of 200 points available.

The UKC Utility Class exercises differ from the AKC in the following ways. The first exercise is called Group Signal and Heeling by the UKC. Several honoring dogs and their handlers are in the ring while the working dog is performing this exercise. The UKC has only one Scent Discrimination exercise (metal), but has organized the Directed Retrieve into two separate exercises. The first, the Directed Marked Retrieve, is performed from the handler's side as with the AKC. In the second, the Directed Signal Retrieve, the handler sends the dog out, stops him, has him turn and sit in a designated area and then retrieve one of the three gloves as directed by the handler.

The fifth exercise is called Consecutive Recalls (not used by AKC). This tests the dog's ability to respond promptly to two consecutive recalls—one with a Drop and one without a Drop—without anticipating the handler's command. The dog scores a zero if he anticipates. The last exercise in the Utility Class is Directed Jumping, which is like the AKC exercise except for the height of the jump. There is no Examination exercise. Scoring is similar with a total of 200 points possible.

The UKC obedience trials are advertised in *Bloodlines*. These are official notice of the event (there are no premium lists) and give the name of the host club, show site, date, time, name and address of secretary, fees, etc. The ad also gives the times that entries will be taken at the show or trial. You must present the dog's registration certificate and three-generation pedigree when entering, and you may be required to present proof of rabies vaccination.

For the many people who have taken all the titles offered in AKC trials, UKC obedience offers a new challenge. For information on how to register your AKC registered dog with UKC so you may participate in their obedience trials, write to United Kennel Club (see Appendix). Also, it is a good idea to purchase the official UKC Obedience Regulations booklet for detailed information, judging and scoring.

Up, up, and away! Boston Terrier going over the high jump. *McKinney photo.*

7

CANADIAN KENNEL CLUB SHOWS AND OBEDIENCE TRIALS

The shows in Canada are generally more informal (some people say more fun) and smaller than those in the United States. Rather than shows that range up to 3,000 dogs, the shows in Canada range from 250- to 1,000 dogs.

CONFORMATION SHOW PROCEDURES

Canadian shows are run much like the AKC shows. The CKC licenses All-Breed Championship shows; Limited Breed shows (which do not proceed to Group and Best in Show); Specialty Championship shows; Field Trial Conformation shows (which are held in connection with a field trial in which those dogs have competed and are similar to the UKC nite hunts and bench shows for coonhounds); Sanctioned Matches (like AKC); and Booster shows at an all-breed show. (The specialty club combines its classes under the term, Booster Show. This is similar to an AKC specialty club designating the breed classes as its specialty show.) All CKC shows are open to purebred dogs of CKC registry at least six months old or Listed Dogs (more about these later). The breeds correspond generally to those registered with the AKC with a few minor differences (see Appendix). Dogs in the Miscellaneous Class are not in competition but are brought into the ring, paraded, and a short history of each breed is given over the public address system.

The Canadian Kennel Club offers some suggestions to American exhibitors with the following breeds noting the variations from practices in the United States:

Belgian Sheepdogs—All the recognized varieties of the Belgian Sheepdog (including the Malinois and Tervuren) are to be entered as "Belgian Sheepdogs." All compete together as Belgian Sheepdogs. There is no separation in classes or judging of each of these varieties.

Dachshunds—All of the six varieties of Dachshund are recognized and registered in Canada as separate breeds. Each variety has its own Best of Breed award and is eligible to compete in the Group. Any Miniature Dachshund not born in Canada is not confirmed as a CKC Champion until he has been officially weighed as prescribed by CKC regulations.

Chihuahuas—For show purposes the Chihuahua is divided into two separate "breeds"—(1) Long Coat, and (2) Short Coat. Each has its own Best of Breed award.

English Toy Spaniels—All varieties are to be entered and compete as "English Toy Spaniels." There is only one Best of Breed award.

Shih Tzu—This breed is regarded as a Non-Sporting breed and competes in Group 6.

Otherwise, classes are quite similar, the main difference being that the designations of dog and bitch become male and female (as in UKC shows). The classes are:

Junior Puppy Class—six months and under nine months

Senior Puppy Class—nine months and under twelve months

Canadian-Bred—six months and born in Canada (corresponds to AKC American-Bred)

Bred by Exhibitor—owned and handled in the ring by the breeder or part breeder (like AKC)

Open Classes—for all dogs over six months

Non-regular classes allowed at championship shows (no points involved) are *Brace Class* (two dogs of one breed belonging to the same exhibitor); and *Team Class* (four dogs of one breed belonging to the same exhibitor). A specialty club may schedule at its specialty show a *Veterans Class*. This class is for dogs over seven years of age on the day of the show. The first place male and female do not compete for points but compete for Best of Breed. Other non-regular classes allowed for specialty shows are *12-18 Months Class, Stud Dog and Get Class*, and *Brood Bitch and Progeny* (dog or bitch and two or more of get or progeny) and *Exhibition Only*.

Just as in AKC and UKC shows, males are shown first. The Winners Male is selected from the winners of each class and a Reserve Winners Male is also chosen. Then the females are shown and the Winners Female and Reserve Winners Female are selected. The Winners compete with the Champion "specials" for Best of Breed. From these the judge also selects a Best of Opposite Sex and a Best of Win-

Siberian Huskies gaiting at an outdoor Canadian show. *Photo by Alex Smith.*

ners. At this point there is a major difference in the procedure. In Canadian shows, after the judge has picked his Best of Winners, he selects a Best Puppy of Breed. If the Best of Breed winner is a puppy, it automatically becomes Best Puppy. If Best of Breed is an adult, all the Puppy Class winners, male and female, are brought into the ring so the judge can select that Best Puppy.

The Best of Breed goes on to compete in its Group. The Groups each have four placements with the first place winners going on to compete for Best in Show. After the judging of each Group, the Best Puppy in each Group is chosen. Here again, if the Group 1 winner is a puppy, it automatically becomes Best Puppy in its Group. If the first place winner is an adult, though, the Best Puppy winners of each breed in the Group are brought in before the judge so he can select Best Puppy in that Group.

After all the groups have been judged, the seven adult winners compete for Best in Show. The exciting climax of the show is not only Best in Show but also Best Puppy in Show, which is selected immediately after the Best in Show judging. I really like the idea of the puppy competition. At AKC matches, the puppy competition is most enjoyable for both competitors and spectators—at a licensed show, it would be doubly enjoyable to see the puppies taking their top awards.

There is one other major difference between Canadian and American Kennel Club shows. At AKC shows, a dog that has won Best of Breed is not required to stay and compete in the Group ring. In Canada, he *must* compete in Group or lose all awards and points, and the owner will face disciplinary action from the Canadian Kennel Club!

POINTS SCORING

To become a Canadian champion, a dog must acquire ten points, but no majors are needed. A dog must take its Winners Class under at least three different judges at three shows. The winners receive from one to five points depending on the number of dogs competing in the breed. The points are the same for all breeds: one point if there are two dogs competing; two points for three to five dogs; three points for six to nine dogs; four points for ten to twelve dogs; and five points for thirteen or more dogs. As in AKC shows, additional points may be won by defeating champions for Best of Breed as this increases the number of dogs competing. More points can be acquired at the Group level, depending on placement. No more than five points are awarded at any one show.

Best in Show judging. *Photo by Alex Smith.*

HOW TO FIND OUT ABOUT UPCOMING SHOWS

The best source of information is the CKC's official magazine, *Dogs in Canada*, published thirteen times a year (see Appendix). It lists coming shows, sanctioned matches, and people or organizations operating as show secretaries. Another way to get information is by writing any Canadian show superintendent (see Appendix) and requesting a premium list. In addition, some Canadian shows are advertised in the AKC's *Gazette* and in *Dog World* magazine.

ELIGIBILITY FOR ENTRY

A dog registered individually with the American Kennel Club and eligible for registration with the Canadian Kennel Club may be entered at events held under CKC rules as a "listed dog" (a listing fee is payable for each show or trial at which the dog is entered). All awards and points earned by the dog while entered as a listed dog will stand to his credit, but it should be noted that the Canadian Kennel Club does not confer a title of any kind on any dog until the dog is registered individually in the records of the CKC. An ILP number does not qualify a dog for entry in a show or trial held under CKC rules.

Registering Your Dog With The CKC

The items you will need to assemble in order to register your dog are:

1. Properly completed Application for Registration (Form RD 175).
2. Original AKC registration certificate of your dog: *Original, not a copy.*
3. Official AKC certified three-generation pedigree: *the original.*
4. Two clear noseprints or a CKC tattoo of your dog for identification.
5. A fee in U.S. funds (less if you have become a non-resident member of the CKC).

So you will know all about all the activities (obedience trials, field trials, as well as shows), it is a good idea to become a non-resident member of the Canadian Kennel Club. The cost of membership includes a subscription to *Dogs in Canada*, including the official pages. Request an application for registration of an AKC registered dog

Typical indoor show ring layout. *Photo by Alex Smith.*

owned by a resident of the U.S.A. (Form RD 175.) Also, buy a copy of the official "Dog Show Rules", and official noseprinting kit (two pre-inked noseprint plates and a pad of numbered noseprint forms). For tattoo information, request a Brochure R3, Information on Identification.

Once you have sent off for your CKC application, membership, and noseprinting kit, obtain your dog's certified three-generation pedigree. The one that the breeder gave you when you purchased your

Junior handlers compete with many different breeds. *Photo by Alex Smith.*

puppy will not do. Neither will one from a pedigree service. *It must be an AKC certified pedigree.* Before you send for the pedigree, make sure that you have your dog's white registration certificate. If you have lost or misplaced it, you can order a replacement when you order the pedigree.

Noseprinting

Although the CKC will accept either a tattoo or a noseprint, I suggest taking the noseprint as tattooing is more complicated. Special tattoo numbers issued by the CKC must be used.

The noseprinting procedure requires two people. One person holds the dog and wipes off his nose. Then the other person applies the inked plate against the nose and presses it on the noseprint form. *Caution:* Be sure to practice this on plain paper before using the forms as you need two *unsmudged* noseprints to send in with your application. The application for registration contains hints on noseprinting and samples of what is and is not acceptable.

Finally, put your noseprints, application, AKC registration certificate, AKC certified pedigree, and fee into a large envelope and send it to the Canadian Kennel Club. Expect to wait six weeks or longer for your registration.

SAMPLES OF ACCEPTABLE NOSEPRINTS

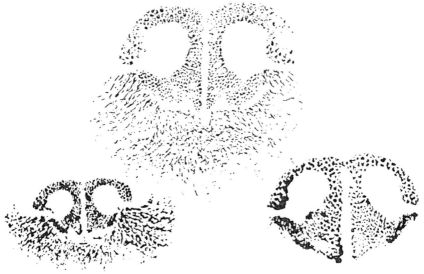

ENTERING A SHOW

When you plan to enter a show, mail your entries *well* ahead to make sure you get them in before the closing date (the mail between the United States and Canada sometimes takes a long time). Allow a couple of weeks and take advantage of the good rate of exchange by sending the fees by postal money order in Canadian funds.

Customs

Don't forget that your dog will need his rabies vaccination certificate from your veterinarian. It has to be within the last twelve months to enter Canada; but when you return home, the U.S. Customs require that it must be dated at least thirty days before you entered Canada.

At the Port of Entry you will need:

1. the signed identification form sent you by the show or trial secretary; and
2. the rabies vaccination certification.

Agree to take the dog out of Canada within ninety days, actually reporting to the Canadian Customs at the time and presenting the copy of the temporary entry form when the dog entered Canada.

OBEDIENCE TRIALS

Obedience trials in Canada are very much like those of the American Kennel Club, but there are some minor differences. I strongly suggest that anyone planning to compete in a Canadian trial should obtain the "Regulations and Standards for Obedience Trials" to set these differences firmly in mind and avoid handler errors.

The maximum total score of all class exercises is 200; a qualifying score is 170, with the dog and handler required to pass fifty percent of each exercise. A title is attained after three qualifying scores at three different trials. These scores must be under three different judges except in some of the sparsely settled provinces where they may be under two different judges. A dog must have a Companion Dog title before he can compete for Companion Dog Excellent and must have a Companion Dog Excellent to compete in Utility. Once attained, the titles follow the dog's name.

The differences in the Novice exercises are in the Heel Free where the point count is forty-five (forty in the U.S.), and in the Heel On-

A Giant Schnauzer clears the bar jump. *Photo by Alex Smith.*

Leash and Figure 8 where the points are thirty-five (instead of the forty in AKC trials).

In the Open Class, the Retrieve on the Flat has a point value of twenty-five instead of the AKC's twenty, but the Retrieve Over High Jump is thirty-five, five points higher than the AKC. The Long Sit and Long Down are worth twenty-five points each instead of the thirty points each for the AKC. On July 1, 1984 the Canadian Kennel Club lowered the jump height to the height of the dog at the withers as in UKC trials.

In the Utility Class there are three Scent Discrimination tests (wood, metal, and leather) with each counting twenty points; whereas, the AKC has two tests which score thirty points each. The Signal Exercise is thirty-five instead of forty points. The CKC has a Group Examination with thirty-five points, whereas AKC now has the Moving Stand and Examination for thirty points. The other difference is in the Seek Back, which replaces the AKC's Directed Retrieve. In this exercise a darker glove (not white) is surreptitiously dropped by the handler during a Heel Free and the dog must later be directed to go back and seek the glove and retrieve it. These are not really great differences, but if you plan to attend obedience trials in Canada, study and practice.

There *is* a major difference in the acquiring of the Obedience Trial Championship. Whereas the AKC title is *only* conferred after a dog has attained the Utility degree *and* accumulated 100 points in additional competition, the title is automatically bestowed on a dog in Canada after he has won his CD, CDX, and UD titles.

Border Collie and handler
executing the Heel Off Lead.
Photo by Alex Smith.

Tips From CKC

Here are some helpful hints for American obedience trial enthusiasts from the Canadian Kennel Club:

1. An owner/owners may enter only *one* dog in the Novice A and Open A Class at any one trial and the dog must be handled by the owner/owners or a member of the immediate family.
2. No licensed handler, no trainer, nor any person who has previously exhibited a dog through his UD (Utility Dog) title in Canada or *elsewhere* shall be allowed to compete in the Novice A Class or the Open A Class.
3. A dog which has won its CD degree in the U.S. or a comparable degree in any foreign country is not eligible for entry in the Novice A Class; he must be entered in the Novice B Class.
4. A dog must be registered individually in the records of the CKC before he may continue to enter the Open or Utility classes. (Miscellaneous Class dogs excepted.)
5. A dog which has won his CDX degree in the U.S. or a comparable degree in any foreign country is not eligible for entry in the Open A Class; he must compete in the Open B Class.
6. A dog cannot be entered in the Open A Class or the Open B Class until he has won his CD degree in Canada.
7. A dog cannot be entered in the Utility Class until he has won his CDX degree in Canada.
8. Dogs in Miscellaneous Class are eligible for competition in obedience trials.

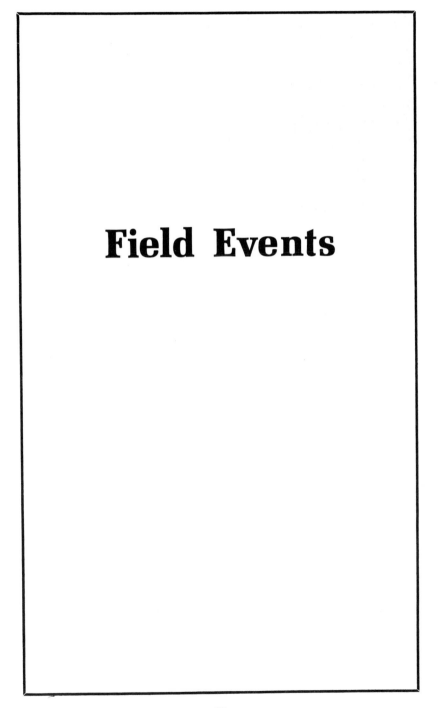

Field Events

8

AKC FIELD TRIALS

Last night's full orange hunter's moon is now a pale imitation of itself, singularly alone in the western sky; in the East the sky is streaked with the first pink rays of dawn. A young man rolls down the window of his van as he turns off the state highway into a big field. A chilly north wind ruffles his hair with the promise of frost soon to come. His glance takes in the wide stretch of open field, high dead grass in clumps still spangled with dew, a stand of trees to the right, the leaves now orange and gold, a body of water past them.

Dead ahead is a collection of parked campers, vans, mini-vans, pickup trucks and station wagons. In or near every one of these is a dog. His own dog whines, then barks in anticipation as acute olfactory senses pick up the smell of birds, rabbits, and other dogs. The damp earth yields its secrets to him. His tail sounds in a staccato beat against the sides of his crate.

"Hurry, hurry," he seems to say. "Let's go. I'm ready." But his owner stretches and yawns, looking over the scene for familiar faces.

Men and women dressed in sturdy shoes and boots, jeans or khaki work pants, flannel shirts and windbreakers are assembled in small groups to chat or drink coffee. Others mingle from one group to another. One man shouts, "Jake, you're here at last," as he spots the new arrival. A whistle hangs down the front of his red plaid shirt; a pheasant's feather curls around his green felt slouch-brimmed hat; his jacket is covered with patches and pins. He hurries toward his friend. Another field trial is about to begin.

In the world of dog sports, the field trial is one of the most exciting and highly competitive. Since field trials simulate hunting, they are held outdoors under natural conditions of different terrain, cover, wind and weather. The people who participate are a hardy lot, as the game bird season for most of the country is fall, and early and late winter. If you purchased a sporting breed, even though you may be a city dweller, you either hunt with your dog or have a secret yen to get out in the great outdoors. Field trials offer you the opportunity to do just that.

Field trials are open to the sporting breeds and the hunting hounds—Beagle, Basset and Dachshund. Coonhound hunts are covered separately. To participate in field trials, one should have a trained dog. There are many good books on training different breeds for hunting and for field trials, and there are many training clubs. It is not the purpose of this book to teach you how to train your dog, but to point you to sports and help you get started and in contact with people who can help.

The purpose of field trials is to test whether a particular dog can do what he was bred for (with proper training). Many people feel that what a dog looks like is not as important as his ability to do what the breed originally did before the very practical purposes of the breed's existence disappeared from our modern way of life. (Breeders have also altered many breeds to produce beauty in the show ring above utility.) After all, nowadays no one *needs* to go out with his dog to hunt rabbit, grouse, pheasant, or duck for the evening stew.

Back in the days when our forefathers hunted with their dogs to provide food for the table, I imagine they all had a secret feeling of pleasure in getting out alone in the woods; a glow of pride when Rover pointed the pheasant or Towser retrieved the duck. There was the meat for the evening meal, and the dog had done what he was born to do. Now, most peoples live in cities, and the woods have been considerably depleted. There are regulated hunting seasons and bag limits. Maybe you go out hunting with your dog, but the idea of competition to see how he stacks up against other dogs also appeals to you. If so, field trials are for you.

Field trialers are people who don't give up easily, who have put a lot of their time into learning about the field trial game and in training their dogs. They work hard and play hard. Training a dog to become a good pointer, retriever, or spaniel trial dog is hard work, and getting to the trials early in the morning no matter what the weather or terrain is hard play. But, they love it. There are men and women of all ages, and even some children. Many families participate together in exercising and training their dogs during the week and packing up the truck, car or van for a weekend of trials.

As in all other sports, whether competition between people or people and dogs, there are only a few winners. The rest lose. But, there is always next time. Some people don't feel competitive. They don't care about ribbons, trophies, intensive training for many months, and constant competitions. They just want to make their dogs better hunters or prove their breeding stock has the necessary hunting instincts of their breed. For them, there are Hunting Retriever and Pointing Breed tests and Working Certificate tests. These test the dogs' ability at different levels and suggest to the owner where he needs to apply more training or perhaps get another dog; or for a breeder, eliminate a dog from his gene pool.

The various trials licensed by the American Kennel Club are held by clubs of the different breeds or by field trial clubs. They publish premium lists which give all pertinent information as to where, when, who the judges are, which stakes are to be run, a complete list of money and ribbon prizes, the date, hour, place of closing of entries, and also of drawing of entries. The trials are open to any AKC registered, unaltered dog six months or older of the applicable breeds—Beagles, Basset Hounds, Dachshunds, Pointing Breeds, Retrievers, and Spaniels, and will be discussed separately. I will first discuss how the trials work, then give information about how to find out about them.

According to *Pure-Bred Dogs/American Kennel Gazette*, over 1,000 field trials are held each year by over 900 clubs. There are also sanctioned and fun trials, so you should be able to find one of these to attend. You will want to go to a trial as a spectator to find out just what it is all about and whether you might like to try it with your dog. Wear comfortable clothes and dress for the season. Although Beagle and Basset Hound trials are held almost every month of the year, most trials are held in cool or cold weather. The trials go on whether it is raining or snowing, so wear waterproof shoes and carry raingear. As a spectator, you will be part of what is called the "gallery." The gallery at any trial is supervised by a field marshal who will tell you where to go. You will meet many friendly people who will be happy to answer your questions. It is better to look for someone without a dog to talk to, as that person will not be so busy.

All AKC field trials are divided into three different types: Member trials and Licensed trials which are for championship points, and Sanctioned trials which are for practice. Member trials are held by clubs which are actually members of the AKC; Licensed trials are held by non-member clubs licensed by the AKC to hold them. No bitches in season are allowed to participate in most of the trials, nor are they allowed anywhere on the grounds.

After watching a Licensed or Member trial as a spectator, you may feel that your dog is well trained enough to at least get started.

If so, I suggest that you enter him in a Sanctioned trial as this is the place to start—not in the actual trial for points. Ribbons are awarded at the Sanctioned trials, and you can find out in a competitive atmosphere whether you and your dog know enough to go into point competition. You may find that you need to study the rule book, do some more training, and attend some more Sanctioned trials before tackling the big ones.

To find out about field trials and hunting tests given under the auspices of the American Kennel Club, subscribe to *Pure-Bred Dogs/American Kennel Gazette.* This magazine contains many useful articles about all the different sports, and in the back of each month's issue are official listings of all the upcoming field trials for all breeds, and hunting and working tests with the name of the sponsoring club, trial dates, secretary, and all information you need for obtaining the premium list.

Another way is to write the AKC Field Trials Division, and ask for the name and address of the secretary of the national association, telling them the breed you have and that you wish to find out about field trials. While you are writing to the AKC, request a copy of the rules and regulations booklet for the type of field trial in which you are interested.

Of course, you may know people with the same breed of dog as yours who participate in these activities. They would be an excellent source of information for you and could probably even help you get started with their club, should you be interested in pursuing field trial activities.

The prerequisites for Field Champion or Amateur Field Champion and what these titles mean are discussed under each of the different types of field trials. When a dog attains his Field or Amateur Field Championship, the title goes before the dog's registered name. Some dogs attain both Field and Amateur Field Championships. In this case, both titles would go before the name. The initials are FC and AFC, or FC/AFC if the dog has both titles. A dog may become both Show and Field Champion, although this doesn't happen too often. Then his titles and registered name would look like this—FC-CH Gundog Rarintogo.

TRAILING HOUND TRIALS

Trailing hounds include the Beagle, Basset Hound, and Dachshund. They track the rabbit or hare, noses to the ground to pick up the trail by scent. When the white cottontail of the rabbit flashes by as the quick, wily fellow scrambles to get off ahead of hounds and people, both hounds and humans feel the adrenalin pump, and the excitement of the hunt tingles through their bodies.

Besides the thrill of the hunt itself, people who go to field trials for the trailing hounds find a lot of enjoyment in the fellowship. Most participants have one or a few hounds which they train themselves, although there are a few professional handlers. Families come in campers, and social gatherings are common. Many people plan ahead and take advantage of fishing, sight-seeing, and other sporting events in the area.

It is easier for a novice to get started in Beagle, Basset and Dachshund trials, as they test natural ability to a greater extent than do the trials for the pointing and retrieving breeds. It is simply a case of pick up your hound and go ahead and get your feet wet. However, if you are buying a puppy so you can field trial with him, Basset and Beagle trialers advise that you select a puppy from proven field trial stock. This way, you are more likely to get one with the proper genetic background because the breeders have selected for hunting instincts as well as good structure.

Joining a local club will give you a good training area with lots of rabbits and you can get involved in all the club's activities.

97

AKC BEAGLE FIELD TRIALS

The Beagle field trial season runs from July 1 of one year to June 30 of the next year. The greatest number of trials are held from spring through fall. Over 400 Beagle field trials are held annually, representing the largest single breed activity at AKC. Beagles compete in trailing rabbits, and the trials are held on grounds which are owned or leased by Beagle clubs, with 80- to 200 acres of fenced land and a clubhouse. Rabbits are raised there in their natural habitat.

The Beagle is bred to be a hunting dog. In the field, he is to find game, pursue it vigorously and show determination to account for it. The purpose of field trials is to test these abilities. A Beagle is graded on the following desirable qualities: searching ability, pursuing ability, accuracy in trailing, proper use of voice, endurance, adaptability, patience, determination, independence, intelligence, cooperation, and competitive spirit. He is faulted for: quitting, backtracking, ghost trailing (no rabbit), pottering, babbling, swinging, skirting, leaving checks (losing the trail), running mute, tightness of mouth (not enough voice on trail), running hit or miss, lack of independence, and bounding off.

A Beagle on the trail. *Photo by Nancy Fuhrman.*

The Beagle in competition is credited mainly for positive accomplishments. Judges are not supposed to credit hounds that run with a lot of style ("showboats"), but don't find and trail rabbits. Credit for working style is given mainly when two successful hounds are performing equally well, but one does it with more style.

Beagle trials are of three types: Brace, Small Pack on Rabbit or Hare, and Large Pack on Hare. The classes are divided into two sizes by height, one not to exceed thirteen inches and one not to exceed fifteen inches, and by sex. The dogs are measured to determine which height class they should go into. So, there is an Open Dog thirteen-inch and Open Dog fifteen-inch, and the same classes for bitches. If there are less than six hounds of a sex entered and eligible to compete in any class, the class is combined. A club may offer non-regular classes, and these are described in the premium list.

To become a Field Champion, a Beagle must have won three first places and a total of 120 points in Open classes with not less than six starters at Licensed or Member field trials.

Field championship points are awarded as follows (there must be six dogs starting in each class):

1 point for each starter—first place winner

½ point for each starter—second place winner

⅓ point for each starter—third place winner

¼ point for each starter—fourth place winner

A fifth ribbon is given for the Next Best Qualified (NBQ) but is not a placement. To illustrate: If there are only the required six dogs in the class, the first place winner receives 6 points, second place-3 points, third place-2 points, and fourth place-1½ points. If it is a large trial and there are thirty starters, the points would be as follows: first place-30 points, second place-15 points, and so on according to the formula above.

According to AKC Beagle Field Trial rules, "A starter is an entered hound that has not been disqualified and that is not measured out for the second series or for the Winners Pack, and that has been cast or laid on a line with its bracemate at the start of its first series heat at a brace trial; or that has been cast at the start of its first series pack at a small pack trial; or that has been cast at the start with the rest of the pack at a large pack trial."

Field trialers get to the trial site in plenty of time, as they have to fill out entry forms, pay entry fees, and report to the field trial secretary who records the numbers. Then they get their hounds measured (if it is a Large Pack trial), and have a number painted on each side of their dogs since the judges have to be able to tell the hounds apart while they are running. In Brace and Small Pack trials, measurement is done only on hounds which advance to the second series or Winners Pack. In Brace trials, the Beagles run in twos, or in trios if there are thirty or more entries in a class. In Small Pack on Rabbit or Hare, the packs consist of four- to seven hounds. If the class has only eight or nine hounds, though, they may run in one pack. In Large Pack on Hare, all entries in a class run as a pack. If there are more than twenty-five starters, the pack may split into two divisions, and the two divisions run at the same time with one advertised judge with each pack.

The time for casting (the actual start of the trial) is always listed in the club's premium list and must be adhered to. Before entries close, the field trial secretary announces any necessary changes of judges, calls out the names of all hounds entered in the class (for Brace Trial), announces that entries have closed, and drawing for running order begins. Handlers must be alert and not stray too far as they must be ready when their hounds are called. Finally the hounds are "cast"—sent out to search for game.

At a Brace or Small Pack Trial, the handler must be with his running hound at all times; but at a Large Pack Trial, the handlers all have to stay together so as not to interfere with the running of the hounds. The handlers are guided by a marshal who is carrying out the instructions of the judges (whose decisions are final). They are appointed by the field trial committee of the club. At a Small Pack Trial, there are two marshals: one guides and supervises the gallery (spectators), and the other, known as the "roving marshal," assists the judges and supervises the handlers. At a Large Pack trial, there are three or more marshals.

In Brace trials, all braces are run and judged. Then the judges announce which hounds they wish to see in the second series. The hound having the highest score is announced as the first hound in the brace, and its bracemate the second highest. Remaining braces are braced in the same manner. The braces are run until one hound, in the judges' opinion, has clearly defeated another. Four placements are made. In addition, a ribbon for NBQ is awarded.

In Small Pack trials, the hounds are either cast to search for game or kept on leash until they are laid on a line when game is sighted (this is up to the judges). The judges may run any pack for as long as they think necessary to select the hounds to be considered for the next series. They will eliminate (order up) any hound interfering with the smooth running of the pack and any whose performance isn't worth further consideration. The series are run until the class is reduced to five- to nine hounds. The remaining finalists are known

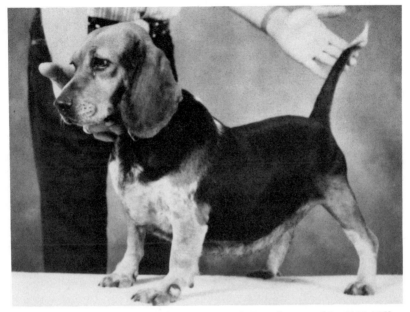

FC Tilley's Blue Nancy, a two-year-old female beagle owned by F.T. Tilley Jr. of Winston-Salem, North Carolina, won the 1989 Purina Outstanding Field Trial Beagle Award. Blue Nancy, who had four first-place finishes in Beagle Federation trials and defeated more than 1,000 other dogs, is handled by Joe and Kim Smith of Rayland, Ohio. *Photo courtesy of Ralston Purina.*

as the Winners' Pack. When running the Winners' Pack, the judges eliminate one or two hounds at a time beginning with the lowest rated one and ending up with the top two hounds. Then these two are run as a Brace until the judges are sure of their choice for top hound.

In Large Pack trials, Open Class Packs are run for not less than three hours. Derby classes (young dogs up to 24 months old) run for not less than an hour and a half. After about two hours of running of an Open Class Pack, the judges begin to eliminate hounds that have little or no score. (They have already eliminated those who displayed bad faults.) Within an hour after the race is closed, the judges' placements are announced.

PURINA AWARDS

The Ralston Purina Company each year makes an award to the Purina Outstanding Field Trial Beagle in recognition of both the hound and his owner's (and handler's) work in achieving success. The winner is determined by points earned in selected events each year, and the owner is given an original oil painting of the winner, a cash award and an engraved wall plaque. If a handler is involved, the cash award and a duplicate plaque are given to him.

AKC BASSET HOUND TRIALS

Basset Hounds are also bred for trailing rabbits. Basset Hound clubs hold about thirty Licensed or Member trials across the U.S. each year. Trials are held on grounds owned by Basset clubs, or the facilities of Beagle clubs are rented. Generally, the males are run one day and the females on another day. The procedures and rules are the same as for Beagles except that Basset Hounds aren't measured. The types of trials are the same: Braces on Rabbit or Hare, Small Packs on Rabbit or Hare, and Large Packs on Hare. However, most trials are for Braces. The premium list states the type of trial and the classes.

To become a Field Champion, a Basset Hound must win sixty championship points in Open All-Age Classes at four (or more) Licensed or Member field trials and must also win at least one first place in such classes. There must be at least ten starters in the classes.

There are four placements and an NBQ ribbon for the Next Best Qualified as in Beagle trials, but the NBQ is not a placement. The points are awarded as follows:

first place—1 point for each starter

second place—½ point for each starter

third place—¼ point for each starter

fourth place—$1/_8$ point for each starter

A field marshal directs the gallery and its movements, announces the braces (in a Brace Trial), and presents them to the two judges. The judges follow the hounds that are trailing the rabbit to decide a winner of the Brace. The rabbit is flushed by the gallery in its movements through the field. When the rabbit is sighted, the gallery cries, "Tally-Ho!" Then the gallery STOPS. The person in the gallery who sighted the rabbit and called "Tally-Ho!" marks the route it took and the handlers of the brace release their dogs. Off the dogs go on their own to trail the rabbit, ears flapping, followed by the two judges (who may be on horseback) and then by the two handlers. The hounds run until both judges are sure of a winner. A hound may compete again and again in succeeding series until he has been defeated. The judges at Basset Hound field trials look for exactly the same qualities as those at Beagle trials, and they eliminate hounds for the same faults.

For complete rules and regulations on Basset Hound Field Trials, write to the AKC requesting a copy of "Basset Hound Field Trial Rules and Standard Procedures."

AKC DACHSHUND TRIALS

Dachshunds were originally bred to hunt badgers and later to trail rabbits by scent and "go to ground" (go into the burrow and flush out the rabbit). It doesn't matter what size your Dachshund is (miniature or standard) or what type of coat he has (smooth, wirehair or long) or whether he is a city or country dog, he can still find rabbits. Since the trial for Dachshunds is a test of natural ability and since there are a very few trials in this country (only about ten a year), it's a good idea to go ahead and enter your dog when you find out about a trial. You will have fun and you won't want to miss the opportunity.

The Dachshund club sponsoring the trial will probably rent the facilities of a Beagle club, as there are plenty of rabbits and the trial must be run on live cottontails. Also, the grounds are fenced.

To become a Field Champion, a Dachshund must win thirty-five points in Open All-Age classes at three or more Licensed or Member field trials. There must be at least six starters in these classes and the hound must take first place at least once. The points for first place in the class equal the number of actual starters; the second place winner receives ½ point for each starter; third place, ⅓ point for each starter; and fourth place, ¼ point for each starter. Thus, if there are nine starters, the first place winner would get nine points, the second place winner 4½ and so on. There is a designation and ribbon for Next Best Qualified, but no placement.

The trial starts at the scheduled time after braces have been drawn. The two judges have selected the course, and they and the field trial chairman call the handlers, dogs (on leash) and gallery out to the field. The marshals have the gallery form a line to walk across the field to flush a rabbit. As in Basset Hound trials, a member of the gallery cries "Tally-Ho!" when a rabbit is sighted, and the first brace of dogs is laid on the line and released to trail the rabbit, giving full cry.

Desirable qualities are searching and pursuing ability, accuracy in trailing, obedience to commands, proper use of voice, willingness to go to earth, endurance, determination and courage, patience, adaptability, independence, cooperation with a running mate, and intelligence. Faults are: quitting (the most serious), pottering, backtracking, ghost trailing, babbling, swinging, skirting the trail, leaving checks, running mute, racing running mates without regard for the trail, running hit or miss, and lack of indendence. Judges credit the Dachshunds mainly for their positive accomplishments.

After the first series is run, the judges tell the marshal which dogs they want called for the second series so they can make their placings. In the second series, each brace is run until, in the opinion of the two judges, one Dachshund has clearly defeated the others. Usually, there will then be a break for lunch, and in the afternoon, the Open All-Age Bitch Class runs in the same manner. There may be a Championship Class in which only field champions run against each other. In this class, if the opportunity presents itself, the Dachshund is expected to go into the burrow after the rabbit by himself and flush it out. Nowadays, usually only the miniature hounds can get into the burrow, but the large dogs *must* dig at the hole and *try* to enter.

For full details, write to the AKC Field Trials Department for "Registration and Field Trial Rules and Standard Procedures for Dachshunds." Also, AKC can put you in contact with the Dachshund Club of America's current secretary, who can give you information.

Dachshunds also may earn a Versatility Certificate (VC) from their parent club for points earned in four of five categories: obedience, tracking, field trials, conformation, and den trials. These suffixes go after the dog's name, as they are not AKC titles.

Left behind! *Photo by Clifford Oliver.*

GLOSSARY OF TERMS

Babbler A hound which barks continuously while trailing or when not on the trail.

Backtrack To run the wrong way on a track.

Bawl Tonguing with long-drawn note, opposite of a chop.

Brace Two hounds drawn to run together in a hunt or trial.

Buck Male rabbit or hare.

Burrow Home of rabbit, underground.

Bye Hound When an uneven number of hounds are present, the odd dog is called the bye hound.

Carry a Line Follow the scent well.

Cast Spread out when searching game, or the swing or circle hounds make to recover trail.

Check Temporary loss of the trail, failure to get scent ahead.

Chop Short chopped barking when hound marks hole.

Couples Swivel-snap fasteners coupling two hounds together.

Cry, Voice, or Tongue All mean the sound of a hound when trailing or running scent. Different from ordinary bark of dogs and varying at different phases of the chase.

Died Hounds which lose a trail are said to die.

Doe Female rabbit or hare.

Drawing Selection of hounds to run together in braces.

Gallery The spectators at a field trial.

Giving Tongue Voice of hound when running a trail.

Gone to Ground When the rabbit has gone into a hole in ground or some other underground shelter.

High Hound The hound scored highest by judges. The top hound in a series.

Lay On Start hound on the scent.

Line Actual track or trail of the rabbit indicated by its scent.

Marshals Officials who carry out judges' and field-trial committee's orders at trials.

Mouthy Tonguing off line. Noisy.

Mute A hound that does not open on line, a silent trailer.

Nose Scenting ability.

Open In a trial, when a hound first gives tongue on a new line.

Ordered Up Judges ask handlers to catch their dogs at a field trial.

Pottering Dwelling too long on scent without any progress.

Run Out When a hound fails to stay with his bracemate.

Squaller Hound with a lighter, faster, crying bawl note.

Starters Hounds actually competing after entry.

Strike To find and start game.

Swing Hounds circling too far trying to recover a lost trail.

Tally-Ho The word that is called when a rabbit is seen in the field, summons both the judges and the handlers with their hounds to begin the chase.

Tongue The hound's voice.

Working a Line Hounds following scent.

(From *This is The Beagle*, George Whitney, DVM, T.F.H., Neptune, N.J. Used with permission.)

10

AKC FIELD TRIALS AND HUNTING TESTS FOR POINTERS

The pointing breeds are: Brittanys, Pointers, German Shorthaired Pointers, German Wirehaired Pointers, English Setters, Gordon Setters, Irish Setters, Vizslas, Weimaraners, and Wirehaired Pointing Griffons. Although these ten breeds are all registrable with the AKC and eligible to compete in their field trials, you will see very few Gordon, English or Irish Setters at AKC trials because of a split between field types and show types. Most setters and many pointers competing in field trials today do so in trials held under American Field rules and are registered with the Field Dog Stud Book (FDSB). Some pointers are registered with both AKC and FDSB. The Wirehaired Pointing Griffon is rarely seen because of its scarcity and is registered as the Drahthaar in the Field Dog Stud Book. Today's show-type English, Gordon and Irish Setters with their lavish coats and plentiful feathering bear little resemblance coat-wise to those bred strictly for field work and are also taller and thinner, lacking the physical ruggedness required for top field performance.

Overall, the continental breeds have become the bird dogs of choice for competition in AKC field trials. These are the Brittany, German Shorthaired Pointer, Vizsla, and Weimaraner. However, a Pointer won the Purina Top Field Trial Bird Dog Award for 1986-87. The very same dog won the award for 1982-83. Another Pointer won that award for 1985-86. In the continental breeds there is no great divergence in type between show and field in looks or conformation. In fact, the Brittanys have won more AKC Dual championsips than any other breed.

Whether you want to field trial or pleasure hunt with your dog (and perhaps test him in one of the pointing breed tests), experienced field trialers and hunters advise buying a puppy from good hunting stock. There should be some field trial champions in the bloodlines in the first two to three generations. It's even better if one of the parents is a field trial champion with a heavy background of these throughout the pedigree.

AKC FIELD TRIALS FOR POINTERS

According to the AKC Field Trial Department, Licensed and Member field trials for pointing breeds are the most numerous of all trials. They are held over the weekend and usually from 80- to 145 dogs compete. There will be a large number of people in attendance— up to about 150—as there are the handlers, the judges, the marshal, all the field trial committee, and family members of most of the handlers, since field trialing is very much a family sport. The trials are sponsored by specialty clubs and offer varying regular stakes and also non-regular stakes (no points), which may include stakes for junior handlers or lady handlers. Not all regular stakes are held at all trials; those offered are listed in the premium list. The premium list will state which breeds may be entered.

There will also be a number of horses, as these wide-ranging dogs must be followed by the judges and handlers on horseback. The horses are made available for rent by the sponsoring club, as are the shotguns. Since this type of trial requires a lot of ground, the trial is held either on state game lands or on large private grounds.

Field championships are broken into two classes: Field Championship and Amateur Field Championship. The Amateur Field Championship is awarded to dogs handled by non-professionals. (A non-professional or amateur is a person who for two years prior to the trial has not accepted any type of remuneration for the training of a hunting dog or the handling of a dog in a field trial.) To attain the title, ten points are required and must be won at three different Licensed or Member trials. Field Champion points are awarded for first place wins in Open Stakes and figured according to the number of dogs starting—more dogs, more points, up to five. Amateur Field Championship points are awarded according to both placement (first through third) and number of dogs entered. There are further requirements according to breed. These are rather complex and can be found in the *AKC Field Trials Rule Book.*

The stakes are run over a predetermined course laid out according to diagrams specified in AKC regulations, and birds are released for each brace in a series. The course is designed so the judges can

High hopes. Will this Vizsla puppy someday be a field-trial champion? *Photo by Ann Nalinzinski, courtesy of Mary Plouffe.*

evaluate the dogs on their hunting sense, ground coverage, independence in hunting, enthusiasm, and use of wind. Open Puppy Stakes are for dogs six months old and under fifteen months and run for fifteen minutes. Open Derby Stakes are for dogs six months old and under two years and run in twenty- to thirty-minute heats. The Gun Dogs (Open and/or Amateur) run at least thirty minute heats. Other regular stakes which may be offered are Limited Gun Dog (Open and/or Amateur), and Limited All-Age. Dogs are run in braces, for which drawings are made and each dog in the brace has his own handler. There may be one or more marshals, one who carries out the two judges' instructions and controls the gallery and others who see that the braces are ready when called and assist in the smooth running of the trial.

A puppy is evaluated on his desire to hunt, boldness and initiative, plus reasonable obedience to his handler. In the Derby, more is expected: a fast and attractive style, ability to find game, pointing the game, and steadiness if the chance comes for the handler to fire a blank shot.

The Gun Dog or All-Age Dog must give a finished performance. He must search for and locate game birds, point the bird, and remain on point while the handler fires his blank pistol. In a Retrieving Stake (required for some breeds), the official gunner shoots the bird and the dog must remain steady until his handler commands him to retrieve the bird, then retrieve it handily. The Gun Dog or All-Age Dog must also point his bracemate when the other dog is pointing a bird. This is called "honoring." The finished Gun Dog or All-Age Dog works with a minimum of handling, and a handler who makes excessive noise is penalized. As in any other field trial, the handler can make errors and accumulate penalties which in turn knock down his dog's score. Any dog that interferes with the smooth running of the trial will be removed from the grounds. Bitches in season may run in these trials if the premium list so states, but are run last.

If you attend a field trial held by a Weimaraner, German Short-haired Pointer or German Wirehaired Pointer club, you will probably witness a Water Test, as these three breeds must pass this test before

Ch. Redemption's Reward, a four-year-old male Pointer won the 1988-89 Purina Top Field Trial Bird Dog Award. "Little Jack" is owned by father and son T. Jack Robinson and Fred C. Robinson of Dayton, TN, and trained by Tommy Davis of Rienzi, MS. *Photo courtesy of Ralston Purina.*

being recorded as Field Champion. The dogs must be passed by two of the approved judges and must retrieve a live or dead game bird from water after a swim of about twenty yards to the bird. The dog must show his willingness to enter the water, swim and retrieve at the direction of his handler, who must be six feet from the water. There is no score, just Pass or Fail.

Once a year each of the pointing breed clubs may hold a National Championship Stake and a National Amateur Championship Stake for its breed. The qualifications for entry are determined by the parent clubs. A German Shorthaired Pointer or a Brittany may attain his Field Championship or Amateur Field Championship by winning the stake and is declared Field Champion or Amateur Field Champion of that breed for the year he won. All other pointing breed winners of these National Championship Stakes are credited with points and designated the National Field or Amateur Field Champion of that breed for the current year. The competition is the toughest imaginable, the competitive spirit of the handlers high, and the enthusiasm and anticipation of the dogs just as intense. This is the most prestigious win of all.

PURINA FIELD TRIAL BIRD DOG AWARD

The Purina Top Field Trial Bird Dog Award, which was initiated in 1963, is the granddaddy of the Ralston Purina Company's awards for field trial achievement. The Purina Award programs have grown to include beagles, coonhounds, herding dogs and retrievers. Each competition is administered by individuals experienced in the respective programs.

These prestigious awards recognize the best and most consistent performers during the past season. The Award programs' goal is to stimulate interest in competition and to give credit to the dogs, their owners and their handlers.

Ralston Purina Company is a leader in dog nutrition and the leading manufacturer of dog foods.

The Purina Top Field Trial Bird Dog Award is administered, judged and scored by an award committee of six prominent and experienced bird dog authorities. The award is based on dog performance in carefully chosen Open All-Age events held during the awards year, which runs from July through April.

Scoring is determined by the number of dogs officially drawn and final placement in each of the more than 50 listed field trials. Bonus points are awarded to winners of selected field trials.

AKC HUNTING TESTS FOR POINTING BREEDS

Many owners of pointing breeds wish to test them in a noncompetitive situation. They usually hunt with them for their own pleasure, but the idea of measurable tests also appeals. The AKC responded to this need by beginning Hunting Tests for Pointing Breeds in 1986. The tests are held by Member or Licensed hunting breed clubs. Premium lists give all pertinent details just as for a field trial. Sanctioned hunting tests may also be held.

The purpose of the tests is to give an opportunity for an owner to demonstrate his dog's ability to perform in actual hunting situations. The judges have extensive backgrounds in field trialing with pointing breeds. Dogs are run in braces, and the order of running is done by draw. The courses may be a single course with or without a birdfield, or a birdfield only. However, the size of the birdfield must be a minimum of five acres; larger is preferable. Pheasants, chukar, quail or pigeons, or a species of upland game bird indigenous to the region, may be used. This also is stated in the premium list.

The tests offered are Junior Hunter, Senior Hunter, and Master Hunter. Each test is divided into five parts: (1) hunting, (2) bird finding ability, (3) pointing, (4) trainability, and (5) retrieving (not applicable in Junior). The Junior Test is run for at least fifteen minutes and the Senior and Master tests for at least thirty minutes. All handling is done on foot, but the judges and a judge's marshal may use horses.

SENIOR HUNTING TEST

In addition to the qualities shown in the Junior hunting dog, the Senior must retrieve, but is not required to be steady to wing and shot. He must honor his bracemate if he encounters him on point.

JUNIOR HUNTING TEST

The Junior hunting dog must exhibit a keen desire to hunt, be independent and bold, have a fast, attractive style, show intelligience and ability to find game, and must establish a point. The handler may fire a blank cartridge from a pistol if within reasonable gun range of a flushed bird after point. The dog should be reasonably obedient.

MASTER HUNTING TEST

To qualify on this test, the dog must give a finished performance, besides showing all the qualities required of the Senior dog. He must be obedient and attentive to his handler, work quietly and retrieve promptly to hand.

No dog that steals a bracemate's point or damages a bird so badly it is unfit for consumption may receive a qualifying score in either the Senior or Master Hunting Test.

The titles Junior Hunter (JH), Senior Hunter (SH), or Master Hunter (MH) go after the dog's registered name after he has passed the applicable number of tests. A dog is not required to work through from Junior up to Master Hunter; he may be entered in the Master Hunting Test straight off if the owner feels he can qualify. A dog must acquire qualifying scores in four Junior Hunting tests to become a Junior Hunter. A dog becomes a Senior Hunter by attaining qualifying scores in five AKC Senior Hunting tests, or in four tests if he has already been recorded as a Junior Hunter. Master Hunter requires qualifying scores at six AKC Master Hunting tests, or five if he has been previously recorded as a Senior Hunter.

Each higher title supercedes the lower one on AKC records. After attaining his certificate in a category, a dog may continue to enter tests in that category but not in any lower category.

GLOSSARY OF TERMS

Back To honor another dog's point by stopping on sight or command.

Back Cast Turn back and hunt to the rear.

Backcourse Area covered in a trial before reaching birdfield.

Birdfield Area where birds are planted in a field trial.

Bird Sense Natural ability to know where birds are.

Blink Avoid pointing a bird.

Bracemate The accompanying dog in a brace.

Breakaway Start of a heat in a trial.

Broke Steady at wing and shot.

Bump Flush of bird by dog.

Call Back Additional performance after completion of first series sometimes requested by judge for determination of placements.

Cast	A part of the race; a movement toward an objective.
Creep	Move slowly on point when bird has not moved.
Flush	To cause bird to fly.
Gallery	Spectators at a field trial.
Hack	Continually giving commands to keep a dog close.
Heel	Walks by person's side.
Honor	Same as back.
Line Running	Running in straight lines without hunting.
Mark	Observe where a dead bird falls.
Marshal	Assistant to the judges in a trial.
Mechanical	Works by direction only, not showing any initiative.
Out of Judgment	Gone from sight too long in a trial.
Pattern	Overall form of a dog's race.
Picked Up	Withdrew from competition after an error.
Pickup	The end of a brace in a trial.
Planted Birds	Man-raised birds released for training dogs or in the birdfield at trials.
Pottering	Spending too much time smelling old scents.
Quartering	Covering ground consistently in a right to left pattern in front of handler.
Retrieve	Bring back a downed bird.
Second Series	Same as Call Back.
Steady	Usually used with "at wing and shot," meaning the dog does not chase birds.
Unproductive	Said of a point where no bird can be found.
Unsteady	Breaks point or breaks at wing or shot.
Wing	The flight of a bird.

(From *The Official Book of The Brittany Spaniel,* Nicky Bissell. Used with permission. Copyright © the American Brittany Spaniel Club, Inc.)

11
AKC RETRIEVER EVENTS

Over 120 retriever clubs across the country hold 200 or more AKC Licensed or Member trials each year. These non-slip retriever trials are for all the breeds of retrievers, plus Irish Water Spaniels. ("Non-slip" means that slip-type collars for release are not used.) The sponsoring retriever clubs may hold trials for one breed or more than one. Expect to see many more Labrador Retrievers (especially the black), but also in evidence are Golden Retrievers followed by a few Chesapeake Bay Retrievers. You may or may not see a Flat-Coated or Curly-Coated Retriever or an Irish Water Spaniel.

Competitors must have well-trained dogs. You should go to a trial or two to see how they work, then get involved with a retriever club and attend sanctioned and fun trials. Retrievers, like pointers, are trained for work from puppyhood. To compete, dogs must be six months of age and registered with the AKC; bitches in season may not compete or be allowed on the grounds.

AKC RETRIEVER FIELD TRIALS

The purpose of a Retriever Trial is to determine the relative merit of retrievers in the field, and trials simulate as nearly as possible the conditions encountered in a day's hunting. Since these trials are held in many different types of terrain in widely divergent parts of the United States, much latitude is given to the field trial committee and the judges in preparing the series of tests. The dogs are expected to retrieve any type of game bird under all conditions. Stakes which carry championship points must be run on both land and water. The premium list specifies the kind of game in each stake. Unless specified otherwise in the premium list, stakes carrying *championship* points must be run on pheasants or ducks. Pheasants, pigeons, or ducks may be used in other stakes.

Retriever field championships are also divided between Field Champion and Amateur Champion (only amateur handlers). To acquire an AFC, a retriever must win a National Championship Stake while handled by an amateur, or a National Amateur Championship Stake, or a total of ten points in Open All-Age, Limited All-Age, or Special All-Age Stakes, or a total of fifteen points in Open All-Age, Limited All-Age, Special All-Age or Amateur All-Age stakes. To acquire a Field Championship (FC), the retriever must win a National Championship Stake or a total of ten championship points. (How the points are determined is discussed in the booklet available from the AKC on field trials.)

Regular official stakes include:

Derby—For dogs under 24 months on the first day of the trial.

Qualifying—For dogs which have never placed or JAMMED (won a Judge's Award of Merit in Open), placed in Amateur or won two first places in Qualifying.

Open All-Age—For all dogs over six months.

Limited All-Age—For dogs that have previously placed or been awarded a Judge's Award of Merit in an Open All-Age or Owner Handled Amateur All-Age Stake carrying championship points, or that have been placed first or second in a Qualifying Stake.

Special All-Age—For dogs that have during the previous and current calendar year up to date of entry closing been placed or awarded Judge's Award of Merit in Open All-Age, Limited All-Age, Special All-Age, Amateur All-Age, or Owner-Handled Amateur All-Age Stake carrying championship points, or been placed first or second in a Qualifying Stake.

Amateur All-Age Stake—For any dogs handled by persons who are amateurs.

Owner-Handled Amateur All-Age—For any dogs handled by an owner or co-owner or member of owner or co-owner's family.

Not all stakes may be offered at any one trial. The premium list will state which ones are offered. Non-regular stakes may also be offered.

A Retriever Field Trial runs for two or three days, and there are two judges for each stake who must concur on all decisions. A National Championship Stake, or National Amateur Championship Stake, held only once a year, will run over four or five days and will have three judges. Thousands of retrievers may start at the beginning of the year while perhaps less than 100 qualify for the National Stakes.

Black Labrador Retriever with trainer. *Photo by Janet L. Yosay.*

The qualifications for the Stakes are decided by the National Retriever Club.

The dogs are tested according to a draw of numbers which is made before the trial. Judges evaluate the dogs on both their natural abilities (memory, intelligence, attention, nose, courage, perseverance, and style), and trained abilities (steadiness, control, response to direction, and delivery). The dog should sit quietly on line or in the blind, walk at heel, and do whatever directed by his handler until sent to retrieve. When ordered to retrieve, the dog should do so quickly and briskly, deliver the bird "tenderly to hand" and then await further orders. The regulations emphasize that accurate marking is of primary importance. The dog must mark the fall of a bird, use the wind, follow a cripple, and take directions from his handler.

A bird thrower throws the bird when directed by the judges. Birds are shot only by an official Gunner, who shoots the bird, then remains quiet waiting for instructions from the judges. At the end of the first series of tests, the judges call back all dogs which they wish to test further, and keep on until they have decided on the winners. Four placements are made.

Any handler using any equipment other than a whistle, making threatening gestures, holding the dog to keep him steady, or noisily or frequently restraining the dog will be eliminated from the stake. The dog may be eliminated for any of the following:

—Prolonged and loud barking or whining on line
—Attempting to retrieve without being ordered to do so
—Interfering with another dog's retrieve
—Refusing to enter rough cover, water, mud, ice, etc.
—Being out of control
—In marked retrieves, returning without the bird, stopping his hunt, or failing to pick the bird up after finding it.

FC AFC CFC Sandy's Slew Man Too, a seven-year-old male black Labrador Retriever won the 1988 Purina Outstanding Field Trial Retriever Award. Slew is owned by William Steadman of Lexington, NC and trained and handled by Gary Unger of Winston-Salem, NC. *Photo courtesy of Ralston Purina Company.*

—Switching
—Failing to find the bird when judges feel he should have
—Retrieving a decoy
—Repeated evidence of having a poor nose
—Not releasing the bird to handler
—Having a hard mouth or badly damaging the bird.

PURINA AWARDS

Ralston Purina also offers the Purina Outstanding Field Trial Retriever award to honor the country's outstanding field trial retriever and stimulate interest in field trial competition. The award is based on the dog's performance in all open events for the field trial season from January 1 through December 31 of each year. All AKC-licensed Open All-Age, Open Limited All-Age, Open Special Limited All-Age and the National Open are included. Bonus points are awarded to finalists and the winner of the National Open. The program is administered by an independent committee of experts in the retriever field trial competition.

AKC HUNTING TESTS FOR RETRIEVERS

In 1985, the American Kennel Club instituted the Hunting Retriever Tests for testing of retrievers in simulated hunting conditions. Many hunters who own retrievers use the dogs primarily for their own pleasure in hunting and do not want to participate in field trials. Instead, they wanted a measurable, non-competitive test of the dog's ability. The tests are held by retriever clubs and licensed by the AKC. The clubs may also hold sanctioned hunting tests for practice.

Junior Hunter, Senior Hunter, and Master Hunter tests are offered. There are no licensed judges and each test is judged by at least two judges experienced in field trials. Ribbons and rosettes (orange) are given, printed with the words "Qualifying Score Hunting Tests." There is a hunting test secretary and hunting test committee, just as there are in the field trials. Premium lists provide all the information needed to pre-enter.

Their purpose is to test the merits of and evaluate retrievers in the field to determine their suitability and ability as hunting companions. Conditions simulate those met in true hunting situations. Pheasants, ducks, or pigeons are used in Junior and Senior tests. Only pheasants, chukars or ducks are used in the Master Hunter tests. The judges have great latitude in designing the tests in order to enhance the hunting situation by using as naturally as possible numerous decoys, camouflaged blinds to conceal guns and throwers, duck boats, and duck and goose calls.

The judges must explain the test set-up and objectives before it starts. Only in the Junior Test are dogs brought on line with collars and leashes. Retrievers should perform equally well on land and in water, and are thoroughly tested on both with each test successively more difficult. They are tested on (1) marking, (2) style, (3) nose, (4) perserverance, and (5) trainability. To earn a qualifying score, a dog must pass all sections of the test in which he is entered with a minimum average of five points in each section and an overall average score of at least seven points. The dog is graded on a scale of zero to ten.

Junior Test

There are a minimum of four single marks, two on land and two on water. The dog may be sent to retrieve no more than twice. A dog requiring more than three casts on more than two marks cannot qualify. The dog should be steady and must retrieve to hand. He may be encouraged to hunt, but excessive noise is penalized.

Senior Hunting Test

There are a minimum of four hunting situations including one land blind, one water blind, one double land mark and one double water mark. One of these should be a walk-up which simulates jump shooting. The handler and dog start walking at the judge's signal. While they are walking, the judge signals for a bird to be thrown. The dog must be steady with no breaking or creeping, and must retrieve to hand. He may be encouraged to hunt. He must honor another dog at least once. Diversions are provided—shots and/or hidden duck or goose calls. Switching is penalized.

Master Hunting Test

This test simulates five hunting situations including a multiple mark over water, multiple mark over land, a land blind and a water

A Labrador Retriever. *Photographed by Janet Yosay.*

blind (one a double) and a multiple mark over land and water. One test includes a walk-up. The judges may devise additional tests, and natural hazards and obstacles are used to a greater degree.

The dog must honor at least once and is scored more strictly than in the Senior Test. There is at least one diversion, preferably two—once on land and once on water. Dogs that switch in this test cannot qualify. The dog must be steady and retrieve to hand once in each of the tests. He may be encouraged to hunt, but scoring is stricter. He must exhibit the willingness to work expected of a finished, experienced hunting dog. A dog fails if he doesn't retrieve, is out of control, switches, retrieves a decoy, or stops his hunt.

The titles Junior Hunter (JH), Senior Hunter (SH), or Master Hunter (MH) go after the dog's registered name. Each higher title supercedes the lower one. The Junior Hunter must receive qualifying scores in four different Junior Hunter tests, the Senior Hunter in five different Senior Hunter tests (or four if he had acquired the Junior Hunter title first), and the Master Hunter in six different Master Hunter tests (or five if he had already acquired the Senior Hunter title). A dog that has earned his certificate in a category cannot compete in a lower category, but can keep competing in the test category in which he has won his title.

For more information, write to the AKC for a copy of "Regulations and Guidelines for AKC Hunting Tests for Retrievers."

WORKING CERTIFICATES

Owners of retriever breeds have still a third option for proving their dog's hunting ability. Working Certificate (WC) and Working Certificate Excellent (WCX) tests are available through parent clubs. They test natural abilities: good nose, perseverance, desire to please, trainability, and intelligence.

Some basic training in retrieving is required. They are a pass/fail test—not a competition against other retrievers, but rather a competition of the dog and handler against a standard. By participating in these tests, people who own show dogs can find out whether their breeding stock have hunting instinct. Many owners who do not have the time or money to compete in field trials find the WC and WCX tests a pleasant form of testing their training.

The titles earned are breed club titles (not AKC) and will not appear on registration papers; however, the dogs must be AKC registered and at least six months old to compete. Each breed has its own requirements.

Basically, passing the Working Certificate shows a retriever's memory, nose, lack of shyness, retrieving instinct and willingness to swim. The WCX is more difficult and tests a dog's training and steadiness to a higher degree.

The Golden Retriever, Labrador Retriever, Chesapeake, and Flat-Coated Retrievers may earn these certificates. For specific requirements and information on where and when tests are held, write to the parent club. (See Appendix.)

GLOSSARY OF TERMS

Blind   1. A structure like those used in duck hunting. 2. A cover behind which dog and handler wait on line. It keeps the dog from seeing the falls or work of the dog he is to follow.

Blind Retrieve   A blind retrieve is one in which the dog isn't allowed to see the fall of the bird so his handler must direct him.

Blinking the Bird   Ignoring the bird when found and leaving it. A serious fault.

Breaking   Going out to retrieve before being commanded to do so. A disqualification in an All-Age stake.

Cast   Direction given a dog when working on a blind retrieve.

Cover   The growth of grass, corn, wheat or soybean stubble and brush where the birds fall.

Freeze   Unwillingness to release a bird on deliver until compelled to do so.

Guns   This refers not to the shotguns themselves but to the men designated to carry the guns and actually shoot the birds at a trial.

Hard Mouth   Badly damaging game in the retrieve, a disqualifying fault.

Honor   To sit quietly on line while another dog does his work.

Line   The spot from which the dog and handler work. A dog that is working is "on-line."

Line Manners   How the dog behaves. Retrievers are expected to be well-mannered.

Mark   The retriever must mark (remember) where he saw a bird fall. Also the mark means the fallen bird. There are single, double, and triple marks.

Popping-up   Looking back for directions on a marked bird before doing a thorough search. This is a moderate fault.

Series   Tests given at a field trial. All dogs compete in the first series, but only the dogs who compete satisfactorily are called back to the second series, etc. The series continue until there is a winner.

Style A dog's manner of performance. A desired performance includes an alert and obedient attitude; fast, determined departure on land and into water; aggressive search for the fallen bird; a prompt pick-up; and a fast return. Outstanding, brilliant exhibitions of style earn extra credit for a retiever.

Switching Birds Giving up on his hunt after a search, leaving the area and going for another bird; also dropping a bird the dog is retrieving and going for another bird.

12

CANADIAN AND NON-AKC TRIALS

UNITED KENNEL CLUB HUNTING RETRIEVER TESTS

In 1984, the Hunting Retriever Club was born; their Hunting Retriever tests are held under the auspices of the United Kennel Club and are open to retrievers registered with the UKC. As with the AKC, the retrievers must be six months old and bitches in heat may not compete. The events are called HRC/UKC licensed hunts and are quite similar to the AKC events, but the nomenclature is different and the rules and philosophy differ somewhat. They differ also in that there is a Hunting Retriever Championship available; whereas, the AKC tests are considered tests only and do not lead to a championship.

The Hunting Retriever Club was formed to test the hunting retriever in true-to-life hunting situations; to make available a Hunting Retriever Championship; to promote conservation of waterfowl and upland hunting birds; and to provide hunters with an ongoing educational program for their training, experience, and sporting competition.

A licensed hunt usually covers two days. Live or dead pheasants, pigeons, ducks or other game birds are used. The handlers, judges, hunt marshals, gunners and birdboy must all wear hunting clothes suitable for the season. Before each test, the judges explain the test objective. HRC tests are non-competitive—dogs pass or fail on their ability to meet preset standards rather than on the handler's expertise. A dog will be eliminated for fighting and may be disqualified for breaking and running into the working area of another retriever.

The hunt may be divided into two different classifications: a Class A Hunt, which has a maximum of thirty Started entries, twenty-five

Seasoned entries, and twenty-five Finished entries; or a Class AA
Hunt, which has a maximum of sixty Started, fifty Seasoned, and fifty
Finished entries.

Points leading to a Hunting Retriever Championship (HR.CH.)
are awarded in each category of tests. To attain a Hunting Retriever
Championship, the dog must obtain a minimum of 100 championship
points. The handler selects which category he will enter. The dog
can attain the championship with a combination of points from all
three categories, working his way up from Started to Finished, or may
attain it competing only in the Finished category if he is of that caliber.
The categories and championship points to be won are as follows:

Started—For passing all four tests in a licensed hunt, 5 championship points are awarded. A retriever may attain only fifteen points
in this category, which means passing all four tests in three different
licensed hunts.

Seasoned—For passing all four tests in a licensed hunt, ten championship points are awarded. A retriever may attain only twenty
points in this category, which means passing all four tests in two different licensed hunts.

Finished—For passing all four tests in a licensed hunt, twenty
championship points are awarded. A hunting retriever may attain his
championship competing only in the Finished category, which would
mean he would have to pass all four tests in five different licensed
hunts.

There is also a title of Grand Hunting Retriever Champion
(GR.HR.CH.) which can be achieved by first earning the hunting
retriever championship, then going on to accumulate another 200
points in the Finished category at licensed hunts. This gives him a
total of 300 points, as the 100 points he earned for his championship
count toward the Grand Championship. The titles are carried as a
prefix to the registered name on his UKC registration certificate and
pedigree.

Started Hunting Retriever

This hunt test is for the young or inexperienced hunting retriever
which may not have had the experience of a season of hunting or has
had only limited exposure to hunting and/or training. There are four
tests: two marked water retrieves and two marked land retrieves. The
dog may be cast twice only and may be encouraged to hunt. The bird
must be delivered in the general area of the handler but not necessarily

to hand. The dog is not required to be steady at the line and may be hand held. Throwing of an object (stone) is allowed, but will lower the score. If the bird is unfit for table (resulting from hard mouth), the retriever fails the test.

Two yellow labradors. *Photographed by Janet L. Yosay.*

Seasoned Hunting Retriever

These hunting tests have longer retrieves on both land and water than the Started tests. They are for dogs that have usually had a couple of hunting seasons' experience and more training time. There are four tests, which consist of at least a double marked land retrieve, a double marked water retrieve, and a walk-up, as well as tracking or quartering tests. The dog must be steady on line and retrieve to hand; the handler may encourage his dog to hunt. If there is a controlled break, the judges will give a lower score. (Creeping is considered a controlled break.) The handler may cast his dog only twice from the retrieving line and, at this level, throwing a stone by the handler will result in the dog failing the test. Once during the hunt, one of the following tests may be used:

Walk-up—The judge signals for the bird to be thrown while the handler and the heeling retriever are walking. This exercise simulates jump shooting.

Tracking—The retriever is required to track, locate, and retrieve a downed bird.

Quartering—The dog is required to quarter and locate the birds within range of the handler as in an upland hunting condition. The dog is not failed if he is not steady to wing and shot, but is scored lower.

Finished Hunting Retriever Test

This is the ultimate hunt for the hunting retriever. To pass the four test exercises is not enough; the retriever must do all the tasks

Dave Watts, professional field trial handler of Cavendish Kennels, Ontario, says gun dog training in winter can be interesting. Shown with a Golden Retriever.

required with both style and accuracy. Judges are looking for natural ability *and* a trained performance. The dog must respond to either voice or whistle command. The hunt has four tests, consisting of a multiple marked water retrieve, a multiple marked land retrieve (either or both of these must include an honor, a tracking, and a diversion retrieve), a water blind retrieve, and a land blind retrieve. The retriever will also be required to either quarter, track, or walk-up, depending on the particular hunting environment.

In this test a handler may encourage his dog to hunt, but the dog must be steady on line and the bird must be delivered to hand. When a diversionary bird is thrown as the retriever is cast or on return, he will be scored lower if he switches, but he must also retrieve the diversionary bird. The handler may cast his dog only one time. The walk-up, tracking, or quartering tests, whichever is used, are the same as in the tests of the Seasoned Retriever, but the Finished Retriever may be required to honor another dog. Triple marks are allowed and there are double marks on both water and land. The judges may require the retrieves to be done in an established sequence.

The United Kennel Club publishes *Hunting Retriever*, a bi-monthly magazine and the official newsletter of The Hunting Retriever Club, Inc. which gives locations of clubs, dates of hunts, etc. (See Appendix.)

The UKC also licenses field trials for coonhounds. These are covered in Chapter 14.

NORTH AMERICAN HUNTING RETRIEVER ASSOCIATION

The North American Hunting Retriever Association (NAHRA) also sponsors hunting retriever tests, although it has no registry affiliations. NAHRA tests are conducted by newly formed clubs (presently found mainly on the East and West coasts with a few in the Midwest). The association relies on individual and club memberships for support, similar to the Hunting Retriever Club/UKC.

Like the HRC/UKC and the AKC, the NAHRA tests are offered on three levels of non-competitive testing. The lowest level is called "Started." The dog must make single marked retrieves on both water and land. He does not have to be steady or deliver the bird to hand.

The second level is called "Intermediate." It requires double marks on land and in water and a very short blind retrieve in water. The dog must be steady and deliver to hand. Trailing and quartering are also required. To pass this test, the retriever must be fairly well-trained.

The third and highest level test is called "Senior." It requires double or triple marks and blind retrieves on water and land. The dog must be steady and deliver to hand. One of the blind retrieves must be mixed with marks and the dog must trail and quarter. A dog must be completly trained in order to pass this test.

Once a year the NAHRA holds a "National Invitational" for retrievers that have earned the most points in the highest level of their tests in the past year. All retrievers that complete this test are named to the NAHRA "All American Team."

NAHRA awards the title of Working Retriever (WR) for a total combination of twenty points in the three test levels. When a dog achieves 100 points (eighty of these earned in Senior level tests), he is awarded the title "Master Hunting Retriever" (MHR).

CANADIAN KENNEL CLUB FIELD TRIALS

Of course, with the popularity of sporting breeds and scent hounds, the same activities are going on north of our border in Canada. Canadian trials are also divided into Licensed and Sanctioned events and are open to unaltered dogs over six months of age registered with the Canadian Kennel Club, or to American dogs for a listing fee with the entry. (For all information on competing in Canada see Chapter 7.) There are trials for Beagles and Basset Hounds, for pointing breeds, retrievers, and spaniels. Instead of a Hunting Retriever Test, Canadians have Working Certificate and Working Certificate Excellent tests.

The events may last either one or two days, and are held on the grounds and terrain simulating as nearly as possible a usual day's hunt. Premium lists are sent out with all the same information as in AKC events. For the most part, the main difference is in the title attained and in the nomenclature of the different stakes. Other differences are: (1) use of dead birds and (2) trials run back-to-back. In Canada, the title attained is Field Trial Champion or Amateur Field Trial Champion and this title goes *before* the registered name (FTCH or AFTCH). If the dog has both titles, they would look like this, FT & AFTCH. If the dog is a dual champion, both show and field, his titles would be CH, FTCH and then the name; i.e., CH, FTCH Gundog Rarintogo.

Beagle Field Trials

Canadian trials are the same type as the AKC: Brace, Small Pack, and Large Pack, and the classes are the same. There are four placements in each class, but there is also a "Reserve" ribbon awarded which is not a placement. In the Derby Class, the Beagles are not divided by sex, and the class is open to dogs whelped between January 1 of the year before to December 31 of the year in which the trial is held.

A Field Trial Championship requires fifty points for thirteen-inch dogs and fifteen-inch bitches and seventy-five points for thirteen-inch bitches and fifteen-inch dogs, plus at least three placements of which two are first place awards. The points are awarded according to the number of starters; the number of entries is divided by place awarded and the fraction is dropped. For further details, see the Rule Book.

In Canadian trials, the measurement of the Beagle is done by three official measurers before the drawing of each stake. If the hound is over eighteen months old, the owner is issued an official Measurement Certificate. Once a hound has this Certificate, he doesn't have to be measured again.

A difference in the running of the Small Pack is that each pack is assigned a color and all hounds in the pack are given a colored collar to wear, which is supplied by the sponsoring club. The colors are red, green, yellow, orange, blue, purple, and gray. The running of all the stakes is essentially the same as those of the AKC.

Pointing Breed Field Trials

In Canada, two additional pointing breeds are recognized: the Pudelpointer and the German Longhaired Pointer. The points required for a Field Trial Championship or Amateur Field Trial Championship are the same as AKC—ten points—and the dog must exhibit ability to honor (also called "back"). The point ratings are Puppy Stakes Winner, one point; Derby Stakes Winner, two points; and Senior Stakes (all stakes except Puppy and Derby) receive one to five points according to placement and number of starters.

Like AKC, the dogs are run over predetermined courses with or without bird fields. They are run in braces by draw on recognized game birds. Times allotted for heats are the same in the different stakes as those of AKC. There are two judges and one judge follows each handler. There is also an official gun for each handler.

The stakes are similar except the Open Puppy stakes are divided: up to eighteen months, and up to twenty-seven months. The Shooting Dog Stake (Open or Amateur) is the same as the AKC Gun Dog Stake. There is also an All-Age Stake (Open or Amateur) open to all dogs over six months of age. There are four placements and ribbons and a Special Merit ribbon (no placement). The judges look for the same things as at an AKC trial. For a Shoot To Kill Stake, the premium list will state whether the shooting is to be done by official guns or whether handlers will be required to shoot their own birds. In the Shoot To Kill Stake, retrieving is required. In Shooting Dog or All-Age stakes restricted to German Shorthaired, German Longhaired or German Wirehaired Pointers, Vizslas, Weimaraners, Wirehaired Pointing Griffons, Brittany Spaniels, and Pudelpointers, there may be a requirement for a demonstration of either land retrieving or water retrieving performance, or both. The judges establish the conditions and must make sure that all placed dogs meet the requirements.

In the Championship stakes, Canada differs a great deal from her AKC counterpart. Winning a Championship Stake does not automatically make a pointing breed dog a Field Trial Champion, but points are counted toward the ten points needed for his title, and the winner and placers receive official certificates. These stakes also differ from AKC in that National, Regional, and Provincial Championship stakes are offered.

Water retrieve at Prince George (B.C.) Retriever Club's Licensed Field Trial. Can. Field Trial Champion and Amateur Field Trial Champion Barty's Sunshine Express, Golden Retriever owned by Dennis and Linda Daley of Prince George, B.C., Canada. *Photo by David Milne.*

Retriever Field Trials

Like the AKC, these trials are for all retriever breeds and Irish Water Spaniels. In addition, Canada has a native retriever, the Nova Scotia Duck Tolling Retriever. As with AKC trials, most of the dogs are Labradors, with a few Goldens and Chesapeakes. The purposes and procedures of the trials are similar to AKC, as are the reasons for elimination of a dog, and what the judges are looking for. In a Canadian trial, however, the judges may opt for the handler rather than the official gun to shoot over the retriever. The Official stakes are also the same, but the Canadians call the Derby Stake a Junior Stake. Nonregular stakes may also be held.

To become a Field Trial Champion, a retriever must accumulate a total of ten points in licensed trials. For an Amateur Field Championship, of course, the handler must be an amateur, and the dog must gain fifteen points. Complete details on which stakes must be won are in the Canadian Kennel Club rules booklet.

The National Championship and Amateur Championship stakes in Canada run the same as in the U.S., and a retriever may become a champion by winning either of the stakes.

Spaniel Field Trials

As in the U.S., these trials entertain mainly English Springer Spaniels, but are designed for all sporting spaniels except the Brittany and Irish Water Spaniels. Unlike the AKC, which has both Field and Amateur Field championships, CKC has only the Field Trial Championship for spaniels. The dogs must acquire ten points earned under two different sets of judges, inclusive of at least one five-point win.

The Official stakes are generally the same as AKC's, except there is no Amateur stake, and the Puppy classes are divided into Junior Puppy (up to eighteen months) and Senior Puppy (up to two years old). Open All-Age is the most important stake, as it is in the U.S. Dogs must demonstrate their ability to retrieve game from water after a swim.

A Canadian spaniel may attain his Field Trial Championship by winning the National Championship Stake; the winner of which is designated National Champion for that year. Entry qualifications are set by the CKC. At a Canadian National Stake for Spaniels, at least six tests or series are run; five on land and one on water. Dogs must run in pairs in at least two of the land series, and in four if possible. There are two judges.

The Canadian Kennel Club's "Field Trial Rules for All Sporting Spaniels" is a remarkably well-written document. The Standard Procedures are reinforced with extra material meant to clarify and analyze the manner in which the Standard Procedures themselves are interpreted. Be sure to write for this publication, no matter where you live or plan to field trial.

WORKING CERTIFICATE AND WORKING CERTIFICATE EXCELLENT

Rather than having the Hunting Retriever tests, the Canadian Kennel Club provides tests for Working Certificate and Working Certificate Excellent for retrievers and Irish Water Spaniels. The primary objective of these tests is to encourage the development and use of those natural working and retrieving abilities for which the retriever breeds were originally bred. These tests provide an additional means to help determine future breeding stock, and to encourage the owners of show dogs to develop their dogs' natural abilities in non-competitive tests.

The Working Certificate test is for all retrievers and Irish Water Spaniels that have not yet won the title of WC. The tests are : 1) Back-

Dan Devos of Cavendish Kennels, Ontario, is shown handling Can. FTCH Gahonk's Leave It To Jessie, Black Labrador Retriever, at the 1985 Canadian National Stake in Saskatoon, Saskatchewan. Jessie was one of Canada's top retrievers in 1985. *Photo by David Watts.*

Can. FTCH, Amateur FTCH, U.S. Amateur FTCH Gahonk's Mississagua Totem, Black Labrador Retriever, with his owner/trainer/handler, Dave Watts, of Cavendish Kennels, Baltimore, Ontario. Totem advanced from Top Canadian Junior in 1975 to Top Canadian Open in 1979. He was Ralston Purina Gold Whistle Winner in 1980, '81, and '82, a record, and in 1981 was winner of the Ontario Retriever Championship Stake. *Photo by G.L. Balogh.*

to-back singles on land and 2) back-to-back singles in the water. The Working Certificate Excellent tests are for those retrievers and Irish Water Spaniels that have won the title of WC before the closing of entries for the WCX tests. The tests are: 1) walk-up test with back-to-back singles on land; 2) honor on the walk-up; 3) water double; and 4) land blind. Two judges judge the dogs in the tests, and the dogs are either passed or failed. Upon satisfactory completion of a test, the dog receives a ribbon (brown) with the CKC crest and the words "Working Certificate Test," or "Working Certificate Excellent Test," and the word "Passed." The letters WC or WCX can then be used following the dog's registered name. Another way retrievers may achieve the titles is to receive a Certificate of Merit at a *licensed Junior or higher stake* for the Working Certificate or a Certificate of Merit at a *licensed Qualifying, Open, or Amateur All-Age stake* for the Working Certificate Excellent. To achieve the titles this way, the owner must apply in writing, giving the details of the placement to the CKC Show and Trials office within six months after the trial, sending in a recording fee with the application.

In general, The Working Certificate test is similar to the Junior Hunter Test and the Working Certificate Excellent test is similar to the Senior Hunter test given by the AKC. The Canadian Kennel Club publishes a three-page flyer giving all the rules and regulations, classification of faults—serious, moderate, and minor—and other pertinent information in detail. Booklets on regulations for Pointing Breed trials, Retriever trials, and Sporting Spaniel trials are individually available from CKC.

To find out about where the various trials are held, check a current copy of *Dogs in Canada*. Entry fees run roughly the same as in the United States.

13

AKC SPANIEL TRIALS

English Springer Spaniels are the only spaniels competing in field trials today, although the trials are meant for all the sporting spaniels except the Irish Water Spaniel. According to the AKC *Pure-Bred Dogs/American Kennel Gazette*, there are forty licensed field trials each year for English Springer Spaniels. Both Cocker and English Cocker Spaniels used to participate in these trials, especially the (American) Cocker, but the last time there were enough of them to fill a stake at a Cocker Spaniel Field Trial was in 1965.

The gallery walks along behind the dogs, handlers and judges, being careful not to disturb the performance of the dogs and keeping out of the way. The brush may be quite heavy, the thickets dense, and you will get caught up in briars if you aren't careful. The purpose of spaniel field trials is to demonstrate the performance of a properly trained spaniel in the field. As in all other field trials, the performance should be similar to an ordinary day's shooting, except done in a more perfect way, and the trial is held under conditions that simulate a day's hunt. The game birds are planted in cover on the course. The trials are held over a one or two-day period, and two judges follow the dogs closely and judge their performance.

Spaniel trials are quite exciting, as spaniels perform as dual-purpose dogs—finding and flushing the game and then retrieving it. A spaniel's first job is to seek, find and flush game, doing it with great eagerness; his second is to bring the game to hand. When a Springer Spaniel boldly attacks rough, thick, bramble-filled cover, this is always positively noted by the judges.

Currently, to become a Field Champion, an English Springer Spaniel must (1) win a National Championship stake (2) win two Open All-Age or two Qualified All-Age stakes or one of each of these stakes at different trials with at least ten starters in either stake, or (3) win one Open All-Age or one Qualified Open All-Age Stake *and* ten championship points in either of these stakes with at least ten starters in each stake with the points running three points for second place, two for third, and one for fourth place. Double points are awarded for these placements in National Championship stakes.

To become an Amateur Field Champion, an English Springer Spaniel must (1) win a National Amateur Championship Stake (2) win two Amateur All-Age stakes at different trials with ten or more starters in each stake, or (3) win one Amateur All-Age Stake *and* ten Amateur Championship points with the points awarded on the same scale as for Field Champion placements, and double points awarded for these placements in National Amateur Championship stakes.

For either championship, the dog must pass a test in retrieving game from water after a swim. For more detailed information on these requirements, please refer to the complete regulations booklet which you may order from the AKC.

The official stakes which may be offered at a Spaniel Field Trial are as follows:

Puppy—Six months up to twenty-four months.

Novice—Never won first through fourth place in Open Stake or Amateur All-Age Stake or first in any other stake (except Puppy).

Limit—Dogs have never won first place in an Open All-Age Stake or two firsts in any regular stake (except Puppy).

Open All-Age—All dogs over six months of age.

Qualified Open All-Age—Dogs over six months that have placed first through fourth place in any stake except Puppy at a trial.

Other, non-regular stakes may be run. The premium list will state which stakes are offered.

A *National Championship Stake* and *National Amateur Championship Stake* may be run once a year for dogs who have qualified. The winners of these national stakes are designated as National Springer Spaniel Field Champion and National Amateur Springer Spaniel Field Champion of the current year.

The Open All-Age Stakes are of first importance in any field trial, and the AKC stresses that an entire day should be reserved for the running of an Open All-Age Stake. For the shooting, official Guns are used, and these men must use a double-barrel, hammerless, or 12-gauge shotgun.

The judges are looking for the following: Control at all times; scenting ability and use of wind; "manner of covering ground;" per-

Springer Spaniel. *Photographed by B.J. Augello.*

severance and courage in facing cover; steadiness to flush, shot and command; aptitude in marking fall of game and ability to find it; ability and willingness to take hand signals; promptness and style of retrieve and delivery; and proof of tender mouth. Although there are only four placements in a stake, the judges may make a Judge's Award of Merit to an unplaced dog for particularly good work.

If you get involved in a Springer Spaniel club, you will find there are many different types of field contests offered. They have training events, fun trials and AKC sanctioned trials. The types of game are pheasants, ducks, chuckar partridges, or pigeons. The stakes at a sanctioned trial may be Puppy (steady and regular), Novice, Novice Handler, and Open and Amateur All-Age stakes. These will prepare you and your dog for the more rigorous point competition.

WORKING CERTIFICATES

The English Springer Spaniel clubs sponsor tests for *Working Certificate* and *Working Certificate Excellent* for all flushing spaniels. These are participated in by show owners and breeders who wish to keep hunting instincts of Springers and other spaniels alive with qualities acceptable to the pleasure hunter. These are non-competitive tests. Passing means the dog is not gun-shy, can hunt well enough to find a bird, and can retrieve on land and water. Pigeons are usually used, but chukars or pheasants may also be used. The Working Certificate Excellent tests are for dogs of more advanced ability.

For more information write to the parent club (see Appendix). The secretary can direct you to a local club in your area and send you detailed information on where tests are held.

GLOSSARY OF TERMS

Blink	Very serious fault whereby a dog avoids game deliberately.
Cast	Usually means the distance a hunting spaniel penetrates the cover when quartering.
Cover	Grass, brush, etc., in the area where one is hunting or working his dog.
Hard Mouth	Bad fault by a dog which injures the game while he is retrieving.
Honor	Steadiness to both wing and shot of game flushed by bracemate in trial or while hunting.
Hup	Command to a spaniel to sit.
Pattern	Degree of perfection which a spaniel demonstrates while quartering.
Steady to Wing or to Flush	A spaniel that stops instantly and remains motionless when it flushes game or if a stray bird flies overhead.
Steady to Shot	The spaniel stops instantly (preferably sits) when gun is fired.
Work a Line, Trail Out	To follow the body or foot scent in cover or on ground to locate moving game.

14

COONHOUND EVENTS

There are six coonhound breeds: American Black and Tan, Bluetick, English, Plott, Redbone, and Treeing Walker. All the breeds except the Plott trace their ancestry back to foxhounds brought over by the English in colonial times. The Plott traces back to boar hounds brought to this country by Jonathan Plott from Germany in 1750 to hunt bears in North Carolina. The breeds excel at hunting raccoons, but some are used to trail and tree bears, cougars, and bobcats.

Coon hunting, a totally American sport, is as old in this country as the first settlements, and as American as apple pie and blueberry muffins. Raccoons are indigenous to North America and are found over most of the continent. The wild raccoon is a nocturnal animal; wily, quick, a fierce fighter. Coons go into town and raid garbage cans and rummage through open garages, raid hen houses and chicken yards on farms, tear up the nests of wild ducks in the corn fields and eat the eggs, but their home is in the woods.

A hotly trailed coon goes up a tree and hides high in the branches among the leaves. The coon's protective coloration makes it nearly impossible to see at night, hence, coon hunters use powerful flashlights. The coon's fierce eyes reflect the light of the flashlight while the hound below barks to his owner that he has "treed" that coon.

Many coon hunters go out on their own with their hounds, but over the last thirty-four years, the licensed "nite hunt" has become one of the most popular organized dog sports in this country. According to *Dog World* magazine, licensed coon hunts draw 150,000 entries a year—more than all of the AKC Beagle, pointing dog and retriever trials combined. Although the hunts themselves are male dominated, a number of women do participate, and many enter their hounds in the bench shows which often precede the hunt.

Coon hunting clubs all over the U.S. and Canada, plus breeder associations for all six breeds, sponsor not only licensed events but also buddy hunts, fun hunts and kid hunts. Some of the youngsters work their own dogs in these hunts while others are given grand champions to use so they can gain experience in hunting. These are non-competitive events and a good opportunity for training young dogs and young or novice coon hunters.

Rural and small town people predominate, but devotees include people from all walks of life. A big event draws hunters from many states and even Canada. The parking area of the clubhouse or fairground is jammed with pickups and campers, motor homes, trailers, vans, and station wagons, all containing crates or dog boxes. It is a noisy gathering with a hub-bub of people exchanging hound stories, greeting old friends, children playing, dogs barking, and a rattling of dishes and pans as a barbecue is prepared.

It is chaos, you think, but organized chaos. Everything and everyone gets sorted out; the bench show starts; the hunt entries close; and casts are drawn. The casts of hunters and judges move out in convoys of pickup trucks to their respective woods—the men wearing either the typical farmer's type cap or lightweight fiberglass hard hats—all with powerful flashlights attached to them, the battery packs at their waists. Each hunter has his hound on-leash.

The night may be starry or pitch black; the woods deep and thick with underbrush, brambles, and wild blackberry vines with sharp thorns. A cool wind carries the smell of evergreens, dead leaves, humus—the forest primeval. Except for the flashlights, they could be in the eighteenth century; four men and their hounds on the trail of the raccoon in the same forests that were hunted back then. The excited hounds snuffle for the scent, then the first hound picks up the scent of the coon, and bawls to his handler, "I've picked up the trail." The second hound chimes in, closely followed by the other two and all are in hot pursuit. Human heartbeats pick up to a tempo that matches that of the hounds. Whose dog will be the first to tree? In this contest no guns will be shot; no raccoon will die, since points are the purpose of this hunt.

Coonhounds are natural hunters but must be trained to hunt only raccoons. The majority of coon hunters train their dogs themselves, and they, in turn, got their own training as youngsters hunting with their fathers or friends.

For a newcomer who wants to get started quickly there are many hounds offered for sale with training ranging from "started" up to Nite Champion, priced according to the amount of training and proven ability. Some sellers offer to ship on ten days' trial, or you can try

Blue Tick Hound treeing the coon. *Photo courtesy of Gary and Sheila Cook.*

the hound in the woods with the seller. If you want to start more slowly, with a young puppy, you will want to join a coon hunters' club in your area to get the training you yourself need, as well as some for the puppy.

Or, you can locate a trainer to train the dog for you. If you get into trouble training your hound and find he is running squirrels, possums or fox, you can have him "trash broken" and trained to hunt only raccoon for about half the monthly charge for full training. There are many advertisements in coon hunter magazines for all these services and for the hounds themselves.

Although there are several registries for coonhounds which license hunts, the largest is the United Kennel Club, Inc. All UKC upcoming events are officially advertised in the UKC monthly magazine, *Coonhound Bloodlines.* The Official UKC "Coonhound Rulebook" is also available from the organization. This gives all registration policies, breed standards, regulations and rules for nite hunts, bench shows, field trials, UKC World Coonhound championships (both Nite Hunt and Show), and information on the Purina Nite Hunt events. If you plan on hunting your coonhound in UKC licensed events, it's a very good idea to get this booklet first.

The magazine lists all the upcoming licensed events alphabetically by states, whether a bench show is also being held, or a water race or field trial. You will also find interesting articles, reports from different breed and hunting associations from all over the country, ads, and official reports on new UKC champions of all kinds.

Another magazine for coon hunters is *American Cooner—The National Tree Hound Magazine.* This is a large magazine, very popular with coon hunters, and besides UKC licensed events, it also features ads on hunts sponsored by other registries.

UNITED KENNEL CLUB HUNTS

Since the United Kennel Club is the largest organization sponsoring coonhound events, its activities will be discussed in detail. The UKC began to license night hunts on wild raccoons in 1953. These events (called "nite hunts") represent the most numerous of the over 5,000 licensed events held annually under the auspices of the United Kennel Club.

Nite hunts are open to all six coonhound breeds for dogs which are registered with the UKC. The hounds must be at least six months old and unaltered. A championship, the UKC Nite Champion (Nite CH.), is awarded to hounds that accumulate 100 UKC points with at least one first place win in a UKC licensed Nite Hunt. To become a Grand Nite Champion (Gr. Nite CH.), a hound must first become a Nite Champion, then win five Champion of Nite Champions events. Only Nite champions compete against each other. Thus, there is Open competition for all hounds not yet champions, competition of Nite champions only, and of Grand Nite champions only. Champions may not hunt in any lower category.

Many UKC registered coonhounds have won their Nite Championship or Grand Nite Championship and are also Show or Grand Show champions (dual champion or dual grand champion). The new registration and pedigree issued by UKC reflect this, and the titles go before the registered name, as Nite Ch. Ch. "PR" Beau's Bugle Ann (dual Champion, Purple Ribbon pedigree) or Gr. Nite Ch. Gr. Ch. "PR" Beau's Bugle Ann (dual Grand Champion, Purple Ribbon pedigree).

In Nite Champion and Grand Nite Champion casts, whichever hound scores the most points wins. The points for Registered (Open) dogs are figured in the following way:

Place	Points
First	40
Second	35
Third	30
Fourth	25
Fifth	20
Sixth	15
Seventh	10
Eighth	5
Ninth	5
Tenth	5

Winners: (1) The dog must have a total score of "plus points" before he can receive championship points and (2) the ten high point winners from different casts will be judged the first ten winners.

Pre-entries are not required. Coon hunters find out where a nite hunt will be and pack up and go.

A UKC licensed hunt is run by a licensed master of hounds and he is usually a member of the sponsoring club. His responsibilities include enforcing UKC rules and regulations; seeing that judging is fair; making sure qualified people are available to take entries; drawing the entries for the cast; keeping the scoresheets; sending the casts out to hunt; giving signed receipts of points earned to the handlers; and making a report of the hunt results to the UKC.

Entries are taken on the evening of the hunt up until the published closing time. Handlers must bring their dog's UKC Registration paper (also called "Bill of Sale") to be presented along with their entries. If there is a bench show in conjunction with the hunt, it is held in the afternoon preceding the hunt. (See Ch. 5.) After entries close, the master of hounds draws the entries from a hat or container, starting first with the Grand Nite champions if there are any, followed by the Nite champions and finally all other Open dogs. A casts consists of three or four dogs.

Non-hunting judges (those who do not hunt that night) are required for the casts of Grand Nite and Nite Champions. Judges who also hunt go out with the Open dogs, although some clubs provide

Gr. Nite Ch. Smith's Hardtime Rocky, a four-year-old male Redtick English Coonhound, poses with owner the Rev. Richard Moore of Queens, NY, after winning the 1988 Purina Outstanding Nite Hunt Coonhound Award. Rocky defeated more than 15,000 other dogs to win the eighth annual award, by far the largest sporting dog program in the country. *Photo courtesy of Ralston Purina Company.*

all non-hunting judges. As each cast is drawn, it is sent out to hunt. Someone familiar with the area takes all four dogs and handlers in a cast to the woods in a truck or van. (Each cast is sent out to a different woods.) The hounds run for three hours per cast and the first dog that strikes (picks up the coon's scent and starts barking) gets 100 points, the second 75, the third 50, and the fourth 25. Hounds have their own distinctive voices, and each handler knows the voice of his own dog. When the first hound gives voice, his handler says, "That's my dog,"; the second likewise; and so on until the last one has opened.,

After all the dogs in a cast are struck, they run the coon and tree him. Three members of the cast have to see the coon unless there is a non-hunting judge. The first dog at the tree gets 125 points, the second 75, the third 50, and the fourth 25. All these points are called "plus points." The judge keeps track on a scorecard. When the cast comes in, whichever dog scored the most points wins the cast. The more coons that are treed, the higher the scores will be, but occasionally a cast will come in without ever seeing a coon. The judges turns the scorecard, signed by the handlers, over to the master of hounds.

Besides the "plus points" for doing things right, there are "minus points" possible for various errors. If a dog accumulates 400 minus points, he is disqualified regardless of how many plus points he has. The minus points are given for treeing off game, treeing when there is no game, leaving a tree, quitting a trail being worked, and other such mistakes. If a Nite Champion or Grand Nite Champion trees off game, he is scratched immediately. He is certainly supposed to know better! Any dog that barks continually at nothing is scratched, as is a dog that is continuously silent on trail. Any dog that fights is immediately disqualified. If a dog is out of control, he is scratched. A dog that fails to hunt within one hour is also disqualified. In addition, any handler who gets out of control—has been drinking and gets disorderly (alcoholic drinks are not allowed), "mouths off" at the judge, is argumentative and rough—is disqualified.

After all the casts have come in, the master of hounds posts the scores onto a master scoresheet, designates the first through tenth placements, and gives the handlers of those dogs receipts for these placements.

Special Events

The two most prestigious annual events are the Autumn Oaks Classic held over each Labor Day weekend, and the World Coonhound Championship Hunt and Bench Show. The Autumn Oaks Classic is usually held three years in a row in one location, then moved to another. It has been held in such places as Coldwater, Michigan; Jasper, Indiana; and Winston-Salem, North Carolina.

Autumn Oaks

The Autumn Oaks runs like a regular nite hunt but pre-entry is required, and the hunt is for Open, Champion and Grand Champion competition. Entry is limited to 500 dogs for the two nights; 250 are hunted each night. One set of awards is made for both nights and special awards are also given.

This event draws upward of 7,000 people from all over the United States and Canada for the combined two-night hunt and accompanying bench show. The weekend is filled with activity in addition to the competitive events. There are booths for each of the chartered breed associations where representatives take memberships and share in fellowship and hound tales. There is a bench show judges' seminar where a judge goes over the fine points of judging using a Grand Champion hound, while another may discuss the coonhound's anatomy. A children's bench show where the youngsters are every bit as serious as Mom or Dad makes every kid a winner with a little trophy for trying. There are balloon races and sacks races, and more.

At least one of the breed associations usually holds its annual meeting and there may be a master of hounds seminar. In short, there is ample opportunity for learning as well as good old-fashioned fun, tall stories, renewing old friendships and making new ones.

The high point winner of the hunt is awarded National Grand Nite Champion of Autumn Oaks for the year. There are awards for National Grand Nite Champion of each breed for the year, and the first through third place winners of the Champion or Champions Hunt are recognized as well as first through tenth place for the registered hunt.

A National Grand Show Champion of Autumn Oaks is the ultimate winner of the bench show. National Grand champions of each breed are selected, there are first through third places in the Champion of Champions Show, and the Best Male and Best Female of each breed are selected in the registered show. Various plaques, trophies and special awards go to the winners.

After a weekend of such extended activity, Dad is bleary-eyed and "plumb pooped out" after crashing through woods and brambles until the wee small hours, so he sacks out in the camper. The kids are too tired to even hassle each other, and Mom is usually the one to drive home. But that's okay, everyone had a great time and a fun holiday.

UKC World Hunt

Once a year the United Kennel Club World Coonhound Nite Hunt and Bench Show Championship is held. This event has special pre-qualifying rules. It has large entries of champions and grand champions, both for hunt and show. The hunts are run according to the Nite Hunt Honor Rules as they apply to champions and grand champions. Only non-hunting judges are used and must be approved by the master of houds. Only UKC World Coonhound Nite Hunt champions may be entered in this World Hunt competition without going through the Regional Qualifying events. All entry fees are paid in advance.

The World Hunt is held in the fall, and the Regional Qualifying events start after January 1. These are located strategically throughout the popular coon hunting areas of the U.S. and Canada. Entries for the Autumn Oaks and World Hunt come from twenty-eight states and Canada. There is no limit to the number of these events a hound may enter trying to qualify, but he may qualify for the four Nite Finals of the World Hunt in only one Regional Qualifying event. An owner may qualify more than one dog. The top ten winners in each event receive special receipts which are sent in along with the entries for the World Hunt. A dog must have a total score of plus points before he can be considered one of the ten winners.

The World Hunt consists of four Nite Finals. On the first night, all eligible dogs are drawn out in casts and hunt for three hours with

Gr. Nite Ch. "PR" Hardwood Dan, a four-year-old male Treeing Walker Coonhound, poses with owner/trainer/handler Paul Sheffield of Baxley, Georgia, after winning the 1989 Purina Outstanding Nite Hunt Coonhound Award. Hardwood Dan defeated more than 16,000 other dogs to win the award, presented annually for the nation's largest sporting dog program. *Photo courtesy of Ralston Purina Company.*

two non-hunting judges and one guide, if needed, for each cast. On the second night, all dogs that hunted the first night except those scratched for ANY reason are redrawn into casts and hunt for three hours, again with two non-hunting judges for each cast and one guide if needed. On the third night, a maximum of twenty dogs hunt alone for two hours with two non-hunting judges for each dog and one guide, if needed. In order to qualify for the third night, the dog must be a cast winner with plus points for both the first and second nights. Should the limit of twenty be exceeded, the dogs with highest total combined cast winning scores with plus points for both nights are ranked until the limit of twenty is met.

On the fourth and final night, the top four cast winners with plus points from the third night are run together in one cast for three hours with three non-hunting judges and one guide, if needed. The dog with the highest total of plus points for this final hunt is declared the year's UKC World Coonhound Nite Champion. This winner's owner receives a wrist watch, a special jacket, a trophy, and a full page of advertising in three coonhound publications. The designation of World Nite Champion will go before this dog's name on his Registration Certificate and pedigree. The other three finalists are awarded special plaques. All four top winners from the third night's hunt receive finalists' jackets. (The final winner's jacket is exchanged for the special winner's jacket on the last night.)

UKC World Coonhound Show

On the last day of the four Night Finals of the World Hunt, the UKC World Coonhound Championship Show is held. The qualifying shows for entry in this event are held at the same time as the Regional Qualifying events for the World Hunt. All registered coonhounds including champions and grand champions are eligible. The shows are held according to the UKC bench show rules as described in Chapter 5.

Only the Best Male and Best Female of Show, Champion, and Grand Champion winners will qualify for the World Show. A UKC Bench Show receipt is given and this is sent in with the entry and fee by the entry deadline for the World Show.

The World Championship Show has two judges. Registered (Open) dogs, champions, and grand champions are all shown together. One judge selects the Best Male and Best Female of each breed of coonhound. Then the second judge, who has not been allowed to watch the first judging, selects from these twelve the UKC World Coonhound Show Champion and Opposite Sex winners. The winner has the designation World Show Champion placed before his/her name on the registration certificate and pedigree. Special plaques and championship jackets are awarded to both the Champion and Opposite Sex winners. The winner also receives a full page of advertisements in three coonhound publications.

UKC FIELD TRIALS

As in all other UKC events, licensed UKC field trials for coonhounds are run for trophies and points only. The field trial is not as popular an event as the Nite Hunt, so we do not see many Field Trial Champions. Most field trials are held in the arid western states where the Nite Hunts are not feasible because of the absence of wild raccoons, but a few are held in conjunction with Nite Hunt events.

One hundred points are required to become a Field Trial Champion and must include one First Tree and one First Line win in Grand Finals at least one time on the same date and in the same trial. To become a Grand Field Trial Champion, a champion must win five First Line and/or First Trees in five different trials plus other requirements (listed in the complete rules).

Dogs run in heats, with a maximum of six dogs per heat. There is a starting judge, two line judges and either one or three tree judges. A live raccoon in a cage which protects him well is placed about twenty-five feet up a pole or tree and left there during the trial. The dogs are taken to the starting line and released on the starting judge's signal. The dogs must follow the trail laid out between line flags (about fifty yards), with line judges behind the flags. A twenty-foot circle is drawn around the pole or tree containing the caged raccoon. The first hound to cross this line gets "First Line." The first hound to bark up the tree gets "First Tree," and there is a tree judge to decide on this portion. The First Line and First Tree dog in each heat advance to a Line or Tree Final. A scent track is laid prior to each new heat.

The larger trials (with over thirty-six entries) have semi-finals. The Line and Tree winners from the heats or semi-finals compete for the same win in the finals. Heat winners receive five points for First Line and five points for First Tree. If there is a large trial, no heat points are given; these points are given to the winners in the semi-finals. In the grand finals, the dog winning First Tree receives fifteen points and First Line ten points. Thus, thirty-five points is the most a dog could earn at any one trial. As always, any dog that fights is disqualified.

The 1984 Autumn Oaks. Judge Ken Duncan goes over National Grand Show Champions of Breed for overall title. *Photo courtesy of Coonhound Bloodlines Magazine.*

Grand Field champions run in their own heat (even if there is only one entered) and run only for prizes or trophies, as no further points are available. Also, a heat must be offered for champions. A Field Champion with no competition must complete the course satisfactorily to receive points toward his Grand Championship.

UKC WATER RACES

A UKC registered coonhound may also become a Water Race Champion. This championship requires 100 points and must include one First Tree and one First Line win in grand finals at least one time on the same date and in the same race. To become a UKC Grand Water Race Champion, a dog must win five First Lines and five First Trees in five Grand Line or Grand Tree finals in water races on five different dates. (For more requirements, see rules booklet.) The points are the same as in the field trials, and the heats are run in the same manner, with semi-finals if over thirty-six dogs are entered. There are the same types and number of judges. Water races usually take place in conjunction with a nite hunt. All the dogs are started at the signal from a starting box or the line, so they are all released at the same time.

Stakes are set at the water's edge and about thirty feet apart. All dogs must pass between these stakes or be disqualified. The raccoon is inside his protective cage and is cranked across the pond by use of pulleys. When he is in the middle of the water—about twenty- to twenty-five-feet out—the starting judge signals for the dogs to be released. The line to be crossed is just before the opposite bank and close to shore. The dogs must swim free and clear of the side boundaries across the pond and under the line, going in the direction of the pole or tree where the coon in his cage has been grabbed out of the water and put up the tree which has the twenty-foot circle marked around it. The first dog across the pond under the line by the shore is First Line winner. The first dog to bark up the tree wins First Tree; he must be completely inside that twenty-foot circle.

PURINA NITE HUNT AWARD

Since 1980, the Ralston Purina Company has sponsored the Purina Outstanding Nite Hunt Coonhound Award. Certain hunts are designated as "A Purina Nite Hunt Event," and points are accumulated at these. Among these events are the UKC World Coonhound Championship, Autumn Oaks, all the Regional Qualifying Events, some of the large sectional hunts and State Championships, plus UKC chartered breed association annual events, and some other breed association events.

The awards committee is made up of representatives from each of the six breeds and has the responsibility of setting the rules, selecting the events, and auditing and approving the final tabulated scores. The UKC keeps records of the points earned and reports the accumulated points monthly in its magazine, *Coonhound Bloodlines*. The competition year runs from September 26 of one year through September 25 of the next year.

The two main awards are a cash prize and an original oil painting of the winning hound given to the owner of the Purina Nite Hunt Coonhound of the Year at the annual awards banquet. Winning this is one of the greatest honors a coonhound can achieve.

OTHER REGISTRIES AND NITE HUNT EVENTS

There are several other registries which license coonhounds and coon hunters' clubs to hold hunts which run like those of the UKC.

These include the United Coon Hunters of America, Inc., the Professional Kennel Club, the National Kennel Club, the World Coon Hunters Association, and the American Kennel Club (which has taken over the American Coon Hunters Association registry and now sponsors events). Their events are advertised in the *American Cooner* in the same fashion and with the same type of information as UKC events. To compete, your dog must be registered with the particular organization, but that can usually be done the day of the hunt.

The big difference between these hunts and those of the UKC is that there are money prizes plus credit toward championships (except AKC). Occasionally, an individual club will hold a "money hunt" on its own.

The United Coon Hunters of America, Inc. (UCHA) holds hunts year-round. Its big event is the Grand National Championship Hunt, which last two days, and a bench show. There is a limited entry; entry fee for one dog is over $100 for the hunt and $40 or so for the bench show. The large entry fees become the prize money and the first place winner might receive as much as $10,000; second place half as much, and so on down through fourth place. The UCHA also holds Tour Hunts which are two-day events with limited entry. First prize for one of these might be around $1,500, with cash prizes awarded through fourth place.

The Professional Kennel Club (PKC) has licensed events in eighteen states, at all of which the awards apply toward PKC championships and the PKC World Championsiop qualifications. The PKC World Championship is for PKC registered champions and dogs that have won $300 for the current year. The events are usually held in the fall with large entry fees—about $250 per dog—and an entry limited to 320 hounds. Awards have been known to total over $50,000, with a very large award for first place. For example, a first place award has run as high as $18,000 to the winner and a tenth of that to the breeder; second place $5,000 to the winner and $500 to the breeder; third place $4,000 to the winner and $400 to the breeder; and on down to the sixteenth place winner with $400 and $40 to the breeder.

In addition, the PKC holds Futurity Finals, which are a two-day event in early fall. All futurities for dogs in any organization work the same way with a whole litter being nominated upon registration for future competition. The PKC event is open to all futurity eligible pups born within the preceding two years. Other requirements are: (1) the dog must win two consecutive casts in a Futurity Qualifying Event or (2) win $300 in PKC events since January 1 or the current year. The dogs compete for hunt awards of first place which can run as high as $15,000 to winner, $3,000 each to breeder and stud owner;

second place, $5,000 to winner and $1,000 each to breeder and stud owner; third place $2,500 and $500 each to breeder and stud owner; down to eighth place—$500, and $100 each. The Futurity Qualifying events are held on two weekends in September, the month before the Futurity, at various specified locations. Futurity monies are paid in on registration of the litter by the breeder, and no further fees are paid for the hunt events. A bench show is also held at the Futurity Finals, for which the entry fee may run around $50 per dog.

A typical PKC Hunt awards thirty percent of proceeds to first place, fifteen percent to second place, ten percent to third place, and five percent to fourth place. The entry fee for these regular hunts is about $20. The events are held in almost half of the lower forty-eight states. For the World Championship Qualifications, two night hunts are held in each region during the same month. The entry is limited, with the fee around $50. All cast winners advance. Typical awards based on a full entry of sixty-four dogs are: first place thirty percent ($960); second place fifteen percent ($480); third place ten percent ($320); and fourth place five percent ($80).

National Grand Show Champion of the 1984 Autumn Oaks, Gr. Ch. ''PR'' Hicks' Kentucky Tara, Treeing Walker female shown by owner Sheila Hicks Cook. *Photo courtesy Sheila Hicks Cook.*

The American Coon Hunters Association (ACHA) had both hunts and bench shows for many years, but the registry is now with the American Kennel Club, which licenses the events. Dogs must be registered with the AKC to compete.

The National Kennel Club (NKC) and the NKC State Champion Hunt and Bench Show are run on similar lines to those of the other clubs.

The World Coon Hunters Association (WCHA) has hunts and bench shows through the year. Their World Hunt and Bench Show is open to UKC, ACHA, PCA, and WCHA registered coonhounds. At the bench show, both awards and prize money are given. The entry fee for a WCHA World Hunt may run around $250 per dog. Typical prizes are: first place $5,000; second place $1,500; third place $1,000; and fourth place $500.

The children have their own special bench show at the Oaks. *Photo courtesy of Coonhound Bloodlines Magazine.*

As you can see, anyone who owns a registered coonhound and wants to hunt can pay his money, take his chances and be very busy every weekend. Coon hunters tell me they go out in the woods with their dogs to hunt a couple of nights a week on their own besides going on licensed hunts. They are people dedicated to their dogs and a love of getting out in the woods at night on a good hunt for those wild and wily raccoons. I have walked into homes where the trophies filled a whole room and spilled over into others. A couple of times when I have been on the way home from competing in a dog show, I have met winners coming home from a coon hunting event. When I saw their gorgeous big trophies, I looked at my six or twelve inch winged victory and thought, "Gee, I must be in the wrong game."

Some of the coonhounds that have won such beautiful trophies are champions or grand champions in both hunts and bench shows with several registries. If so, the name and all the titles would look like this if they were all spelled out: UKC Nite Champion, Show Champion "PR," NKC Nite Champion, Show Champion Beau's Bugle Ann; or UKC Grand Nite Champion, NKC Grand Nite Champion, PKC Grand Nite Champion, ACHA Nite Champion Beau's Bugle Ann. What a busy lady! And besides, being a female, Bugle Ann is going to spend time in the whelping box, too.

You can see that with the big prizes in the various coon hunting events, the people who pay the fees to enter such stiff competition are going to have dogs that are very well-trained, with good basic instincts bred into them. But, this is a sport in which anyone can participate, given a coonhound with good instincts and basic training in the woods.

GLOSSARY OF TERMS

Bawl   Long-drawn note of a hound's voice, opposite of chop.

Cast   Group of hounds and handlers sent out to hunt together.

Chop   Short, chopping bark.

Dog box   Crate or box with vents and door used to transport dog to hunts.

Drawing   Selection by draw of hounds to run together in a cast.

Go to the Timber   Go out into the woods to hunt.

Hunting Judge   In some casts at hunts the judge may also be one of the handlers of a hound in the cast.

Non-hunting Judge   The judge does not hunt but only judges the performance of the hounds. Always used in Nite Champion and Grand Nite Champion casts in all licensed hunts.

Off Game   Game other than raccoon.

Open   When a hound first gives tongue on a new track.

Scratched   Disqualified from further participation in hunt.

Strike   To find the game (coon).

Tongue   Voice of a hound.

Trashing   Running "off game" (any game other than raccoon).

Voice   The sound of a particular hound.

15
TERRIER TRIALS

Most people don't realize that they can participate in sport with their terriers. They think trials are for the sporting breeds or hounds; terriers just catch mice and rats, or dig holes in the yard if there are moles. Not so. Since 1971 when the American Working Terrier Association formed to promote the working abilities of terriers, terrier trials have been growing. Both dogs and owners find the competition to be a lot of fun.

Originally, working terriers were bred for hunting. The dogs had to go to ground (hence the name "terrier") and either bolt the quarry (drive it from its den), draw the quarry (drag it out of its den), or hold the quarry at bay (trap it in the den and bark or growl to signal its location so the people above ground could dig down to the quarry). Doing these things requires relatively small dogs with a tremendous amount of courage, skill, and gripping jaws. After all, small dogs going after such game as foxes, otters and badgers, as well as small vermin had to be very game and plucky. Except for the Miniature Schnauzer, all AKC registered dogs of the terrier group are either very old terrier breeds or go back to the original terriers of the British Isles.

Trials sponsored by the American Working Terrier Association are open to Dachshunds and any terrier that can get into a nine by nine inch hole. They must be registered with the AKC, or have an ILP number, or be registered with any recognized kennel club. Airedales and Soft Coated Wheaten Terriers are too large, but you will see a few Kerry Blue and Irish Terriers (the long-legged breeds) if they are on the small side. Predominantly, there are Cairn, Australian, Border, Jack Russell (who have their own registry), and Fox Terriers, all of which do very well at these trials. You will also see some Lakeland and Welsh, Bedlington, Norwich, Norfolk, West Highland White and Scottish Terriers, and the little Toy Fox Terriers which are registered with the UKC.

Association clubs that hold trials may be found anywhere in the United States, but are predominant in the East Coast states of Alabama, Florida, Georgia, Maryland, New Jersey, New York, North and South Carolina, Pennsylvania and Virginia. Putting on a terrier trial is quite inexpensive as an acre in a country setting is sufficient and the artificial earth is easy to construct. Most trials will have as many as 100- to 150 terriers competing in all classes. No training is required for a novice dog to compete, as the trials test natural terrier instincts. Trials are held from early spring through November.

To find out about clubs or trials that may be held near you, write to the American Working Terrier Association. (See Appendix.) It sends out a newsletter four times a year, and a subscription is included with membership dues. When you locate a trial within driving distance, plan to go and participate with your terrier. Entries are usually taken the day of the trial. Wear casual clothes and comfortable shoes, things you won't mind getting a little dirty. Take a picnic lunch, cold or hot drinks, a crate to keep your dog in when he isn't competing, his water and bowl, a lead and collar, and be prepared to have a good time.

In order to present similar conditions for all dogs in competition, club members construct an artificial "earth." A trench is dug and a nine by nine inch three-sided wooden structure is placed in the trench

Working terriers leaving the starting box. *Courtesy of Elizabeth Harrington.*

to form a tunnel. At the end of the tunnel is a cage protected by a wire barrier. The standard quarry placed in the cage are hooded rats, which are quite bad tempered. At no time can the dogs gain access to the quarry due to the cage. Also in this den area is a trap door for lifting out the dog and for the judge to observe the dog at work. Earth and brush are placed over the tunnel and den (cage) to make it look as natural as possible. Artifical scent is laid and is renewed after each dog competes.

THE CLASSES

The classes are Novice A for puppies up to twelve months, Novice B for dogs one year and older that have never qualified in a trial, and Open for dogs that have earned 100 percent in the Novice Class or are experienced at hunting game. A dog that earns 100 percent in the Open Class is awarded a Certificate of Gameness from the AWTA. (This is not an AKC certificate.) More advanced competition is available in the Certificate Class. The Canadian Kennel Club recognizes AWTCA titles. When a title is attained, the owner may send proof to the CKC, pay a recording fee and use the title after the dog's name.

Novice

For the Novice Classes the tunnel is ten feet in length with one turn (see Figure 1). No dog may wear a collar or anything on his body as it could get hung up while he is in the tunnel.

In the Novice classes, the handler and dog start ten feet back from the entrance hole. At the signal to release, the time starts. The dog must find the entrance on his own and enter and traverse the ten feet to the cage in one minute. When he gets to the caged animal, he must work continuously for a minimum of thirty seconds. Working means barking, digging, scratching, whining, or chewing. He may change his form of action but it must be continuous with no pauses of inactivity.

The judge sits at one end of the tunnel by the den area. He has a stopwatch and peeks in the porthole to observe the dog. At the end of thirty seconds, the dog's time is up and he is removed through the porthole. To pass, the dog must score 100 percent. The dog loses points if he isn't sure where the entrance hole is; you may help your dog, but this lowers his score. Judges are very lenient in letting novice

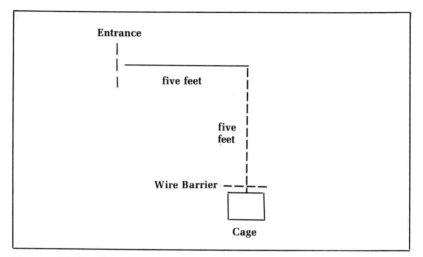

Figure 1. Novice Class Course.

dogs learn as this is the only way for them to gain experience and find out what's really going on. They won't pass this first time if they have to be helped and encouraged, but they will almost certainly pass the next time.

Open

For the Open Class, the tunnel is thirty feet long and has three ninety degree turns (see Figure 2). From the starting point, the open

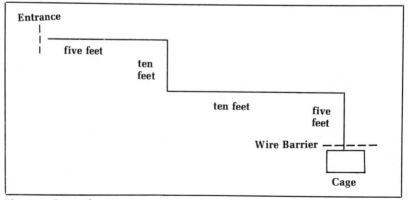

Figure 2. Open Class Course.

dog has thirty seconds to reach the end of the tunnel and must work the game continuously for one minute. It is only from this class that the Certificate of Gameness is awarded, and the dog must score 100 percent with no help from his owner in finding the entrance to the earth.

There is no limit on the number of times a dog can run in this class; they compete for the joy of it. However, once a dog has won his Open title, he is eligible to compete in the Certificate Class.

POST-TRIAL ACTIVITES

After the trial is over, practice is usually allowed using a wooden tunnel on top of the ground. Also after the trials are over, there may be races (both straight races and hurdle races), and conformation competition. These complete a day of fun for both dogs and owners.

TERRIER RACES

The races are divided by height so that the short-legged and long-legged terriers are competing against their own kind. The race course

Jack Russell Terrier going after the quarry. *Courtesy of Jeff Darling.*

is 100- to 125-feet long, enclosed with fencing. An animal pelt (or a fox tail) is used as a lure and is reeled up by the person standing behind a wall of hay bales with an opening for the speeding lure and dogs to pass through. Four to six dogs at a time are placed in starting boxes and shown the lure. Merry terrier eyes get brighter and short tails go like sixty. Then the boxes are opened and they're off! They are scored on passing through the opening in the hay bales to catch the lure. A lot of cheering goes on with the owners often more excited than the dogs. Once the dogs are past the hay bales, each owner has to hurry to retrieve his dog before he tears up the lure, which is needed for the next heat of terriers. Usually the first and second place winners from each heat will compete in a runoff to determine the overall winner.

For the race with hurdles, four hurdles are used and the rest of the race is conducted in the same manner as the straight races. The hurdles may be made of brush, wood, drain pipes, or sometimes even miniature stone walls are put up across the path. Actually, the hurdles may be constructed of whatever comes to hand, or may be made of wood and taken to the trial specifically for this purpose.

THE CONFORMATION SHOW

There is also a conformation show as part of the trial, and usually a sanctioned Jack Russell Terrier judge is used (or someone who is familiar with that breed and all AKC terrier breeds). For this particular show, which resembles an AKC "B" or fun match, the judge is looking both at the conformation or structure of the dog, and also at the suitability of his coat for working undergound. The classes are divided into male and female and usually consist of four- to six-months, six- to twelve-months, and adults. Most of the terriers entered in the conformation show are Jack Russells, which are divided by height in the adult classes—ten- to twelve and one half-inches and twelve and one half- to fifteen-inches.

With three different types of events occurring on the same day, whether you are a spectator or a participant, you will have a full day of fun and excitement. If your terrier was at his first trial as a novice dog, he will have learned a lot and will be raring to go the next time.

16
FOR SIGHTHOUNDS ONLY: LURE AND OPEN FIELD COURSING

The sighthounds (also called "gazehounds") are ancient breeds which were originally bred to sight and course (chase) live game, hunting on their own or in groups with hunters. Their purpose was either to kill for food or to eliminate predators. Since there is no longer a need for such dogs to help man bring down large, swift game for food, man has devised *artificial* lure coursing which simulates the hunt. In addition, there is open field coursing on *live* jack rabbits, but this is legal only in a few states.

The ten sighthound breeds recognized by the American Kennel Club and the American Sighthound Field Association (ASFA) are: Afghan Hound, Basenji, Borzoi, Greyhound, Ibizan Hound, Irish Wolfhound, Pharaoh Hound, Saluki, Scottish Deerhound, and the Whippet. For the purpose of lure coursing trials, the hound must be at least one year old by the day of the trial. Hounds which have been spayed or neutered may participate.

For centuries, coursing of hounds has been a spectator sport as hunters watched while hounds pursued their prey. After hunting methods improved, coursing survived because of human fascination with the beauty and drama of the swift, graceful and noble sighthounds. In the early 1700s, rules for formal coursing meets were drawn up in Europe. Country gentlemen as well as nobility were enjoying coursing while the American colonists struggled to clear the wilderness and build homes. Naturally, it took some time for us to catch up.

But lure coursing can be enjoyed today by Mr. or Ms. Every American. Almost without exception, any sighthound can be trained to course after a lure. If you have a sighthound, you and your hound can find tremendous enjoyment in this sport. It doesn't matter whether you bought your puppy as a companion or show prospect. All the sighthound breeds have had the coursing instinct bred into them for centuries. If fact, drawings of Greyhound-like dogs have been found on the walls of tombs of the ancient pharaohs. Many lure coursing hounds are also shown in conformation and obedience trials, and attain their show championships as well as titles in lure coursing.

By all means, find out where a lure coursing trial will be held in your area and go. You may know someone who courses his hound; the breeder from whom you bought your hound may course hounds or know about trials or a local club. If you strike out on information, write to the ASFA (see Appendix) and you will get a quick reply. Once at a trial, you can learn more about clubs, their events, and practice sessions. The contest is not only one of speed; the hounds are judged in five categories: enthusiasm, following (the lure), speed, agility, and endurance.

No matter where you go to course your sighthound in field trials, you must first train and condition him; you must get your dog in top shape as coursing is a most strenuous sport. A visit to your veterinarian for a complete checkup is the place to start. Most sighthound owners start training on their own and then go to practice sessions with a club, finally entering sanctioned trials for practice before they go to actual field trials.

Training the hound will probably be easier than conditioning as most sighthounds quickly become interested in the lure. My lure coursing friends start their hounds with a strip of rabbit fur tied to a line on a fishing pole. They play with the hound with this, running along in front of him. He jumps and dives at the bobbling piece of fur and plays tug-of-war. Some hounds become quite uncontrollable in their enthusiasm once their interest has been aroused.

This is where conditioning comes in as a hound may become so enthusiastic and excited at a trial that he pushes himself beyond his endurance, thus badly injuring himself. Even death may result. So, start with light workouts and progress slowly on a regular and consistent program, building up to the strenuous workouts of coursing. A dog's footpads need to be toughened also. This can be done with roadwork on gravel, and there are also products available to apply to the pads to toughen them and heal raw or cracked pads.

The ASFA publishes a pamphlet called ''Guidelines for Lure Coursing Practice.'' In this, the association recommends optimum conditions for training novice hounds, since aggressive hounds are not desirable, nor are those that chase the other hounds instead of the lure. Also, a course diagram for practice has been carefully worked out and requires only six pulleys so the hounds are not far away from the handlers at any point in the course. Stopping places are marked for young puppies or hounds starting to tire.

It is recommended that the practice sessions be conducted by someone with coursing experience and an experienced lure operator. Each hound is run by himself and some require several practice sessions before they develop a keen interest. The ASFA feels that hounds should complete the course alone *many* times at different practice events before running with any other hounds (e.g., six courses at three different meets). It is stressed that the most critical period in the hound's preparation for lure coursing is his first few courses with other hounds. At this time a novice hound can be ruined by another interfering with his course, so the hound chosen to run with novices must be selected very carefully—he should be one that will *never* interfere or fight.

Some "Dos and Don'ts" of ASFA practices are:

1. Don't run a novice hound with any other hound until you are sure that he is ready.
2. Don't run a hound that's tired.

TALLY-HO! Borzois, at the start of a lure course. *Photo courtesy of Diana Darling.*

3 . Don't run puppies on a regular course until they are at least *ten months old*. A puppy may run a short, straight course alone.

4 . Do play rag games with your hound before and after coming to a lure course.

5 . Don't be upset if your hound doesn't run well or maybe not at all. Go to several practices before giving up hope. Many good lure coursing hounds did not run well the very first time. Remember that this is a *fun* activity.

6 . Don't feed your hound before running.

7 . Check your hound's physical condition for minor foot injuries, signs of over-heating, etc. as you leave the field.

AMERICAN SIGHTHOUND FIELD ASSOCIATION LURE COURSING TRIALS

Currently no lure coursing trials are licensed by the American Kennel Club, although this has been under discussion. Currently the events in the United States are held under the auspices of the American Sighthound Field Association, which was founded in California in 1972. Lure coursing events are held by clubs that are members of the ASFA (presently just over 100 clubs), usually in the states where they are located, but sometimes in another adjoining state if the coursing club wants to hold a trial there and can find the facilities. For instance, Illinois clubs sometimes hold trials in Indiana, which does not have any clubs. Hawaii has a club but few entries since dogs entering Hawaii have a three-month quarantine period. Alaska does not have a club; and of the forty-eight contiguous states there are no coursing clubs in Alabama, Arkansas, Idaho, Indiana, Louisiana, Maine, Mississippi, Montana, Nevada, North Dakota, Rhode Island, South Carolina, South Dakota, Tennessee, Vermont, West Virginia, or Wisconsin, because not enough sighthound owners in those states have learned about lure coursing and applied to form a club.

The site may be any big grassy area away from people and traffic, with fencing along any highway. It need not be flat or treeless. It may be a cow pasture, a farmer's field, or a park. Two trials are usually held at one location over a weekend; one on Saturday and one on Sunday. This is because there aren't that many lure coursing trials available and many people travel hundreds of miles to participate. Over 300 trials are held each year, drawing about 10,000 total entries.

The events are open to all ten sighthound breeds. Registration is open to hounds which are registered with the American Kennel

Club, National Greyhound Assoication, the Canadian Kennel Club, or any AKC recognized foreign registry, or which have an AKC Indefinite Listing Privilege (ILP).

Two titles are available: Field Champion (FCh) and Lure Courser of Merit (LCM). The titles go *after* the dog's registered name. A hound must be a Field Champion before he can compete for LCM. On completion of a title, a certificate is automatically mailed to the owner. There are also certificates for Dual Champion (show and field champion) and for Dual Titlist (obedience and field champion). These are not automatically sent and must be applied for by the owner.

To become a Field Champion requires 100 points, two first placements, or one first and one second with *qualifying* competition (at least one first with two hounds qualifying, or second out of three hounds qualifying). The judges score hounds on five categories. These categories and the maximum points available are:

Enthusiasm	15 points
Follow	15 points
Speed	25 points
Agility	25 points
Endurance	20 points
Total Maximum Points	100

There are five placements, and championship points are awarded for each stake for each breed as follows:

First Place—four times the number of dogs participating (maximum of forty points).

Second Place—three times the number of dogs participating (maximum of thirty points).

Third Place—two times the number of dogs participating (maximum of twenty points).

Fourth Place—one times the number of dogs participating (maximum of ten points).

Fifth Place—Next Best Qualified (NBQ) ribbon, but no points. This is a reserve award.

To become a Lure Courser of Merit, the hound must first be a Field Champion. From the Field Champion Stakes he must earn 300 points and four qualifying firsts against competition. An alternate way is to win a qualifying first place when there is only one dog in a stake. For example, suppose there is one Open dog and one Field champion of a breed and there is no other competition. The Best of Breed winner (if he wins by running in the run-off) has defeated another dog, and the first place now counts. Remember that these trials are ASFA titles, not AKC.

The breeds do not compete against one another except in the Best in Field course—when all the Best of Breed winners compete. So, if all breeds were present, there would be a total of ten hounds competing for Best in Field. In the regular stakes, Afghans run against Afghans, Borzois against Borzois, Whippets against other Whippets. The regular stakes offered in all licensed trials for each breed are: *Open Stake* for hounds that do not have the Field Champion title; and *Field Champion Stake* for Field champions only. The Field champions cannot compete in any lower stake. The *Best in Field Stake* is usually offered at trials, but it is a non-official stake run at the option of the sponsoring club. Other non-regular stakes may be offered, such as Puppy, Veteran, Kennel or Breeder stakes. Non-regular stakes do not carry any championship points.

Premium lists give all the information about where the trial will be held, when, how to get to the site, the entry fee, time entries close, field committee, entry limit (if any), awards, stakes offered, trial hours, time of roll call, course plan, and other pertinent information. The course is varied with both sharp turns and straightaways, and should be interesting but not hazardous to the dogs. The minimum length of the course is about 500 yards, but it may go over a mile, depending on the trial site. The course is usually reversed for the finals, then again for Best of Breed and for Best in Field.

The lure used is made of strips of white plastic trash bag which may be combined with strips of rabbit fur. If the course is run on a field of snow, black or green plastic is used. The lure is attached to the end of a strong nylon cord, such as fishing line. A common method of running the lure is to use a battery-powered starter motor connected to a reel. The line is strung out over the course, making turns around low pulleys spiked down into the ground. The cord is about two inches from the ground. The lure operator uses a variable speed control or an on/off switch on the motor to reel in the lure at speeds up to sixty miles an hour. Some clubs use gasoline-powered generators.

If gate entries are also taken on the trial date, the entries will close half an hour before roll call which can be any time from six to ten A.M., but is always shown in the premium list. The purpose of roll call is to determine who is present of those entered and if they are capable of being run. Examination is done by the field trial committee to see if any hound is sick, lame, or if any bitch is in season. None of these will be allowed to run. If a hound is lame or in season, and in some cases, if the hound is sick, the entry fee is refunded.

Muzzles are not required, but some Whippets and Greyhounds do run muzzled since they are used to it on the race track. Coursing blankets are usually furnished by the clubs, as are the slip leads (the premium list will so state), but most lure coursers have their own sets of blankets and their own slip leads for their dogs. The blankets are of blue, pink, and yellow—as bright as possible—and are not actually blankets at all, but sturdy material secured with elastic in a size to fit the hound. These are for identification purposes so the judges can distinguish one hound from another.

Any dog that is not present at the roll call is scratched and the entry fee is not refunded. After roll call, there is a random draw by breed. Each breed is run in trios (threes). After the draw order is done, colors are posted so each handler knows which color his dog is to wear, which dogs he is to run with, and which course is to be run.

The order of the runs has been determined; clouds have boiled up overhead with a threat of rain. The first three to run are Afghans. They stand at the starting point with their handlers holding them, waiting for the signal. The excitement of the hounds is shared by their handlers. One man stoops to kiss his hound's head. The woman on the left has difficulty restraining hers. The third owner watches intently, waiting for the signal, legs braced, holding the quick release slip collar with both hands. Her hound trembles in anticipation of the chase and strains forward.

"Tally-Ho!" cries the huntmaster. And they're off, silken ears flying, coat flowing, in their double-suspension gallop, the white lure always ahead of them. Once slipped, the hounds are completely on their own with only their inbred instincts and training to guide them.

The two judges sit on a platform raised above ground level about ten- to twelve feet for an overview of the course. A canvas canopy shields them from the first drops of rain. The first hound in the blue blanket cruises by completely suspended in mid-air. The course takes a sharp turn and the hound shows his agility with a sudden shift in direction. The other two are close behind in hot pursuit of that bobbling white lure. The three hounds know it's just a piece of plastic, but that doesn't dampen their enthusiasm for the chase any more than the now-steady rain. Soon the chase is over; the three Afghans return to their owners as they have been trained to do; and the next three get ready for their turn.

All the preliminary courses are run for each breed, with the order of the breeds optional with the organizing club. After all the preliminaries ("prelims") are run, a random drawing is held to determine which hounds will run together in the finals, which are run in the same breed order as the preliminaries. After each course, the field secretary posts the judges' scores onto a master scoresheet. There are usually two judges per breed; however, only one judge may be used.

Each judge awards each dog points for his course, and after the hounds have run the two courses—preliminary and final—the sums of the two runs are added together. The total judges' scores determine the placements. A qualifying score is a minimum of fifty percent of the maximum judges' points available. If there are any ties, these are run off at the option of the handlers. In other words, if a handler feels his dog is too tired, he can forfeit the placement instead of running off the tie. An average dog will score from fifty- to sixty points from a judge; sixty to seventy-five for fairly good runners, higher for great runners. The dogs that run but quit, or just aren't with it, will score in the thirtys and fortys.

After the run-offs, the Best of Breed runs are made between the Open Stake Winner and the Field Champion Stake Winner of each breed, again in the same breed order as the prelims, finals, and run-offs. When a Best in Field Stake is offered, all the Best of Breed winners run against each other, and the highest scorer receives the award. Very beautiful rosettes are given for first placements, ribbons for all other placements, and a rosette and trophy for each Best of Breed and Best in Field.

There are three categories where a dog may be "participating" and not earn a score: excused, dismissed, or disqualified. A hound will be excused for failure to run, dismissed for playful interference with another dog's course, and disqualified for aggression toward another dog. An excusal does not affect a hound's record, but two dismissals within six trials will result in a hound being disqualified, which means he cannot compete until he is retrained and reinstated. The privilege to compete may be reinstated by the board of directors upon completion of (1) a minimum of one calendar month of retraining as appropriate, (2) certification by two licensed judges stating the hound is running cleanly, (3) a letter to the board of directors from the owner of the hound applying for reinstatement, and (4) a decision by the board to reinstate said privilege.

In the ASFA, an all-breed judge is one who is licensed to judge all ten breeds. A regular licensed judge may be licensed in certain breeds and provisional in others. To move from provisional to regular licensed judge in a particular breed, the applicant must judge the performance of seven or more hounds per trial in that breed at a minimum of three trials and under three or more different licensed judges. A provisional judge can judge three breeds, but can never judge alone.

The huntmaster has the responsibility of notifying any handler if his dog has been excused, dismissed or disqualified. The huntmaster is also responsible for making sure the judges, the lure operator, and handlers are ready. When all are ready, he signals the lure operator to start the lure moving. When it is moving a good distance (twenty- to thirty feet), he signals for the trio of dogs on line to be released by calling, "Tally-Ho!" Any dog released before the "T" of "Tally-Ho" may be penalized from one to ten points per judge in that course. This is called a "pre-slip" and the huntmaster must notify the judges of this. Some hounds get so excited that they are very hard to hold and lunge in anticipation, creating a pre-slip. Handlers have to know their hounds and guard against this. In addition, a course delay penalty can be earned by either hound or handler. Failure to arrive at the line on time, or failure to catch the hound right away at the end of a course results in a course delay penalty. Usually, a $5 fine is imposed on any handler whose hound is accidentally loose during a course.

A trial called the Grand Prix is always held in the East (New Jersey, Maryland or eastern Pennsylvania) toward the end of November. The Grand Prix has a perpetual trophy for every breed and Best in Field. It can be retired by winning it three times. In the West, a trial called the Turkey Run is held on Thanksgiving weekend. This is a very popular event and draws a very large entry.

Besides these popular regional trials, there are the Regional Invitationals and the International Invitational held each year. At these the best in the country compete since, as the names state, they are by invitation only. There are big trophies at these trials and the entry fees are higher. The International Invitational is normally held the first weekend in June and is rotated to different locations around the country. A perpetual trophy is offered only for Best in Field.

A trial called the Grand National is always held in the Denver, Colorado, area on the second or third weekend in September; however, no ASFA points can be offered at this trial as it is not sanctioned by the association. A perpetual trophy is offered for the Best in Field winner.

Although the American Sighthound Field Association is made up of member clubs and does not accept individual members, any owner who wants to get into lure coursing with his sighthound can join a local or regional club if there is one close enough. It is not necessary to join a club, however, to enter a trial. If you live in a state which

Borzoi, Kristull Rhythmic Polecat CDX, LCM, Can CD, Can FCHX, TT. *Photo courtesy of Diana Darling.*

does not have a club, and there are enough owners interested in start-ing one, you can write to ASFA for information. The association publishes a bi-monthly magazine called *Field Advisory News* which contains official news, articles, results of trials, trial schedules, new titles, and advertising. From this magazine you can obtain information on where to write for premium lists (see Appendix).

CANADIAN KENNEL CLUB LURE COURSING

In Canada both sanctioned and licensed lure coursing trials are held under the auspices of the Canadian Kennel Club. As in all other trials, the licensed ones are for championship points and the sanc-tioned ones are for practice. These trials are open to ten breeds which are recognized by the AKC and are CKC registered or registerable (see Chapter 7).

Trials are held by individual lure coursing clubs or specialty breed clubs. All the major provinces of Canada along the U.S. border have clubs, with Ontario's being the largest. There is very little difference between CKC trials and those of the American Sighthound Field Association. The premium lists give the very same types of information; the trials are run exactly the same; the hounds' placements and judges' points and scoring are the same; the hounds must be one year old by the day of the trial and may be altered; and the regular stakes are the same—Open and Field Champion. Non-regular stakes may also be held. Best in Field coursing and awards are held at the option of the trial-giving clubs. The championship points are figured in the same way.

The differences include: the Canadian course has a minimum of 450 yards in length; there must *always* be two judges; the title of Field Champion (FCh) requires 100 points and one first or two seconds, but there has to be one other dog competing even if he doesn't qualify. The highest title is Field Champion Excellent (FChX), but first, the hound must be a Field Champion of record. He competes in the Field Champion Stakes to earn an additional 200 points and a total of at least five first placements with competition. These first placements can include first placements won while attaining his Field Championship. The titles, FCh or FChX, go after the registered name.

Non-regular stakes (with no points) may be offered at the trials. These may be: Puppy—for ages six months to one year; Kennel—open to any two hounds entered in regular stakes and kenneled by the same person; and Veteran—open to any hound seven years or older on the day of the trial. The Veteran Stake is a mixed-breed stake.

For a copy of the booklet, "Field Trial Rules and Regulations for Lure Coursing," write to the Canadian Kennel Club. You will find schedules of the field trials for the coming three months in *Dogs in Canada*. Entry fees run about the same as in the U.S. and all trials are two- or three-day events.

OPEN FIELD COURSING

Open field coursing is the real thing—running sighthounds on live game: the jack rabbit. This is where the grace, beauty, speed, and agility of the hounds out in the open spaces is combined with the thrill and drama of the real chase. Watching these superb athletes in all-out pursuit of the fast-moving jack rabbit, both rabbit and dogs in their double-suspension gallop, you are transported to the ancient days of Egypt, Babylon and Persia. You can't help falling in love with the sight and the sport.

There are only a few states (California, Colorado, Minnesota, Washington, Wyoming, Nevada, and New Mexico) where such hunting of the jack rabbit is legal. As a further restriction, hundreds or even thousands of acres are needed, preferably wide open range. The courses themselves may vary from several hundred yards to several miles, depending on how long it takes for the hounds to catch the jack rabbit, or for the rabbit to escape. Twenty-five years of record keeping by the National Open Field Coursing Association shows that seventy percent of the jack rabbits escape, according to the NOFCA president, John Cogan. All the above states except Nevada and New Mexico have open field coursing clubs which are members of the National Open Field Coursing Association, headquartered in California. This association is an outgrowth of the Sighthound Coursing Advisory Committee, formed in California in the early 1960s. In 1970, the Open Field Coursing Association was founded, and expanded into the National Open Field Coursing Assocation (NOFCA) in 1973. All sighthound breeds registered with the AKC, CKC, National Greyhound Association, or AKC recognized registry except the Basenji may apply for registration and run in the NOFCA trials (see Appendix).

NOFCA publishes a newsletter for owners of all NOFCA-registered sighthounds which has all the information on trials and entry fees, and a coursing schedule for the season. The coursing year runs as the calendar year, but the courses are usually held from October to April.

The titles to be obtained are Coursing Champion (CC) and Courser of Merit (CM), also called Award of Coursing Merit. The titles go after the hound's name. The title of Coursing Champion require 100 points, at least ten points from a breed stake, ten points from a mixed-breed stake, and also one first or two seconds, and one unassisted take (kill) or two assisted takes. To become a Courser of Merit, the hound must earn all 100 points competing against his breed, plus one first or two seconds in regular breed stakes with one unassisted take, or two assisted takes from either breed or mixed stakes.

The points are earned in exactly the same way as in lure coursing trials with the same five placements. The first through fourth placements and points are the same, but the NOFCA fifth placement also carries points—half the number of dogs competing with a maximum of five points. No hunt can be held with less than five dogs, and the regular stakes are Open Mixed (all-breeds) and Open Breed. The non-regular stakes (which carry no points) may be Puppy, Veteran, Breeder, Champion, etc. The procedures are the same as in lure coursing a with random draw of three running together in a course.

The differences between lure and open coursing are: handlers always furnish their own blankets and slip leads, and not all dogs run two courses. They all run preliminaries; but to advance to the finals, the hound must meet the following criteria: (1) win his course or (2) any hound whose score is equal to or greater than the average of the course winners may also advance contingent on the judge's decision. (There is only one judge.)

For finals, there is a random draw again. There are no run-offs to break ties; instead the points are split. The judge scores a hound's performance in the following way:

Desire	10 points
Speed	25 points
Agility	25 points
Endurance	25 points
Touch or Take	15 points
Maximum Points	100 points

The pre-slip penalty is from zero to ten minus points, while in lure coursing trials the penalty is one to ten.

Since the courses are run on live game, the game must be flushed out by the dogs, handlers, judge, and gallery walking through the fields. In front are the three dogs with their handlers, with the huntmaster close by. Behind these walk the gallery (all other handlers and spectators). The person who sees the jack rabbit calls "Rabbit!" and gives the direction, right, left, or behind. The sudden leaping of a very large rabbit, perhaps right at your foot, can be quite startling, so much so that an inexperienced person can become suddenly mute and forget what he is supposed to do. The rabbit may even go in the opposite direction.

The judge places himself where he has the best visibility. The course varies due to the type of locale. In California, coursing is done in wide open, flat unimproved pastures or cultivated alfalfa fields where the entire course is visible. This is also true of Minnesota and New Mexico where visibility is lost only when the hounds run out more than a mile, so binoculars are necessary. If the course is run in hilly country, the judge will post himself at the highest point so that he can see what happens on the other side of the hill. Bright colored hound blankets are important for identification.

When the huntmaster sees the rabbit, he must determine whether it is actually a jack and if the course is runnable—no huge gullies or too near barbed wire fencing. If so, he gives the jack a thirty- to fifty-yard head start then calls, ''Tally Ho!'' If one of the three hounds is sighted on the game, it is considered a course. Each handler is responsible for seeing that his dog is sighted on the game.

In running the course, a new jack rabbit may pop up. Any hound that switches to the new rabbit loses the course, unless all three dogs switch. The judge must see the kill (or take), and also note whether one hound alone has taken the jack, or if the other hounds were involved.

When the course is over, the dogs *must* come back to the handlers. The reason for this is that the dogs will generally come back the same way they went out, whereas a handler going out to retrieve his hound may go out over new ground and flush another rabbit. If the hound takes too long in returning, a handler may go out to retrieve him only *if* he has permission to do so from the huntmaster.

Pharoah hounds such as this one compete in lure coursing. *Photo by Deloris Reinke.*

Two hunts are always held on a weekend. Handlers either camp out in RVs or vans, or they stay at a motel. Since the events take place out in the middle of nowhere, motels may be thirty or forty miles away. Roll call may be before daylight with the temperature down in the single digits, but everyone has to be up and off in the wee small hours to get there on time and most have already driven for hundreds of miles to get to the general area. Obviously, this is NOT a sport for anyone who is not in almost as superb condition as his hound; it is extremely important that both of you be in excellent condition. You may have to walk eight to ten hours in the field, climb fences, help lift your hound and other people's hounds over these (and some hounds weigh as much as people), or get your hound under barbed wire fencing. There are holes, gullies, and rugged terrain. A hound or handler can severely hurt himself. Dogs are trained to go under the strands of barbed wire fencing; better to tear holes in the coursing blankets than in their bellies. The first time out a hound may step on prickly pear cactus and wind up with needles in his pads. He generally will not step on prickly pear again.

Take at least a gallon of water for yourself and your dog, lunch, a first aid kit, a change of clothes (from cold to hot), and wear good hiking shoes. It is a good idea to back pack all of this since you will wind up a long way from your vehicle. Expect to be out on the open range from very early in the morning when it is very cold, to hot afternoon miles and miles from civilization—no concession stands, no portable toilets, no veterinarian on call. In case of rain, you will need boots and a slicker. Also, it is each handler's responsibility to make sure his hound has a strong collar and leash, as much, much more time is spent walking than in coursing.

If your hound advances to the finals, he has run two courses for the day, besides walking many miles. He will be very tired that night, but due to his remarkable recuperative powers, after a good meal and a good night's sleep, he will be raring to go the next morning. You would think the handlers would all drop into an exhausted sleep as soon as they have had dinner, but, no, they sometimes talk half the night. These are healthy, tough, competitive outdoors people who love the hunts almost as much as their gifted sighthounds.

Other Competitive
Events

17
OTHER KENNEL CLUB EVENTS

U.S. AND CANADIAN TRACKING TESTS

Tracking tests are offered by both the American Kennel Club and the Canadian Kennel Club. The titles awarded by both clubs are Tracking Dog (TD) and Tracking Dog Excellent (TDX). In both countries, both of these titles are placed after the dog's registered name, and a dog must attain the Tracking Dog title before he can attempt Tracking Dog Excellent. If the dog is already a Utility Dog, the initials UDT or UDTX would go after the registered name in both countries.

Passing the tracking test requires a great deal of training; therefore, very few dogs have attained either title. Tracking Dog trials test scenting in general, whereas the trial for Tracking Dog Excellent tests scent discrimination and time. The purpose of these tests is to demonstrate the dog's ability to recognize and follow human scent, and to use this skill in the service of mankind. The dogs are tested at outdoor trials under varied scenting conditions and over a variety of terrain. Dogs and owners are usually rugged outdoor types.

This is not a competitive sport—the dog is either passed or failed with no scoring for placement with other dogs. The tests are meant to demonstrate the willingness and enjoyment of the dog. By the nature and conditions of the tests, only a few dogs can be tested in a day, so there is usually a long waiting list for dogs to get their chance to prove their tracking ability.

The AKC and CKC tests are quite similar, although the Canadian track for TD is somewhat shorter than that in the U.S., and the TDX track is somewhat longer. The AKC TD track must be not less than 440 yards nor more than 500 yards. The CKC TD track must be at least 400 meters (about 433 yards) and not more than 450 meters (about 487 yards). The AKC TDX track must be least 800 yards but not more than 1,000 yards; whereas, the Canadian TDX track must be not less than 900 meters (about 975 yards) but not over 1,000 meters (about 1,400 yards). Both the U.S. and Canadian Tracking Dog tracks have just one track, and the Tracking Dog Excellent tracks have two diversionary tracks laid by other track-layers crossing the main track in order to confuse the dog and make his job more difficult.

In both countries the track is plotted the day before the tests. The track-layers and two judges meet and the judges select the fields where the track is to be laid, mapping it on a chart. Two starting flags, 30 yards apart, are set in place. Then the courses are set and stakes are put at each turn on a given course. On the day of the Tracking Dog tests, a half hour before the test begins, the track-layer, wearing the glove he is going to drop at the end of the track, moves from turn to turn pulling up the stakes as he goes (leaving the two starting flags). At the end of the track, he drops his glove. Neither the handler nor the dog knows the course.

In the Tracking Dog Excellent tests, the track is laid at least three hours before the dog is to start and only one starting flag is left in place. The track-layer drops one personal article at the starting flag and three other different personal articles at designated places along the course, the last of which may be a leather glove or wallet. The track-layer pulls up all the stakes on the course except the starting flag.

Dogs in the tracking test wear a harness with a twenty- to forty-foot leash attached. The handler follows the dog at a distance of twenty feet, but must not guide or lead the dog in any way; if he does, the dog will be immediately failed. The dog will also fail the AKC's TDX if he goes over fifty feet onto one of the diversionary cross tracks. In Canada, the dog is allowed twenty meters (about sixty-five feet).

Sometimes, unforeseen things happen at a tracking test which may cause even a very well-trained dog to forget all about the track. When a fox, groundhog or squirrel, or a covey of game birds is accidentally flushed, the dog must resume his tracking in a reasonable amount of time or he is failed. However, if this should happen, the dog can try again at another test.

For the AKC TD Test, applicants go through a process called certification because the number of tests given are so limited. This process screens out dogs that aren't quite ready. To apply, write a letter to the AKC asking for names and addresses of tracking judges in your area. Then contact the judge and make arrangements to meet him with your dog at a field he has approved. Either the judge or someone appointed by him will have the track laid and aged for about a half hour before you start your dog tracking. If your dog performs well in this preliminary test, the judge will certify in writing that he is capable of doing well at a tracking test. The judge will provide four certificates valid for twelve months based on the one certification. One certificate should be attached to each test entry form. If during this time your dog fails at four successive tracking tests, and thus does not earn the tracking degree, he must again be certified.

To find out about where tracking tests are held, read the AKC's *Gazette*, which gives dates of tests, sponsoring clubs, locations, judges' names, and deadlines. In Canada, premium lists are sent out by the club holding the tests. Write to the CKC for information or find the listings in *Dogs in Canada*. You may wish to observe a test, where you will be welcome, as there are usually several spectators in attendance.

CARTING

Among some of the more breed specific events available to participate in are Water Rescue and Carting tests. Some of the breeds that were developed originally to assist their masters by pulling carts loaded with goods to market, or assist on the farm are the Bernese Mountain Dog, Saint Bernard, Bouvier des Flandres, Rotweiller, Collie and the Newfoundland. The national clubs for most of these breeds sponsor drafting events to test and develop the inherited abilities of their dogs. The dogs are tested to demonstrate their obedience to the handler, willingness to be harnessed and pull the wagon, toboggan or travois over a maneuvering course. The dogs are asked to pull at a normal speed, slow, halt, back, work in circular patterns, 90-degree turns, narrow areas, and to stay while the handler is away from the cart and dog. Dogs can be tested at two levels of work: individual or as a team of two or more dogs hitched to a cart.

WATER RESCUE

Water rescue tests for Newfoundlands are sponsored by the Working Dog Committee of the Newfoundland Club of America who award titles for this work. The tests are divided into two levels of proficiency, junior "Water Dog" (WD), and senior or "Water Rescue Dog" (WRD). To obtain the WD title the dog must demonstrate six basic obedience and water rescue abilities. 1) complete a basic obedience performance, 2) make a single water retrieve of a "boat fender" at least thirty feet from shore, 3) carry the end of a line fifty feet out to a stranger in the water so he may be rescued by people on shore, 4) a retrieve of an object indicated by the handler floating on the water fifty feet from shore, 5) haul a boat with a rope attached for a distance of fifty feet in wading depth water without assistance from the handler, and, finally, 6) swim away from shore with the handler and then drag the handler back to shore on command.

In the senior division the dog must perform six exercises that demonstrate he has genuine ability to save lives in the water. 1) Standing in belly deep water the dog is asked to retrieve a small weighted object from under the water three feet in front of the dog. 2) He must carry a line out to a stranger in a boat and tow the boat ashore with the line. 3) The dog and handler then go out in a boat and the handler throws a paddle at least 20 feet away from the boat and sends the dog to retrieve it. 4) The dog is directed to retrieve one of two objects floating on the water to the handler and then retrieve the second one on command. 5) The life ring is considered an advanced life saving exercise. The dog is to go to one of three swimmers who is splashing and calling for help. Carrying a life ring with a short rope, the dog is to ignore the other two swimmers and go directly to the person calling for help and haul him back to shore by the rope on the ring. 6) Last, the dog is in the boat with the handler and one other person fifty feet from shore and the handler falls or jumps from the boat and calls to the dog for help. The dog must jump into the water and tow the handler to shore.

CANINE GOOD CITIZEN CERTIFICATION

The AKC Board of Directors approved the Canine Good Citizen Test effective September 1, 1989, for all AKC registered dogs. The dogs are evaluated on the basis of a pass-fail system. To qualify for the certificate issued by the AKC, the dog must pass ten individual tests done on leash that reflect situations you may encounter in everyday life. As stated by AKC, "the purpose of the Canine Good Citizen Test is to demonstrate that the dog, as a companion to man, can be a respected member of the community and can be trained and conditioned always to behave in the home, in public places, and in the presence of other dogs in a manner that will reflect credit on the dog. The Canine Good Citizen Test is not a competitive program, but rather a program of certification; it seeks to identify and recognize officially those dogs that possess the attributes that enable them to serve effectively as personal companions and as member in good standing with the community."

Contact the American Kennel Club for rules and additional information.

18
SLED DOG EVENTS

From the snowy frozen plains of Siberia, the Alaskan tundra, the vast white-laden lands of Canada, and those of Greenland and Labrador emerged the Arctic breeds of dogs. Surely, the Nordic gods must have pitied the human beings who lived through howling blizzards, extreme cold, and snow drifted higher than their heads. Perhaps they nodded to each other and agreed that they must atone to these people by creating wonderful heavy-coated dogs with plumy tails, little grinning smiles, sweet temperaments, and large, strong, compact feet—all the attributes that would enable them to pull sledges, help with the hunts, and provide a means of transportation for the human inhabitants of northern climes.

The heritage of these dogs goes back thousands of years into those misty and mystic times when men began to make up stories about their gods and how everything all started. History records the triumphs of these dogs in enabling man to reach both the North and South Poles, and thereby begin bringing civilization to the desolate frozen lands of the Arctic and Antarctic.

As early as 1873, the Royal Canadian Mounted Police used dog team patrols to bring order to the northern frontiers. Dog teams pulled the sledges loaded with mail throughout Alaska and Canada. In January 1925, diphtheria broke out in Nome, Alaska, and there was not enough antitoxin to prevent an epidemic. A relay of twenty-two native and mail teams raced through the rugged interior of Alaska from Anchorage and across the frozen Bering Sea to bring the serum to Nome. A statue of Balto, leader of one of the relay teams, now stands in New York City's Central Park.

The first formally recorded race between sled dog teams was in 1908—the running of the All Alaska Sweepstakes, a distance of 408 miles from Nome to Candle and back. It was won by John Hegness with a time of 119 hours, 15 minutes, and 12 seconds. The 1910 race was won by John (Iron Man) Johnson driving Siberian Huskies with a time of 74 hours, 14 minutes, and 37 seconds—still an unbroken record time.

ISDRA

The sport of sled dog racing was accepted with great enthusiasm and spread through the United States and Canada. In 1966, the International Sled Dog Racing Association, Inc. (ISDRA) was founded to serve as the central governing body for the sport. It lists members in forty-two states, nine Canadian provinces, seven European countries, and New Zealand. Among its purposes are: promoting public interest, encouraging cooperation between race clubs, creating standardization of race rules and procedures, and aiding in securing financial sponsorship of ISDRA sanctioned events. The association also works closely with national kennel clubs and the International Olympic Committee in establishing standards for races throughout the world. A certain flexibility in rules and regulations is necessary, not because of any change in the traditional elements or basic tenets of the sport, but

Noel Flanders and her six-dog team.

because of new techniques and materials. Of paramount concern are humane treatment of dogs and the safety of race contestants.

ISDRA sanctions sprint races, freight races, gig racing, and weight pulling. Most races are sponsored by a local sled dog club and held in a rural section of the state or province. In order to make the events as exciting as possible to attract large numbers of spectators, sponsors invite large numbers of sled dog racers. Sponsors such as dog food or supply companies, beverage companies, and truck manufacturers offer cash purse prizes, trophies, and/or dog food for the winning teams in each race held during the two or three day event.

The ISDRA has a point championship award program. The race or weight pull must be sanctioned by the ISDRA and drivers and weight pull handlers must be members of the Association to earn these championship points. The complicated formula of awarding points consists of several factors: size of purses for winners of different races, length of trail, type of class, number of drivers, and placement. (No points are awarded beyond fifteenth place.) The awards are gold, silver, and bronze medals for first, second and third places respectively; certificates are given to the top three placers in events which do not qualify for medals. Regional certificates are awarded to the top three placers in each region where applicable.

Races are held from mid-December to the middle of March in such places as Manitoba, Ontario, Alberta, Quebec, Saskatchewan, and British Columbia in Canada; Alaska, Montana, Colorado, Northern California, Minnesota, Michigan, New Jersey, North Dakota, Wisconsin, Wyoming, Illinois, Pennsylvania, Vermont, Utah, Idaho, New York, Ohio, Maine, Oregon, and New Hampshire in the United States. If you live in or visit any of these states or Canadian provinces, try to attend a sled dog race. It will help you to appreciate the events more fully if you know what goes into a racing team, how the classes are determined, and more about the race itself.

THE RACES

The modern sled dog race is a closed court event on a groomed trail of varying distances, usually with the start and finish lines at the same location. Each race is run in heats over a one, two, or three day period with the best overall time determining the winner.

On the first day the drivers draw for position, put on their numbered tabards, and leave the starting line at timed intervals. If one team overtakes another, it has the right-of-way and the overtaken team driver must give way to provide a clean pass.

Siberian Husky owned by
Phil and Denise
Burkhalter.

Sprint Races

The most popular type of racing today in this fastest-growing of winter sports is the sprint race. Sprint teams are divided into classes based on the number of dogs in the team and trail distance. These classes are:

Unlimited Class—The driver must start with at least seven dogs, but most start with twelve to sixteen dogs. The trail distance varies from a minimum of twelve miles at the beginning of the winter racing season to twenty-five to thirty miles in major races toward the end of the winter.

Eight Dog Class—The team is composed of a minimum of four dogs and a maximum of eight. Trail lengths vary from seven to twelve miles.

Six Dog Class—The team may have a minimum of three dogs and a maximum of six, trails running from five to eight miles long.

Three Dog Class—The team must have at least two dogs and a maximum of three. Trails are three to five miles long. This class includes both children and adults competing.

Freight Class—The freight classes consist of eight-dog, six-dog or three-dog teams with trails varying in length depending on class. The sled is weighted with cargo, usually fifty pounds per dog in the team. (Freighting dogs are usually larger animals more comfortable running at a steady, fast trot. Alaskan Malamutes excel in this class.)

Limited team events include the *Junior Class* with qualifying ages of children varying from region to region. There may be a *Pee-Wee Class* with children as young as three years old competing in dash races with one dog pulling a sled. The distance may be from 100 yards up to a quarter mile, under direct supervision of parents and trail personnel.

Cross Country/Long-Distance Races

The most famous of these races is the Iditarod, which covers 1,100 miles from Anchorage to Nome, Alaska. Many people call this the "Last great race on Earth." The race goes along the Iditarod Trail, now a national historic trail, which started as a mail and supply route. The race was first organized in 1971 by Joe Remington, called the "Father of the Iditarod."

Dogs and equipment are readied for a race.

Each team is examined by veterinarians before the race and also at each of twenty checkpoints along the way. If any dog has a medical problem, he is flown to Nome or Anchorage for treatment. The race tests both human beings and dogs to the utmost as they go through blizzards, extremely rough terrain, howling winds, temperatures that dip to as low as minus thirty, forty or even fifty-three degrees F., with a wind chill that is even lower. In addition, there is always the chance of a dangerous encounter with herds of wild moose.

The winner of the Iditarod receives a purse of around fifty thousand dollars in prize money, and a silver bowl. A humanitarian award goes to the musher who takes the best care of his dogs during the race. There is also a good sportsmanship award.

Most middle-distance and long-distance races vary from twenty-five or fifty miles up to as long as 500 miles. In these races there really isn't any limit to the number of dogs on a team. Drivers who prefer these races want to test the long range endurance of their dogs and themselves. The dogs best suited are Nordic breeds with an inheritance of centuries of work and survival in harsh climates. Pre-season training begins months before the first snow and is carefully planned to develop strength and endurance. Hundreds of miles of conditioning are necessary for team and driver prior to any middle- or long-distance competition. The drivers/owners have large kennels of dogs they have bred and trained from puppyhood.

There are always checkpoints along the trail and spectators can actually keep score as they watch the teams arrive at the checkpoints. During the race, drivers give their dogs snacks, food, water, and rest breaks. The drivers are required to carry, in addition to food, such survival equipment as a sleeping bag, snow shoes, first aid supplies, and fire-making supplies. Since the races go on into the night, lights

Racer in Tri Athlon.

are also carried. As in a marathon run, strategy plays an important part—when to rest, when to push on, how to take advantage of the weather.

Gig Racing

Sled dog racing requires an ingredient—snow—that is completely absent in some of the United States and other countries. To maintain the heritage of Nordic dogs in those milder climates, there are ISDRA sanctioned gig (rig) races which permit the dogs to compete. A gig may also be used to train northern dogs during the non-snowy seasons.

A gig is a three-wheeled cart with a locking brake and steering mechanism, available in aluminum weighing thirty to fifty pounds, or in steel weighing 90- to 200 pounds. The weight and number of dogs determines which gig is used. The lighter weight ones are used for the actual race. These have ballbearing wheels, which once in motion keep moving. Racing is restricted to times when the temperature is below sixty degrees F. for safety's sake, as these heavy-coated dogs become quickly overheated at higher temperatures.

These races are divided into the same classes as sprint races. Usually, there will be eight-, six-, and three-dog senior classes for adults, a three-dog Junior Class for twelve- to fifteen-year-olds, a one-dog Junior Class for children seven to twelve, and a Pee Wee Class for four- to seven-year-olds.

THE DOGS

A first-time spectator at a sled dog race may be a bit surprised at the different types of dogs in the teams. Yes, the Arctic breeds recognized by the AKC and CKC are present—Alaskan Malamutes, Siberian Huskies, and Samoyeds. But, as one woman said, "You can race anything with four legs and a tail that will run for you." Other purebreds that appear on teams include Irish Setters, Dalmatians, and American Coon and Fox Hounds, not to mention Collies. Also, there are mixes of hound/Husky, and hound/Labrador Retriever (for speed). One of the most popular and fastest dogs in the sport today is the Alaskan Husky, originally bred in the remote villages of Alaska for speed and stamina. It is a mixture of Arctic dogs with some outcrosses.

All the top performing dogs share certain characteristics: strength, slightly roached backs, well-angled shoulders, deep chests (good lung capacity), compact, tough feet, and protective coats. Today's racing dogs are on the small side, averaging twenty-four inches at the shoulder and weighing fifty pounds or less. These dogs have no useless fat; they are the long-distance athletes of the dog world and their owners carefully monitor the weight of each dog, keep their quarters very clean, and have excellent relationships with their veterinarians, whom they see often.

The dogs chosen for the team must be team players, as no driver has time to break up dog fights, and they must not be skittish or frightened by noise and commotion. The dogs are started in training at an early age.

EQUIPMENT

Racing sleds are about eight feet long, weigh under forty pounds, and are handmade from white ash, hickory, or birch wood lashed together. They are flexible and easy to maneuver. There is a brake, but in addition, all drivers are required to carry a snow hook secured by a rope to the sled. It is used to dig into the hard-packed snow as a temporary anchor.

The dogs are hitched to the sled in pairs by a lightweight polyethylene rope gangline known as the Alaskan racing hitch. Harnesses (made of nylon webbing) are custom-fitted for each dog, padded around the neck and down the center of the chest. For distance racing the harness is padded all the way up to the ribs for greater comfort.

The drivers carry two bags: one for extra snaps, collars, gloves, snacks, etc.; the other is a dog bag, which fits into the sled basket and is used to carry a tired or injured dog.

THE DRIVERS AND TRAINING

As in all other dog sports, the participants in sled dog racing represent every occupation in the country. This can be very much a family sport since there are races for both adults and children. And women do very well as drivers. In 1985, for the first time, a woman, Libby Riddles, won the grueling Iditarod; and in 1986, another woman, Susan Butcher, won, repeating her win in 1987 and 1988, and finishing second in 1989.

The drivers have to be almost as superb athletes as their dogs since it takes an incredible amount of strength to handle the dogs, and the driver doesn't get to ride much. When he does, he is usually pushing the sled with one foot ("peddling").

A driver starts off his future sled dog pulling a small piece of wood so the dog gets used to having something following him. Gradually, a little more weight is added. A sled dog doesn't have to be able to pull huge amounts of weight, he only needs to go as fast as he can with a reasonable amount of weight. The driver is supposed to offset the weight by pushing the sled, and also keeping the slack out of the gangline, to avoid a lot of shock on the dog's harnesses.

The harness fits the dog snugly around his neck and lies evenly over his back, coming across his last rib and ending at his tail with a small loop. The tugline connects to this loop and also a neckline, which is hooked to the dog's collar. With these, the driver keeps the dogs going in a straight line.

Having a good lead dog is an invaluable asset. Lead dogs can sell for as much as $5,000, if an owner will indeed part with him.

Since only a few drivers can secure outside financial assistance from sponsors, and even consistent winners earn only enough prize money to cover expenses, most participants in sled dog racing are dedicated hobbyists who do it for love, excitement, and a sense of accomplishment. They invest huge amounts of time and considerable money in their kennel of dogs, equipment, truck and dog boxes for transportation, veterinary bills, dog food and supplies, expenses for transportation and lodging while at the events, and entry fees. Care and training go on year-round, but the average musher attends five to ten races in a season. (Sometimes Mother Nature doesn't cooperate and there is no snow. And personal crises and illness cause other cancellations.)

According to ISDRA statistics, a typical three-dog team has trained for at least 100 accumulated miles during the fall months before entering the winter competitions, and many of the eight-dog and unlimited teams average over 200 miles per training season. For middle-distance and long-distance racing, even more hundreds of miles of conditioning and training are required to develop strength, endurance, and mental confidence.

Mush Toward Olympics

The sled dog racers hope to become part of the Winter Olympic Games in 1992. If so, these will be the first canine events in any Olympic games and will be an exciting addition.

Children compete in a Pee Wee class race.

Tips For Spectators

The ISDRA puts out a pamphlet about sled dog racing and lists these tips for spectators:

• Bring your camera and take all the pictures you want. But, remember that the chemicals in Polaroid film are poisonous to dogs. Use flash bulbs with discretion—don't use too close to a starting or moving team. Make sure you don't startle the dogs or interfere with the team's progress. Stay in the position you have selected until all teams have passed your post, then move.

• Never bring your pets to the races, or if you must, leave them in the car. Your pet will be safe there and won't bolt onto a course and cause a race to be lost.

• Never offer a competing dog treats. Always ask before petting. The dogs have important business to attend to—winning a race!

• Keep small children in hand. The dogs are eager to run and may leap or rear up in anticipation.

• Stay clear of the trail. Anyone too close may distract the dogs and cause them to bolt or balk.

If spectators keep these few precautions in mind, they can have a day of unique and exciting entertainment.

CANADIAN KENNEL CLUB SLED DOG PROGRAM

Canada also has a sled dog program. Canadian Kennel Club Sled Dog titles are awarded to sled dogs that pass certain requirements. Once attained, the letters SD (Sled Dog), SDX (Sled Dog Excellent), SDU (Sled Dog Unlimited) go after the registered name. The purpose of these races is to encourage participation and to recognize a dog's abilities, such as desire, intelligence, agility, strength, and attitude toward master and team workmanship in sled dog events. These races are run under International Sled Dog Racing Association (ISDRA) rules.

For the Sled Dog title, the dog must run at least three successfully completed races with a total accumulation of fifty miles and must be registered with the Canadian Kennel Club. After completing the Sled Dog title, a dog may compete for Sled Dog Excellent. For this, the dog must have a total accumulation of 100 miles (not including the fifty miles run for the Sled Dog title) and three successfully run races. The Sled Dog Unlimited title has a prerequisite that the dog have his SDX title. He must accumulate at least 300 miles (besides the 100 for SDX) in not less than three successfully run races. For more information, write to the Canadian Kennel Club (see Appendix).

WEIGHT PULLING CONTESTS

Weight pulling is not a new sport; it is, rather, an old sport that is gaining new popularity. These contests are sponsored by sled dog associations, weight pull clubs, and national breed clubs like the Alaskan Malamute Club of America. The ISDRA sanctions weight pulls in conjunction with its races, and the new International Weight Pull Association also sponsors them (see Appendix). The clubs have different rules but are similar to those of the ISDRA and all basically require a dog to pull the weighted sled sixteen feet in sixty seconds. Only one dog is needed to compete, not a whole team. All dogs must be one-year-old, and bitches in season may not compete.

Competing breeds include Poodles, Pit Bull Terriers, Alaskan Malamutes, Siberian Huskies, St. Bernards, Basenjis, Mastiffs, Alaskan Huskies, Newfoundlands, even the Bichon Frise and just about every type of dog, purebred or mixed-breed that you can imagine. The dogs are started in training when they are about three months old. At this time a trainer will put a very small harness on a pup and have him drag around a small piece of wood while playing with him. At this stage, it is important for the pup to have fun or he will become bored and more difficult to train later on. The trainer increases the weight as the dog grows and progresses. Some trainers use a small car tire, progressing to more tires or larger ones.

The harness used is specially constructed with a wooden dowel at the tail area. The harness is designed to ride low along the ribcage so that the weight is evenly distributed. The sled is built low to the ground and on runners for snow. When snow isn't available, a six-wheeled vehicle is used. The sled must be capable of carrying a load of 2,700 pounds (1200 kg.), and is pre-weighted with dog food, bricks, sand bags, or even cases of beer.

The course is sixteen feet long and about ten feet wide. A one minute time limit is set even though the actual pull may take only five or ten seconds. When a dog completes his pull, he is led from the chute even if the minute isn't up. The full minute is given to allow the dog time to figure out what he is to do, whether he can do it, whether he wants to do it, and how to do it, and finally, to do it.

The styles of handlers and dogs are quite varied. While one handler may quietly call his dog, another may shout and slap the

Weight pulling contests begin with lightly loaded carts that are built up gradually to several hundred pounds.

Samoyed. *Photo courtesy
of Karen T. McCarthy.*

ground. The dog can be encouraged in this fashion but he cannot be
touched. A dog must have a very strong desire to please his handler
and love to pull in order to excel. The dogs respond in different ways
to this encouragement. Some lean into the harness to start the load
moving and walk into the finish line. Others jump into the air. When
pulling sleds, the best trained dogs spring forward to start the load
moving, then keep their heads low, continuing to pick up momentum
until they cross the finish line.

There are two stages to the pull, a pre-contest in which the dogs
are weighed and qualify for a class, and then the classes. The classes
for ISDRA pulls are:

60 pound (27 Kg) Class—For all dogs 60 pounds or less.

80 pound (36 Kg) Class—For all dogs over 60 pounds up to and
including 80 pounds.

110 pound (55 Kg) Class—For all dogs over 80 pounds up to and
including 110 pounds.

Unlimited Class—For all dogs weighing more than 110 pounds.

This heavy-duty harness is used for weight pulls.

To qualify for the 60-pound Class a dog must pull 250 pounds maximum, 300 pounds for 80-pound Class, 350 pounds for 110-pound Class, and 400 pounds maximum for the over 110-pound Class (Unlimited).

The pulling chute is ten- to fifteen-feet wide and is at least forty feet, but not more than sixty feet, long. It is open at both ends to accommodate the sled and pull. A fenced barrier separates the spectators from the chute. The surface of the pull is level and snow is as hard-packed as conditions allow. After each pull, the track is leveled and groomed for the next dog. A holding area behind the pull chute is provided for waiting contestants.

At the start of the competition, each division is set at a determined weight level and increments of 50- to 100-pounds are added as decided by the chief judge. There may be many pulls before a winner is announced. An owner may elect to pass only twice in a row.

The dog pulling the most weight in his division is declared the winner. If there is a tie, the dog that completed the pull in the fastest time is declared the winner. At ISDRA sanctioned pulls, International Championship Points are awarded and gold, silver, and bronze medals are given to the three top point placers. Also, most of the weight pulls have cash awards to the winner which may be as high as $2,500.

Some examples of winning pulls: Unlimited won by a Mastiff pulling 3,130 pounds; 110-pound Class won by the same dog pulling 2,880 pounds; 80 pound Class won by an Alaskan Malamute pulling 2,680 pounds; 60-pound Class won by an Alaskan Husky pulling 2,080 pounds.

International Weight Pull Association

The contests of this association are organized so that all breeds can compete on an equal basis. A relatively new organization, it has members in eighteen states from Alaska to Florida, and in four Canadian provinces. Competitions are held on both snow and on wheels where there is no snow. Its rules are similar to those of the ISDRA, but additional weight categories are fifty pounds and under, and thirty-five pounds and under.

The IWPA confers International, National, State/Province, and Breed championships at each weight level. There are also titles to be won:

Working Dog—Must pull ten times its weight on snow, or twelve times is weight on wheels on four occasions.

Working Dog Excellent—Must pull fifteen times its weight on snow, or seventeen times its weight on wheels on four occasions.

Working Dog Superior—Must pull twenty times its weight on snow, or twenty-one times its weight on wheels on four occasions.

For the address of IWPA, see Appendix C.

HOW TO LOCATE EVENTS

The best way to find out about where and when races will be held is to write to ISDRA or subscribe to one of the racing publications. One published by ISDRA nine times a year for members is called *INFO.* Two others are *Team and Trail,* and *The Mushers' Monthly News* (see Appendix). These have advertisements of upcoming races (and weight pulls), some with entry forms included. Another way to locate a racing event would be to contact a breeder of the Nordic breeds (Alaskan Malamutes, Siberian Huskies, or Samoyeds). In the actual racing areas, many local veterinarians know who the racers are, as they see them frequently. Another possible source of information is the chamber of commerce in cities in the snowy states where races may be held.

GLOSSARY OF TERMS

All right!, Let's go!, Hike!	All are commands to move forward.
Bolt	To leave the trail or be out of control.
Checkpoints	Various stations along the course where race personnel check the teams coming through to insure that all drivers complete the entire course.
Chute	The fenced off section of the trail immediately beyond the starting line.
Gee	The command which tells the dogs to turn right.
Haw	The command which tells the dogs to turn left.
Holding Area	The area of the race site where the dogs are staked out prior to the race.
Leader(s)	The dog or dogs at the front of the team that are trained to respond to the driver's commands. When two dogs are used, it is called a "double lead."
Musher	A dog team driver.
Point Dogs (Also called swing dogs)	The pair of dogs directly behind the lead dog(s) which support the leaders in taking commands.
Stake-out-chain(s)	A means of retaining dogs at a race or training area before they are hooked up to a driver's sled.
Stoved	A dog that is lame or does not feel well.
Straight Ahead	A command used when there are alternative trail crossings and the driver wants his dog to go in a straight line.
Team Dogs	All dogs between the leaders and the wheelers.
Wheel Dogs	The dogs directly in front of the sled. They help the driver to pivot the sled around corners.

19

HERDING TRIALS AND TESTS

Herding dogs are still in demand in this and other countries for working livestock, whether sheep or cattle. Herding trials provide a way for owners and breeders to competitively prove the worth of their herding dogs.

One of the members of the herding dog group, the Border Collie, has been bred for hundreds of years for work, with intelligence and herding instinct the criteria for using a dog in a breeding program—not beauty. The Border Collie has its own registry and these dogs are used more for herding worldwide than any other breed. Australian Shepherds also have their own registry, where the stress is on herding ability and working qualities. Aussies also participate in many trials.

Many dogs of the herding group, although now bred mainly for show, obedience, and companion dogs, still retain all the instincts for which their ancestors were exclusively bred. From the Collie and Puli down to the little Shetland Sheepdog and Corgi, these dogs were originally bred to work stock. After hundreds of years of fulfilling their genetically programmed destiny by herding sheep or driving cattle, these breeds began to be recognized for show in their own home countries, and then in the United States. In order to make the dogs more beautiful for the conformation shows, breeders began to turn their attention to the finer points, and began to look for prettiness rather than for working qualities when considering studs and dams for their breeding programs. Even so, there are still plenty of dogs of these "prettier" breeds working on ranches and farms today.

In the last few years, there has been a resurgence of concern for preserving the intelligence and ability for herding for which these breeds were intended. Herding instinct tests and trial programs have been put in place by national breed clubs, and herding trial groups have sprung up across the country to make sure that these dogs still have the herding instincts when considering them for reproduction. Participation in these tests is exciting for the owners and awakens a latent inbred, retained instinct to go out and do their work in many herding dogs that have never seen a sheep or duck.

To find out where a sheepdog trial is being held, contact one of the organizations listed in the Appendix. Plan to spend the whole day; take a picnic lunch; don't take your dog if you are a spectator rather than a participant, but do take the whole family as it will be informative, fun and exciting.

AUSTRALIAN SHEPHERD CLUB OF AMERICA TRIALS

The trials held under the auspices of the Australian Shepherd Club of America in its Stockdog Program are also open to other breeds. The purposes of the Stockdog Program are to preserve and promote the inherited instinct of the Australian Shepherd, and to stimulate interest in the natural working ability of the breed through the use of certification programs and rigorous trial competitions. Outstanding working dogs are recognized in three areas: Working trials, Ranch Dogs, and Working Dogs.

Working Trials are conducted at three levels: training, fun trials, and sanctioned trials (the only level in which dogs may receive scores toward certification). All aspects of ASCA Working Trials are regulated by the ASCA Stockdog Committee using well-established rules and regulations. Dogs may show their versatility by competing in any of four classes consisting of ducks, sheep, hogs, or cattle. The duck competition enables the city dweller to test his dog for herding instincts.

The Ranch Dog program is for dogs that demonstrate a marked ability to be of assistance in everyday ranch work. The Working Dog certification is given for an unusual type of work, including all phases of stockyard work, auctions, and rodeos.

Sanctioned trials have the regular divisions and classes plus non-regular classes which don't count toward ASCA titles. When these trials are open to all breeds, they are called "all-breed trials." The trials are hosted by member clubs. The divisions open for dogs competing for certification are:

Started Trial Dog—for dogs six months or older that have not earned a Started, Open, or Advanced Trial Dog Certificate for the class being entered.

Open Trial Dog—for dogs that have been certified Started Trial Dogs for the class being entered, but not Open or Advanced.

Advanced Trial Dog—for dogs that have been certified Open Trial Dogs for the class being entered. Dogs certified Advanced Trial dogs may continue to compete in this division for that class.

The classes are: a) ducks, b) sheep/goats, c) cattle, and d) hogs. Non-regular classes which may be offered are run after the regular classes.

Titles that may be awarded are Started Trial Dog - STD (Class of stock), Open Trial Dog - OTD (Class of stock), Advanced Trial Dog - ATD (Class of stock), and Ranch Dog - RD (Grade).

Each dog must progress through the titles—Started, Open, and Advanced—in that order for a particular class of stock for the trial dog titles. Two qualifying scores at different trials are required for each title under two different judges in each class and division. Qualifying scores are comprised of scores from course and style as defined for each division and are:

1. Started Trial Dog—sixty-nine percent or more of the total points (69/115).
2. Open Trial Dog—seventy percent or more of the total points (87½/125) and forty percent of the total course score (14/35).
3. Advanced Trial Dog—seventy percent or more of the total points (87½/125) and fifty percent of the total course score (18/35).

Dogs are excused from competition for overdriving, mauling, incompetent work, abuse of livestock, excessive gripping, and wearing any training aid attached to the collar. The course is run to show the judge different abilities a dog should have for the level of class entered. Aussie trials consist of pen work. The dog takes the stock (three to five head) from a small take pen through two obstacles at the other end of the arena and re-pens the stock in the take pen. There is a difficult center chute for Open and Advanced dogs.

The course is judged on taking from the pen, drive, obstacles one and two, the chute, and re-penning for a maximum course score of thirty-five. Style is scored on natural working style, amount of handler assistance, attitude and obedience of dog, degree of training (amount of direction given), dog's stock savvy (thinking for himself), bark (quiet workers score highest), grip (where dog grips and how), and workability of stock (easy, cooperative stock score lower than more uncontrollable stock). Total style score can be ninety, and combined maximum score is 125. In the Advanced Class, if the dog passes the center chute, there is a fifty percent penalty off the total score.

Dog and handler also are working against a time limit. Circling the pen too many times, a weaving or uncontrolled fetch, and too many tries at an obstacle cause point deductions. Every trial is different in both facilities and stock, so each trial is new and interesting.

There is also a modified outrun course which begins with an outrun. The fencelike obstacles are positioned slightly differently; the central obstacle is a panel obstacle rather than a chute; and the intermediate and advanced sheep and duck classes have a free-standing pen.

Premium lists are sent out with all information. If entry limits aren't reached at sanctioned trials, day-of-trial entries are taken. After entries close, there is a random drawing of the order of runs, then the judge or course director gives any special rules or advice.

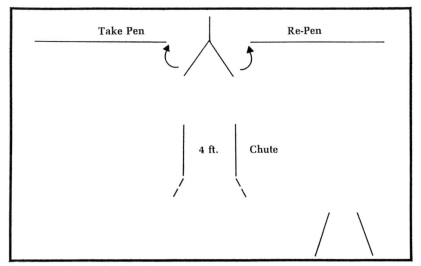

Figure 1—A typical course layout.

Ranch Dog

Any club member who has Australian Shepherds that have shown themselves of great assistance to their owners in everyday ranch work may apply to the ASC of A to have a Ranch Dog Inspection. The dog must be a valuable asset and a necessary part of handling livestock or fowl for the owner, and must demonstrate his talent to an ASC of A approved judge. Spayed bitches and neutered males may compete.

The applicant must describe the type of work to be done, the terrain and obstacles on the course, and the type and number of stock or fowl to be worked. A relatively small fee is charged.

The dogs are judged on attitude, style, obedience, task, and handler with a possible total of 100 points. Average is fifty to seventy-four points; Good, seventy-five to eighty-nine points; and Excellent, ninety to 100 points. Teams of two dogs are judged on separate score-sheets. The owner provides room and board for the judge.

For the Australian Shepherd Club of America Stockdog rules, and information on a club or trials in your state or region, write to Michelle Sage, Stockdog Secretary (see Appendix).

BORDER COLLIE TRIALS

The first recorded sheepdog trial was held in Bala, Wales on October 8, 1873. Ten dogs competed and the trial was attended by 300 people. The winner was a Scot and the dog was Scottish bred. From there, the trials spread to other countries, but it was in Scotland that the high standard for intelligence of the Border Collie breed was set by breeders and shepherds. The canny Scots knew how much time and money the hard-working dogs could save them, as one Border Collie can help a rancher move several hundred head of sheep, doing the work of eight men. The Border Collie alone has the true "eye," which controls the sheep.

In the United States today, there are several Border Collie organizations to jealously guard the standards of working ability set for the breed, and to sponsor sheepdog trials. These are: the American Border Collie Association, the American International Border Collie Registry, the Border Collie Club of America, and the North American Sheep Dog Society. The latter is an affiliate of the International Sheep Dog Society of Great Britain.

Working Certificates

Border Collie clubs provide opportunities for attainment of the Working Certificate, permitting the use of WC after the dog's name. Typical requirements for the WC are those of the Border Collie Club of America (based on North American Sheepdog Society requirements).

First, the dog must be registered with one of these four associations (ABCA, BCCA, AIBC, or NASDS); second, the dog must be certi-

A Border Collie and handler working sheep.

fied by a recognized sheepdog trial judge at a recognized sheepdog trial; and third, the dog must be considered of proven working ability by the judge. The dog's working ability is judged in the following five areas:

1. *Gathering* a group of animals (sheep or comparable livestock), making not less than a 100-yard outrun, cautious approach, careful lift, and straight fetch.
2. *Driving* a group of animals in a specified direction to a designated point for at least twenty-five yards away from the handler.
3. *Penning* the group of animals on command.
4. *Style*—doing the work in quiet Border Collie style, with no gripping or pulling wool and using eye for control.
5. *Judging*—according to the BCCA Standard of Working Ability.

The BCCA stipulates that should a Border Collie breed be recognized by the AKC for show (conformation) purposes, the AKC must recognize the Working Certificate, and no dog shall be permitted to become a conformation champion unless he has been certified as a working stockdog.

Sheepdog Trials

Sheepdog trials for Border Collies were the first trials held in the United States, and all trial programs for other breeds are patterned after them. A minimum of three sheep, with a maximum of five, are used for each dog. A total of fifty sheep may be used at a typical trial. The trial classes and point schedules vary somewhat according to the sponsoring association or club, but generally, the classes are divided into Novice and Open. The Novice class is designed strictly for novice dogs and handlers who have *never* competed in Open classes. There may be a Pro-Novice class for a combination of either a beginner handler and trained dog, or a beginner dog and an experienced handler. The Open classes are for everyone who wishes to compete in them, but are usually entered by experienced handlers and trained dogs. Successfully competing in Open classes requires years of work on the part of both dog and handler.

There are many local and regional trials and also state championship trials. Some trials are called National Championships, but no special requirements of previous wins are necessary, except for the "handlers trial" which is held in the fall. Dogs that compete in this trial must have finished at the top of a qualifying trial within the preceding year.

An example of judging and possible points at a Border Collie trial are:

General (5 points)
Overall impression of dog's work

Temperament (10 points)
Adjustment to people and environment	3 points
Intelligence	2 points
Obedience	2 points
Attitude toward work	3 points

Eye (30 points)
Concentration	15 points
Control of livestock	15 points

Style (15 points)
Freedom of movement	4 points
Tail carriage	3 points
Speed and stamina	4 points
Courage and caution	4 points

Gathering (30 points)

Outrun	15 points
Pause and lift	5 points
Fetch	5 points
Balance	5 points

Driving (10 points)

Approach	5 points
Control of livestock	5 points
Grand total	100 points

Some trials include another ten points for shedding (also called shagging). This entails having the handler leave the dog to bring the sheep from the pen to the shedding area a short distance away from the pen. The dog must then separate one or two sheep from the others and drive them away from the rest of the sheep to the judge's satisfaction.

Another schedule and possible points might run as follows:

Gather (outrun-10, left-5, fetch-10)	25 points
Driving (7.5 each drive and gate)	15 points
Shedding (separate 2 sheep from flock)	5 points
Penning	15 points
Single Sheep (separate 1 sheep from flock)	5 points
Maximum Total	65 points

Just as many trials do not include shedding or single sheep, many trials have additional gates, bridges, or chutes for the sheep to be driven through. However, all trials include the elements of outrun, lift, fetch, drive, and pen. Also, each dog (and handler) starts with the total possible points and then points are deducted along the way for every mistake. Because of this variety, every trial is different, interesting, and challenging for dog and handler.

At the start of the run, the handler and his dog stand several hundred yards away from three or four sheep. (See course diagram.) Already the dog senses the sheep and excitedly implores his handler to let him go work the "woolies." The sheep, however, have no idea yet that the dog is there. At the signal from the course director, the handler lets his dog go, giving him a command to go to the left (come by) or the right (away-to-me). The dog streaks out on his outrun to position himself cautiously behind the sheep without causing them to bolt. Now, as the handler calls or whistles, the dog performs the

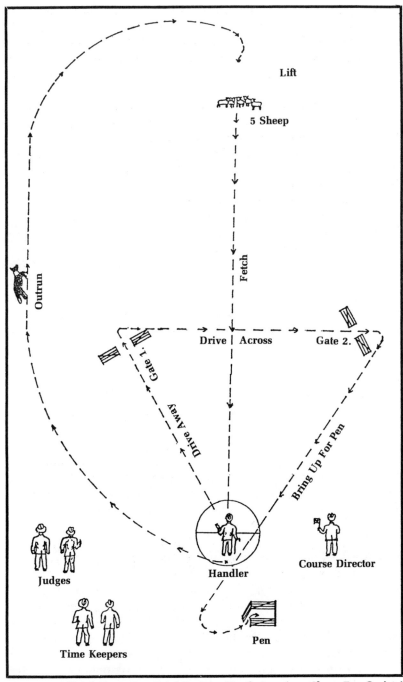

Figure 1—Official Sheep Dog Trial Course (North American Sheep Dog Society)

lift, starting the sheep in motion. The dog must maintain control with eye contact to keep sheep moving in as direct a fetch back to the handler as possible, or points are deducted. If an animal moves in the wrong direction, the handler will call instructions to the dog to tell him which way to go to get the sheep all going in the right direction.

Once the dog has the sheep in front of the handler, the handler directs the dog by voice and signal to drive the sheep 100 yards directly across the course through another gate. Then the handler leaves the spot where he has stood through the entire run (in front of the judge), and stands by a chute which is fifty or sixty yards from the second gate. The handler may not touch the sheep, but may use his shepherd's staff to pound the ground to help the dog force the sheep through the chute and into a pen.

Most Border Collie trials provide for work at a pretty advanced level. They are held at farms and ranches or at fairgrounds in conjunction with county or state fairs, and are usually sponsored by a local Border Collie club. Training clinics are also available. To find out where trials are held in your area, write to the North America Sheepdog Society (which sends out flyers with information on upcoming trials and clinics), the Border Collie Club of America, or the American Border Collie Association (see Appendix).

Border Collies are real pros in the field.

AKC HERDING BREED CLUB PROGRAMS

While Border Collies have always been bred for work rather than conformation, the herding breeds of AKC registry have been bred mainly (but not exclusively) for show, companion, or obedience work. However, several parent clubs now have programs to test herding instinct, and some even conduct trials and award herding titles. This signifies a renewed interest in preserving the heritage of these breeds and encouraging breeders to test their stock for herding instinct when considering them for their breeding programs.

The first herding breed club to start a program to test for herding instinct as well as establish a trials program with titles was the Bearded Collie Club of America in, 1983. They were followed shortly thereafter by the American Working Collie Association (smooth and rough-coated Collies) and the Belgian Tervuren Club of America. In 1986, the American Herding Breed Association was formed to provide the same opportunities to other breeds to earn the Herding Instinct Certifications. Its trial program was set to begin January 1, 1988. In 1987, the American Shetland Sheepdog Association followed suit with its herding instinct program.

Herding Instinct Certification

Basically, all the associations have similar requirements and guidelines for herding instinct tests. These are strictly "pass/no pass" tests developed to test the inborn ability and desire of a dog to work livestock. If a dog of another breed than that of the sponsoring club is entered in a test which is open to all herding breeds, the program chairman of the parent club of that dog's breed must sanction the test (in other words, approve the tester and the test guidelines and then receive results of the test before it issues a Herding Instinct Certificate and allows the dog to use HC after his registered name).

The herding instinct test does not require previous training. Any person with just one dog of a herding breed may particiapte. However, the dog must be registered with the AKC, the UKC, have Indefinite Listing Privilege (ILP), or be registered with a foreign registry, and must be six months old in order to qualify. They may be spayed or neutered. Dogs that fail the test may be tested again on another day. Some tests are open to all herding breeds, while others are exclusively for one breed.

Each dog is tested individually. Usually, about twenty-five to thirty dogs are tested in a day, with a limit of forty per tester per day.

Some breeds are tested on ducks.

Three head of ducks, sheep, goats, or cattle are required for each dog. Usually, ducks or sheep are used. There must be enough stock to allow rest periods, as the safety and humane treatment of the livestock are of prime concern.

The arena is fenced in and should be at least forty by sixty feet for ducks and sixty by eighty feet for sheep. Each dog is tested wtih lead dragging or off-lead, and is given a maximum of fifteen minutes to fulfill requirements for passing.

The experienced tester is crucial since most of the dogs may have never encountered livestock before. When the owner enters the area with his dog on-lead, the tester will ask him a few questions about the dog's background and the owner's experience. Depending on the responses, the tester may do all the handling or closely guide the owner. The tester must know techniques to help awaken a dog's instincts, develop proper habits, and be able to recognize potential problems. He or she gives participants the necessary guidelines and carries a long bamboo pole to block a dog from coming too close to the stock if necessary.

To qualify, the dog, after a brief period of introduction, must show sustained interest in herding the livestock by either circling or attempting to gather them, or following them to drive them, for at least five of the fifteen minutes. So long as there is no threat to the livestock, barking and feinting as though to nip do not keep a dog from passing. The dog may be loose-eyed or show a lot of eye, and a variety of approaches and styles are acceptable.

If a dog shows no interest at all, fails to show sustained herding instinct, or leaves or attempts to leave the working area, he will not pass. Any dog that strongly and consistently shows aggression toward the livestock, attacks an animal, or grips it, will not pass and must be removed from the work area *at once.* Uncontrollable dogs and those that cannot be tested with lead dragging or off-lead will not pass. If a dog shows such fear of the livestock that he cannot be tested, he, of course, cannot pass.

If you participate in a day of testing, you may go home with a sunburned nose, a scraped shin, and dust in your hair, but your dog will have had a pleasant day, and if your dog passed the test, you will have experienced the thrill of learning if your city-bred dog still has the inborn instinct for what he was originally bred to do. You can put that HC after his name, and you might both have had such a positive experience that you will decide to go in for active training to compete in herding trials.

Herding Trials Program

Before participating in an actual trial, you will need to train your dog on livestock with someone who is an experienced trialer, or, best of all, with a herding club. These clubs have been springing up all over the country in the past few years. By writing to any of the associations already mentioned (see Appendix), you can find a club near you. Herding club newsletters (including the AHBA newsletter) and herding magazines provide calendars of events where information about upcoming trials can be obtained.

The AKC herding breed clubs mentioned in this chapter and the American Herding Breed Association have arrangements whereby a dog may qualify in other trials and receive credit toward a title so long as the owner applies ahead of time for approval and the forms to take to the trial for the judge to fill out and sign as to the dog's qualifying score. For example, a Bearded Collie may participate in an Australian Shepherd Club trial or a Border Collie trial (if it is open to other breeds) and get credit toward a herding championship with the Bearded Collie Club if he qualifies.

Generally, the courses are quite similar and are Border Collie-type outrun courses like the one shown for NASDS trials. Courses may vary slightly according to the sponsoring club.

Scoring also may vary from one organization to another, but the dogs are always graded on the outrun, lift, fetch, driving, and penning of the livestock. The judging is rather subjective, as a great deal of interpretation is allowed.

Judges for the North American Sheepdog Association, the Australian Shepherd Club of America, and local or state sheepdog societies are eligible to judge at the trials sponsored by these associations with others approved on a case-by-case basis. The regular classes are Started (beginner or novice) and Open (for trained dogs and titled dogs). The Open Class may be divided into Intermediate and Advanced. The stock must be at least three per dog of either ducks, sheep, goats, or cattle.

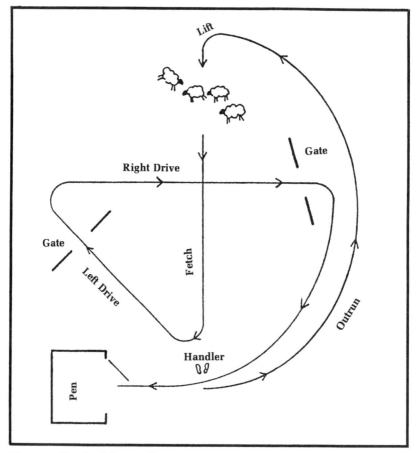

Figure 2—Standard Outrun Course

Herding Titles

The Bearded Collie Club of America, the American Working Collie Association, and the Belgian Tervuren Club of America all have a Herding Trial Champion (HTCh) title available. They all require fifteen points for attaining the title under at least two different judges, but there are slight requirement differences for the classes and courses. The points are figured according to how many dogs compete in a class, or if there are no classes, in the trial. They all must defeat at least one other dog for a point to count. The point schedules are:

	20 or more dogs	10 to 19 dogs	less than 10 dogs
first place	5 points	4 points	3 points
second place	4 points	3 points	2 points
third place	3 points	2 points	1 point
fourth place	2 points	1 point	0 points
fifth place	1 point	0 points	0 points

In the case of dogs that win High in Trial, all the dogs in the trial are counted. If there were thirty dogs, the points would be for thirty dogs instead of only those he defeated in his class.

Both the Belgian Tervuren Club and American Working Collie Association require that a dog take at least one three-point major placement before the dog can be awarded the title of Herding Trial Champion. The American Working Collie Association also has less advanced herding degrees: Herding Trial Dog (HDT) and Herding Trial Dog Excellent (HTDX). The HTD is earned by getting two qualifying scores in started classes under two different judges. The HTDX is earned by getting two qualifying scores in intermediate and/or advanced classes under two different judges. These trials must be on general outrun courses, and these titles go after the dog's name. Each of these titles earns the dog one point toward his HTCh. In addition, the Belgian Tervuren Club allows one point toward its HTCh for a dog's attaining his Herding Instinct Certification.

The American Herding Breed Assocation program will provide for a progression of titles of Herding Trial Dog—HTD I, HTD II, and HTD III—earned by qualifying as in obedience trials.

Because of so much work by so many dedicated people in these herding clubs, herding dogs of every breed have more opportunities for both testing and trial competition than they have ever had in the past. Human participants are challanged and fascinated by herding trials, and the dogs thoroughly enjoy the activities.

AKC HERDING TRIALS

In 1989, the American Kennel Club initiated a Herding Program. Two major divisions are included: non-competitive tests for dogs with little or no prior herding experience; and competitive trials for dogs with substantial training. The program is open to all AKC herding group breeds. The first of these events was held in January, 1990.

The tests provide for two non-competitive titles, Herding Tested (HT) and Pre-trial Tested (PT). To earn an HT, a dog must pass both a Preliminary Test and a Principal Test. Ducks, sheep or cattle may be worked. The dog must show five minutes *cumulative* herding work within a fifteen-minute test period. Dogs are evaluated according to type of instinct or working style: driving, gathering, or boundary. After passing the Preliminary Test, the dog may be entered in the Principal Test. Here the owner must have minimal control and the dog must show five minutes *sustained* herding in a fifteen minute test. After a dog has passed both tests the HT may be placed after his registered name.

The Pre-trial Test (PT) requires that dog and handler move the stock around a larger arena in both directions, and then pen the stock. The HT is not a prerequisite. If the dog is a boundary herder, the test begins with a boundary exercise before the stock are moved and penned.

At the competitive level, three titles can be earned: Herding Started (HS), Herding Intermediate (HI), and Herding Excellent (HX). A dog must pass the test for each level three times at different trials under three different judges, scoring at least sixty percent of the total points and at least fifty percent of the points in each category. Four placements and High in Trial (HIT) are awarded.

At each level three "courses" are offered: course A for driving dogs that move the livestock ahead of the shepherd; course B for fetching dogs that bring the stock toward the shepherd; and course c, a modified continental course, for boundary herding dogs that were developed to drive flocks from one point to another within boundaries, that is, without letting any of the stock stray into a neighboring field or flock. The size of the arena depends on the course and class, with the boundary course being the largest.

Dogs that have earned the HX title may continue to compete for a Herding Championship (H.Ch.). fifteen points must be earned by placing in the Advanced class, including two firsts, one which carries three or more points. The number of points are determined by the number of dogs competing.

For more information write to the AKC for "Regulations for Herding Tests and Trials."

PURINA FIELD TRIAL HERDING DOG AWARDS

The Purina Outstanding Field Trial Herding Dog Award was established in 1988 to honor the finest herding dog in the country.

The award program and its specified point system are administered by an independent committee of five prominent experts in herding dog competition. The program is open to any herding breed and is based on dog performance in carefully chosen open events, run according to International Sheepdog Society rules.

The 1989 winner received $1,000 in cash plus other prizes. Second- and third-place owners received $500 and $250 cash, respectively. Says George P. Cook, director of professional programs for Ralston Purina, "To see participation increase by thirty percent from the first year to the second year of the award is testament to the importance of herding dogs. We look forward to a long and successful program."

CANADIAN KENNEL CLUB STOCK DOG TRIALS

The Canadian Kennel Club held its first Stock Dog Trials on May 13 and May 14, 1989. The herding instinct tests are in the planning stage.

The Canadian trials are similar to Border Collie and Australian Shepherd trials, but are adapted to the needs of Canadian dogs and their handlers. To attain a title, the dog must be duly registered with the CKC. There are two titles at present, the Started Stock Dog Certificate, (SSC) and a second level, the Open Stock Dog Certificate. The dog qualifying for these levels may have the letters SSC or OSC used after his name. A third level is planned—Stock Dog Excellent (SDX).

The progression is similar to the three legs of obedience trials. A qualifying score is 65 percent of the 200 total points. For the SSD, a dog must qualify in three trials under at least two different judges. The first trial can be worked on a long line (minimum of twenty-five feet). For advanced levels, the dog must work strictly on his own. To compete in the Open trials, a dog must win his Started Dog title. To win his Open title, he must also qualify in two trials under two different judges.

The course used by the Canadians is similar to that of the Australian Shepherd Club of America, with a take pen, a catch pen, and three obstacles. Five cattle or sheep are used. The trial may be on cattle or sheep, depending on which the sponsoring club wants to use. The CKC specifies the breeds to be used on cattle as: Australian Cattle Dog, Rottweilver, German Shepherd Dog, Bearded Collie, Welsh Corgi, Australian Kelpie, Puli, Bouvier des Flendres and Belgian Sheepdog. The breeds used to herd sheep are Bearded Collie, Border Collie, Australian Kelpie, Rough and Smooth Collie, Shetland Sheepdog, Briard, Old English Sheepdog and Puli.

Scoring

The scoring is done in two sections, 1) the course and 2) the dog's style according to its breed. The latter ensures that each breed gets his rightful judging, since a Corgi is going to work stock in a completely different manner than a Bouvier or German Shepherd.

Maximum course points are:

Take from pen   10 points
(2 points per animal)

Drive   10 points
(Quiet, steady, efficient work. Splitting herd or losing control to be penalized.)

Obstacle #1   10 points
Obstacle #2   10 points
Obstacle #3   10 points
(2 points per animal that negotiates the obstacle correctly without handler helping.)   _____

Maximum total   50 points

Maximum style points are:

Natural working style   25 points
(I.e., natural and correct heeling style of heeling breeds; the wearing and fetching ability of the Puli, Collie, and Sheltie; the steady driving ability of the Rottweiler, German Shepherd and Australian Cattle Dog, etc.)

Attitude   10 points
(Degree of interest in work assigned the dog and his concentration of the stock.)

Handler Assistance   10 points
(Working without assistance assures 10 points. Points are deducted according to how much handler assists.)

Dog's obedience   10 points
(How the dog responds to commands and his desire to work as one with his handler.)

This Collie passed his herding instinct test. *McKinney photo.*

Degree of training   10 points
(Distance of cast dog has and degree of direction.)
Dog's stock sense   10 points
(How dog handles situations where he has to think for himself.)
Force   5 points
(Dog should force if necessary in the manner that is natural to his breed; i.e., grip, feint, bark, using eye, etc.)
Workability of stock   20 points
(Easy, cooperative stock are scored lower than difficult stock that make the dog work.)
Maximum total   100 points

The Canadians are off and running with their stock dog herding program, which allows not only the breeds designated as herding dogs to participate, but also the Rottweiler from the working group. (The Rottweilver originated back in Roman times as a drover; so in Canada, at least, the breed is back at its old work of driving cattle.)

GLOSSARY OF TERMS

Approach   Manner in which dog comes in to the stock. A smooth approach is most highly prized, with the dog moving very steadily with no bouncing around, weaving, or jumping in aggressively.

Away-to-me   Traditional Scottish command to move the dog counterclockwise with respect to the stock.

Balance   The ability of the dog to position himself so that the stock moves in the desired direction.

Come By   Traditional Scottish command to move the dog clockwise.

Close Running   A dog working as close as possible to the stock.

Driving   Taking the livestock away from the owner, or at right angles to the owner, either naturally or upon direction.

Eye   An intense, unwavering gaze used to control stock, often accompanied by a crouching or stalking approach. (1) A dog showing the above qualities to a marked degree is said to be strong-eyed. (2) A dog showing eye, but without the crouching approach is said to be medium-eyed. (3) A dog that does not keep his eyes riveted to the stock is said to be loose-eyed. He may also glance around or at the owner from time to time. Most dogs that bark while working are loose-eyed.

Fetching   Bringing the animals to the owner. Also called "gathering" or in Australia, "heading."

Heading   Nipping at the heads of livestock to turn or control them.

Heeling   Nipping at the hind legs or heels of livestock to move them.

Lift   The movement toward the stock that starts them in motion.

Outrun   The path the dog takes from the handler to the opposite side of the stock in order to fetch them.

Power   The confidence or strength of will that a dog has to move stubborn stock, often without nipping.

Shag (also called shed)	Splitting of the herd or separation of one sheep from the rest of the herd.
Weak	Lacking boldness and confidence to stand up to stubborn or fighting stock.
Wearing	The weaving motion that a dog makes to keep the flock grouped.
Wide Running	Keeping a good distance from the stock while working.
Wool-pulling	Biting at the bodies of sheep, tearing out hunks of wool.
Woolies	The sheep.

Roy, a six-year-old, black and mottled Border Collie owned by Thomas Wilson of Gordonsville, Virginia, won the 1989 Purina Award for Outstanding Field Trial Herding Dog. Roy defeated hundreds of herding dogs from around the country to capture this second annual honor. *Photo courtesy of Ralston Purina Company.*

20

SCHUTZHUND

Schutzhund is the German word for protection dog. Schutzhund trials were developed in Germany in the early 1900s to test the German Shepherd Dog, and have now become fairly popular in the United States. The Schutzhund dog is tested in three areas—tracking, obedience, and protection—and three progressively more difficult levels of competition lead to the Schutzhund I, II and III degrees. These titles go after the dog's name as SchH I, II or III, but do not become part of the dog's AKC registered name since Schutzhund is sponsored by other organizations. There are other degrees available such as FH (Fartenhund), the most advanced tracking degree; VB (Traffic Sure Companion Dog); BH (Companion Dog); AD (Ausdauer) drafting; and WH (Watch Dog). The Canadian Kennel Club also recognizes the Schutzhund titles. When a title is attained, the owner of a CKC registered dog may send proof to the CKC, pay a recording fee and receive certification to use the title after the dog's name.

There are several Schutzhund organizations and clubs in this country, but they are not found in every state. All of the all-breed Schutzhund clubs accept mixed breeds as well as purebred dogs at their competitions; each conducts its own trials. The organizations are: United Schutzhund Clubs of America (USA), which is an SV (Schaeferhund-Verein) organization, which means "German Shepherd Dog Club." And there is the DVG, the German all-breed Schutzhund organization (see Appendix).

Besides these organizations, there is the International competition. Whereas the requirements for Schutzhund I, II and III vary somewhat from country to country and organization to organization, the International rules are standard. While the tracking level is rather

225

Belgian Tervuren scaling a six-foot vertical wall with a retrieve. *Photo courtesy of Linda C. Franklin.*

elementary, the obedience and protection requirements are very difficult and demand the utmost in control, which is why few dogs earn the International title.

To find out about Schutzhund trials to attend as a spectator, or about clubs of the different organizations, ask breeders of German Shepherds, Rottweilers and Doberman Pinschers, in particular, as these are the breeds most involved in Schutzhund.

Dog Sports Magazine has information about Schutzhund trial dates, trial results, training articles, information on Search and Rescue, Police K-9's and SWAT units, breed columns and more. (See Appendix.)

The magazine *Schutzhund USA* is the official publication of the United Schutzhund Clubs of America. Subscription to the magazine includes membership in the USA Club. It reports results of all USA trials, has special articles on training, health and nutrition, directory of clubs and much useful information.

When you locate a Schutzhund trial, pack a picnic lunch, gather the family, and plan to spend the day. Wear comfortable shoes and take rain gear if it looks rainy, as the trial goes on anyhow. The trials are held in large arenas such as polo or rodeo grounds, stadiums, and fairgrounds.

THE SCHUTZHUND COMPETITORS

The sport of Schutzhund has not spread to all states in the United States. There is good reason—Schutzhund is not the sport for every dog and handler.

The Dog

The German Shepherd Dog predominates in the sport, which is entirely understandable as Schutzhund was developed to test this breed. However, other dogs of the protection heritage breeds also compete—Doberman Pinschers, Rottweilers, Bouvier de Flandres, Belgian Tervuren, and Giant Schnauzers. You might see a Pit Bull Terrier, a Labrador or Golden Retriever, or even a Miniature Pinscher at a Schutzhund trial, and one or more of these breeds might attain a Schutzhund I title. But, generally speaking, the five large breeds do best because of the many years of breeding for the qualities that are suited to Schutzhund work.

The Handler

The owner/handler must assume a great deal of responsibility when he trains a protection dog. First, he must take care to select a dog that is sound in body and temperament, since training clubs will not accept for training a mean dog that is unsound and unsuited for the sport, nor will they take on an irresponsible owner. Second, the handler himself must be well-conditioned, as the sport is strenuous for both the human and the animal.

Just as in any other dog sport, Schutzhund enthusiasts are found in all occupations. These are not lazy people; in fact, they work extremely hard training their dogs. The challenge is cited as one reason for dedication to the sport, and also the incredible bonding that develops between dog and handler. The majority of American Schutzhund competitors train and handle their own dogs, many of whom also have AKC obedience titles and may even be AKC comformation champions.

Once a person locates a good Schutzhund candidate, the next step is to join a training club. This is an activity club that usually holds its training sessions for three or four hours on one weekend day. The next day, and every day during the week, the handler spends fifteen to thirty minutes a day on one or the other of the three phases of Schutzhund.

Since the minimum age for any Schutzhund trial is fourteen months, there is no reason to push a young dog. Light continuous training must be done, but a trainer should wait until the dog is full grown, at full weight and full mental capacity before starting intensive training. A dog usually attains his Schutzhund I title around two- to two and a half years of age, after about eight months *minimum* of hard training. Most trainers feel a longer training period provides a more secure, confident basis for the dog's first trial.

Since Schutzhund is a German-derived sport, many of the judges are from Germany and most handlers learn to give the German commands. It is believed that the more guttural sounds of the German language are better understood by the dogs. However, the language used for commands is the handler's preference. When the handler and dog are ready for competition, the owner must obtain a working trials scorebook which is taken to each trial so his results may be officially recorded.

GLOSSARY OF STANDARD COMMANDS

English	German
Come	Hier
Down	Platz
Fetch	Bring
Go Out	Voraus
Heel	Fuss
Over	Hopp
Out	Aus
Sit	Sitz
Stand	Steh
Track	Such

THE TRIALS

All levels of Schutzhund I, II and III include three parts, and all three parts of the trial are conducted on the same day. (Schutzhund A, a preliminary class for those who are not ready or interested in earning a title, includes only two parts: obedience and protection.) Competitions are usually held in a large arena with the tracking portion done in an open field.

Trials are held on local and regional levels. The premier American events are the American National Championships. A top event in the world of Schutzhund is the German Championship (Deutsche Meisterschaft). Dog/handler teams must meet specific qualifications to compete. Also, the European Championship Trials for German Shepherd Dogs are held each year in different countries (Italy, Hungary, Holland, Germany), and have special requirements.

Minimum age requirements are 14 months for Schutzhund A and I, 16 months for Schutzhund II and Tracking Dog (FH), and 18 months for the Schutzhund III level. For a one-day trial with a single judge, the entry limit is 10 dogs. If more dogs are entered, the trial may last for one and a half or two days, or additional judges may be used. In the latter case, one judge would judge tracking and another obedience and protection.

The judges are given a great deal of latitude in their decisions. Also, they may conduct temperament tests, pressuring the dog, maybe walking between him and his handler, or pushing him with their knee. Any dog failing such a temperament test, showing aggression or fearfulness, is excused from participation in the trial.

At the end of the trial, prizes are awarded. First place goes to the dog that scored the highest number of points regardless of what level of Schutzhund he competed in. Other placements are awarded according to points scored.

Scoring

Each of the three categories (tracking, obedience, protection) is worth 100 points. A passing score of 70 points is needed for tracking and obedience, while 80 points are needed to pass protection. Therefore, Schutzhund I, II, and III have a possible 300 maximum points. (Since Schutzhund A has only the obedience and protection phases, the maximum score is 200, and both phases are graded as in Schutzhund I.)

Scoring breakdown for each 100 points is:

96-100	V (Excellent)
90-95	SG (Very Good)
80-89	G (Good)
70-79	B (Satisfactory)
35-69	M (Insufficient)
0-35	U (Unsatisfactory)

Total point ratings out of the possible 300 are:

286-300	V (Excellent)
270-285	SG (Very Good)
240-269	G (Good)
220-239	B (Satisfactory)
110-219	M (Insufficient)
0-109	U (Unsatisfactory)

Average total scores run from 232 to 237 for Schutzhund I and II, to 252 for Schutzhund III. Scores of 260-265 are considered satisfactory, not excellent, but good. Many dogs compete repeatedly at the Schutzhund III level to obtain the highest possible scores and also to advance to championship competition.

Tracking Testing, Part A

Tracking is done in the morning with the track being aged twenty minutes for Schutzhund I, thirty minutes for Schutzhund II, and fifty minutes for Schutzhund III. Tracks are laid by the handler for Schutzhund I, and by another person for Schutzhund II and III. This phase is similar to the AKC and CKC tracking test described in Chapter 17 with a person walking a prescribed route of several hundred yards and dropping a number of articles which the dog must locate (2 articles for Schutzhund I and II, and 3 articles for Schutzhund III.) During actual tracking, the handler uses a long line, or the dog works off-lead. In either case, the handler must stay thirty feet behind the dog except when the dog locates an article. The distance for each track is 300-400 paces for Schutzhund I, 400-500 pace for Schutzhund II, and 800-1000 paces for Schutzhund III.

Points are deducted for faulty starts, lack of concentration, repeated encouragement, sloppy picking up of object or dropping it, tracking with nose high, soiling of track, not finding article, and continued circling of corners. However, overshooting corners is not considered a fault since the wind often carries scent past a corner.

Obedience Testing, Part B

This phase is similar to AKC obedience at the CDX level in Schutzhund A and I, except that guns are fired and groups of people milling about offer distractions in the heel off-lead, and the additonal

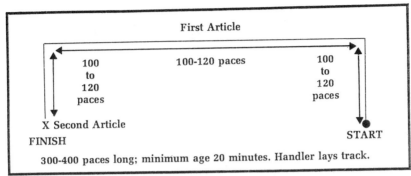

Figure 1. Schutzhund I Typical Track

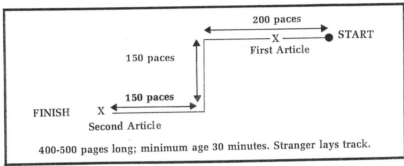

Figure 2. Schutzhund II Typical Track

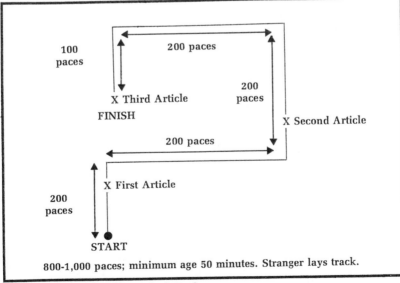

Figure 3 . Schutzhund III Typical Track.

"go out" exercise is included, which is done at the Utility level in AKC obedience. In all three levels of the obedience trials, the following exercises are included: heel off-lead, walking sit, down with recall, retrieve on flat, retrieve over one-meter jump, go out with down, and down under distraction. The heel on-lead is included only in Schutzhund I and II. It is during the heel off-lead that a blank gun is fired twice to test for gun shyness. If the dog runs from the shots, he must be disqualified from the trial then and there. In the "down under distraction" portion (always the last exercise in the obedience phase), the dog is downed by the handler and the handler goes to stand about forty paces away with his back to the dog. Then, the next dog does the first seven exercises of the obedience trial while the downed dog remains in place until his handler releases him.

Schutzhund II adds the climbing jump over a scaling wall and retrieve, which is also required in Schutzhund III. Schutzhund III drops the heel off-lead, but adds a walking stand-stay and running stand-stay. Schutzhund I has eight exercises; Schutzhund II has nine; and Schutzhund III has ten.

As in all obedience trials, points are deducted for less than perfect work: forging ahead or lagging behind in heeling; handler hesitation; dog lying down or standing rather than sitting; dropping a retrieved object, playing with it or chewing it; not retrieving (gets a zero); refusing to jump; lying down too soon on a down, or hesitation in doing so; handler helping dog to climb and jump the scaling wall; and any sloppy work. Each exercise is graded from perfect down to zero.

Protection Testing, Part C

In the protection exercises there are a number of simulated attacks by a person taking the role of aggressor (the trial helper) who wears padded leather pants and a padded sleeve which the dog bites. The dog is trained to bite only the sleeve. When the dog is on the sleeve, the agitator strikes the dog with a bamboo or willow stick to test the dog's courage and willingness to continue when counter-attacked. The helper is permitted to strike the hindquarters, sides and withers of a dog. When the helper stands still, the dog must watch and bark but not bite. The purpose of the protection program is not to produce a "killer dog," but a dog that responds to a direct threat in an appropriate manner.

In Schutzhund I the hold and bark are worth five points, the surprise attack thirty-five points, and the follow and hold (courage test) a full sixty points. Schutzhund II includes the surprise attack

Belgian Tervuren, Ch. Chimina's Etiene De La Corps UDTX, Sch.III, AD, FH Int. in a Schutzhund III Trial. *Photo courtesy of Linda C. Franklin.*

and courage test (thirty points); and Schutzhund III includes the surprise attack, pursuit, and courage test (forty-five points). Ratings are given by the judge for fighting drive, courage, and hardness during this tests. The ratings for courage are "a" (notable), "vh" (present), and "ng" (insufficient).

When a dog charges the helper and attacks, biting hard on the sleeve, he shows external signs of an inherent fighting drive. If a dog dodges the blows, he must not give up fighting, but immediately attack again with courage. If the dog runs back to his handler or doesn't hold the helper in place after the courage test, he cannot receive the "a" (notable) distinction for fighting drive. A judge may disqualify a dog if he displays weakness of character even if he has passed a temperament test before the trial began. Dogs which cannot be controlled by their handlers, or which do not let go during a fighting situation until their handlers physically interfere, cannot pass the trial.

The agitator in all classes appears as menacing as he can, yelling and waving his arms as he simulates an attack on dog or handler. Under the DVG (German) rules, if a dog will not cease biting the agitator (out) on command, he will not be granted a title. The NASA rules require that the dog automatically release the sleeved arm when aggression ceases.

In all three classes of Schutzhund protection, the dog must locate the aggressor/agitator behind blinds that are set up in a field. In Schutzhund I there are two blinds to be searched, and in Schutzhund II and III there are five blinds. When the aggressor is found, the dog must bark aggressively, but not bite except when attacked or on command. In Schutzhund II and III, the dog must guard the agitator (keep him from moving) while the handler searches the blind. Then the handler and dog escort the aggressor, walking for fifty paces down the field while staying about fifteen feet behind him.

Occasional retracing in searching blinds for the helper is not considered faulty. Points are deducted if a dog's barking is weak or if he doesn't bark at all, also if the dog bumps the handler or bites hard during the hold and bark section.

Schutzhund Advanced Tracking Degree—Fartenhund (FH)

This degree is the most advanced in tracking and resembles the American and Canadian TDX tests. A dog must be sixteen months old before he can compete in this trial and must already have a Schutzhund I degree, a Companion Dog (BH) degree for the German (DVG or USA) tests, or a Traffic Sure Companion (VB) degree in a NASA trial.

The track is approximately 1500 paces long (minimum distance is 1000 paces), is laid by a stranger, is at least three hours old with ninety degree turns, has four dropped articles, and has three misleading tracks (where the track is crossed by a stranger's path). The four articles are carried on the tracklayer for a least a half-hour so they will be well scented.

A perfect score is 100, with a minimum of 70 required to pass. The judge is looking for the sure tracking dog that stays on the track he started on and doesn't change to a fresher trail. Before the exercise starts, the handler tells the judge whether his dog will pick up or point out each object found. He must do one or the other, but not both: this is considered a fault. The dog must work the track from start to finish at a calm, regular pace; work well through all angles of the course; not be misled by the decoy tracks; and must not pick up any object that was not dropped by the tracklayer.

The handler follows behind the dog, leaving slack in the tracking lead, with the judge and tracklayer well behind him (about fifty paces). When the dog finds an article, he must either pick it up in his mouth or clearly point it out. He may sit, lie down, or stand to point it out. Then the handler goes to the dog, takes the article, and raises it in the air. Now, he may praise the dog, and the tracking continues straightaway. Should a dog switch over to one of the decoy tracks and continue for as much as twenty-five paces or so, the exercise is terminated and the dog fails. (See diagram.)

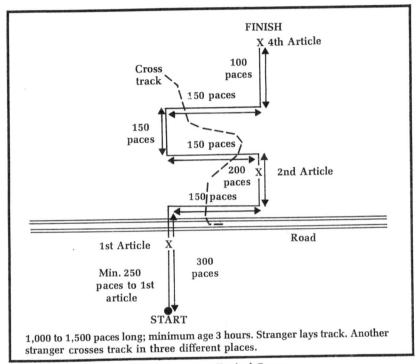

Figure 3. Fartenhund (FH) Tracking Dog Typical Course.

Traffic Sure Companion Dog (VB), Companion Dog (BH), and Watch Dog (WD)

These are tests of obedience on- and off-lead. The dogs are required to heel, sit, stay, walk, down with recall, down under distraction in one section, and pass a test of heeling and conduct in a traffic situation. The dog is either passed or failed and is eligible for this test at the age of twelve months. Dogs of any size and breed may take the test. The same two rules apply for taking the Watch Dog (WD) test, which is also a pass/fail test. The procedure is the same for Companion Dog on heeling. There is a sit-stay, down with recall, retrieve of an object, down under distraction, guarding possessions test, and a test of the dog's watchfulness.

Ausdauer (drafting)

In this competition, the dog must cover a twelve and a half mile course in under two hours while maintaining a trotting speed throughout the distance. Since the dog must pull a cart and handler, this requires a great deal of preparation and conditioning time. This is also a pass or fail test.

Carting. Belgian Tervuren, Ch. Chimina's Etiene De La Corps, UDTX, Sch.III, AD, FH, Int., pulls owner, Linda C. Franklin. *Photo by Marilyn Hankes.*

21

PRIVATE SECTOR COMPETITIONS

Besides the sports already covered, there are some events which are sponsored by the private sector and not held under the aegis of a national kennel club or dog sports association. These include Frisbee® (flying disc) competition, the Gaines Annual Obedience Classic competition, the Purina Annual Invitational Dog Show, and three newer sports, Flyball, dog agility, and the Purina® Hi Pro Dog Runs.

SPORT WITH FRISBEES®

Sport with Frisbees® has grown by leaps and bounds since humans have teamed up with their dogs to play the game. Incidentally, Frisbee® is the name of the flying disc manufactured by the Wham-O Manufacturing Company.

Dog owners are cautioned to have their animals checked by their veterinarian before getting them started in Frisbee® activities since all athletes must be in condition—human or canine. Although sport with Frisbees® can be enjoyed by any dog and his owner, there are some breeds that take to it better than others. A large, heavy dog or a low-slung, short-legged dog won't be able to make the fantastic leaps of a Whippet, but anyone can participate at home or in competition for fun and exercise. Besides the Whippet, other successful breeds include Australian Shepherds, German Shepherds, Dobermans, Border Collies, retrievers, pointers and Beagles. Generally, the working, herding and sporting breeds that are more athletic, and some of the sighthounds, do best at catching the flying discs.

Irv Lander, executive director of the Ashley Whippet Invitational says: "The sport of Frisbee® -catching for dogs is a relatively new

237

one, although one really does not know when it first started as an alternative to dogs fetching balls and sticks. Since Frisbee® -catching for humans really came into being in the late fifties, it is possible that a dog intercepted an airborne throw between two friends playing catch and it became a regular play activity in the park or at the beach.''

It was really popularized with the entry on the national scene of an amazing four-legged athlete known as Ashley Whippet, a purebred Whippet owned by Alex Stein. This team made history when they leapt uninvited and unannounced onto Dodger Stadium's field in 1974, thrilling a capacity crowd during the Dodgers-Reds game, and an at-home television audience in the millions. Fans and viewers alike loved it, and a new sport was born.

In 1977, Gaines dog food became the sponsor of this competition, which created the opportunity nationwide for thousands of talented canines and their owners to compete for fame, if not fortune. It is now called the Gaines Cycle Ashley Whippet Invititational, Cycle being one of the major brands of Gaines dog food.

Entry to the competition is free and free Frisbee® discs are supplied to all contestants. There are separate awards for both experienced and novice contenders, as well as awards for the smallest dogs. The competition is open to all canines, mixed-breeds or purebred, male or female, large or small.

There are approximately 100 local competitions and 40 state finals, which anyone can attend. Although there are winners at local and state finals on the basis of scores, they are, in reality, practice

German Shepherd Dog catches a frisbee. *Photo by Daryl Breese.*

sessions for the regional finals where anyone is eligible, regardless of whether they have competed previously in a state or local final, or whatever their score happened to be if they did compete.

Regional finals are held in seven major cities with a semi-finals in the morning at a parksite, co-hosted or co-sponsored by the particular community's recreation department and Gaines. The top three scorers from the semi-finals then compete either on the same evening, or the next afternoon at a major league baseball stadium in that city to determine the winner and runner-up. Both receive an all-expenses paid trip to the World Finals. World finalists are treated royally and compete over a two-day period, followed by a gala dinner in their honor hosted by Gaines. The first, second, and third place winners receive U.S. Savings Bonds of different denominations. Everyone gets complete World Finals outfits, including shirts, shorts, sox, jackets and caps.

Spectators are welcome at all levels of competition and there is no charge to them. Only in the stadiums do normal ticket prices prevail. A guidelines booklet details the general rules of competition and conduct. Interested parties can obtain information as to where to compete in Gaines Invitationals' local, state and regional competitions by sending a stamped, self-addressed envelope to Gaines Cycle Ashley Whippet Invitational, Box 725, Encino, California 91426. Also, anyone who already has a dog he would like to train or is interested in getting a dog that could perhaps become another Ashley Whippet, can obtain a free training manual by sending a stamped, self-addressed envelope to Gaines Frisbee® Booklet, P.O. Box 8177, Kankakee, Illinois 60902.

The Competition

The competition format for local and state finals may consist of either Basic Throw and Catch, or Freeflight, or both. If both are conducted, scores for each are added together to determine the winner and runner-up. Male dogs compete first, followed by females. No females in heat may compete, nor dogs whose overly-aggressive behavior presents a hazard to other contestants or spectators. Also, anyone who abuses a competing dog is disqualified. In both Basic Throw and Catch, and Freeflight, each contestant is allowed ninety seconds to complete as many throws as possible. If both these forms are used, sixty seconds is allowed in each.

Basic Throw and Catch has a chalked circle with a seventeen yard radius. In the center of this is a "thrower's box," four yards square.

The thrower must be inside this box. The dog doesn't have to be in the circle when the disc is released but must bring it back each time to the thrower's box. Scoring is one point for any catch (mid-air or not) where the dog lands inside the circle; two points for any catch where the dog lands outside the circle but one or more paws touched the ground at the time of catch, and three points for any mid-air catch where the dog lands outside the circle and no foot touches the ground at time of catch.

For *Freeflight*, the contestant may throw from any location and doesn't have to wait for the dog to return the disc to him. There are at least two judges who award points on a one to ten scale in each of three categories: showmanship/execution, leaping ability, and degree of difficulty. In Freeflight, the dog and his owner work as a well-trained team with difficult tricks and pass patterns. Sometimes the dogs jump over their owners (while they are standing) or catch more than one Frisbee® at a time.

The 1987 Invitational was won by Jeff Gabel of Suffield, Connecticut, and his dog, Casey, a black Labrador Retriever/Setter

German Shepherd Dog, Yote, catches a frisbee disk. *Photo courtesy of Doug Milham.*

mix. First runner-up was Bill Murphy from Lubbock, Texas, with his dog, Boo, an Australian Shepherd Dog; second runner-up was Mark Wood from Columbus, Ohio, with his dog, Zach, a Lab mix; third runner-up was Chris Barbo from Kent, Ohio, with his dog, Kato, a Lab/Setter mix.

GAINES OBEDIENCE CLASSIC

Gaines Dog Foods also sponsors the Gaines U.S. Obedience Classic, also know as the "Superdog Competition," which has been held since 1976, with three regionals plus the Classic each year. The Classic is a competition designed to determine which of the country's finest obedience-trained dogs are tops in Novice, Open, and Super Dog classes. (Super Dog is Open and Utility combined, and is truly the most exciting obedience event you will ever see.) An outstanding event for exhibitors and their dogs, the Gaines Classic provides interest and excitement for the public as well. It is always a thrill to watch a really good obedience dog perform, but a closely contested event featuring top dogs from several states is something that shouldn't be missed.

Although exercises and judging at the Gaines Classic are done as they are in licensed obedience trials, there is one significant difference: the scores for each dog's individual exercise are posted as soon as the dog leaves the ring.

Three routes exist for entry into a Classic: (1) Any dog placing in the top ten in a regional class automatically has a spot at the Classic. (2) The remaining thirty slots in each division can be filled by dogs that have not exhibited at a regional but have earned at least three scores averaging 195 or better in licensed AKC trials, or whose scores averaged 195 or better at a related regional competition. (3) A dog is also eligible for entry if he has earned the AKC's Obedience Trial Champion title (OTCh).

The three regional contests are held early in the year, starting as early as late April, with the Classic in November or December. The regions are Eastern, Western, and Central. The entries in the regionals are also limited. Rosettes, plaques, and cash prizes are awarded. Each regional is a three-day event with three shows. The three divisions and their entry requirements are:

Division I—Super Dog—Earned a confirmed Utility title in the U.S. prior to closing date, three scores averaging 193 or better in Open B and three scores in Utility A or B averaging 193 or better at licensed trials prior to the regional.

Division II—Novice Dog—Earned a confirmed Companion Dog title in the U.S. prior to entry closing and cannot have completed the third leg on a CDX prior to the regional, with three scores averaging 193 or better in Novice A or B competition at licensed trials.

Division III—Open Dog—Earned a confirmed Companion Dog Excellent Title in the U.S. prior to entry closing date, but cannot have completed the third leg toward a UD prior to the regional date, plus three scores averaging 193 or better in Open A or B in licensed competition before the Regional.

The Gaines Classic is held over a three-day period and is comprised of three shows: Red, White, and Blue. Each show has a Novice, Open, Super Open, and Super Utility class, each with a different judge. Every Novice and Open dog must compete three times—once in each of the three shows. Super dogs must compete six times—three times in Super Open and three times in Super Utility. The scores from all classes in which a dog has competed are totaled and averaged to determine the top dogs in each class.

The first day of the Classic brings the thrill of eight rings in action at once and exciting mid-day exhibitions, such as dog relay racing, various types of service dog demonstrations, Frisbee® catching exhibitions, and more. These mid-day demonstrations are repeated on the second day.

The second day provides the additional excitement of seeing how the dogs standing high in the rankings will perform, and whether they will do well enough to achieve a placement. Competition is further stimulated by the sizeable cash prizes, trophies, and rosettes offered for the highest individual scores in each class and for Sunday's best—the highest scoring dog of the day. The award ceremony, following the close of competition late Sunday afternoon, is a stirring event as winners and their dogs receive recognition for their outstanding performances.

Some of the great memories of the Classic include the team of Russell Kipple and his Golden Retriever "Tonka" who won three Super Dog Awards. There was also the team of OTCH Meadowpond Stardust Reggie and his owner, Fred Einhorn, who won the Super Dog Award for the second time in 1987. What made this an especially wonderful event was the fact that the runner-up for this award was "Reggie's" daughter, OTCH Stardust Ruby Slippers with her owner, Laurie Rubenfeld of Monsey, New York. They were separated by only 1½ points out of a possible 1200 at the end of the competition!

PURINA INVITATIONAL DOG SHOW

It had to happen: sooner or later someone would sponsor a yearly bang-up, no other like it, super dog show. In 1986 the Purina Company did it—they launched their annual invitational.

To compete in this event, a dog must be rated among the top show dogs of its breed or variety for the previous year according to the records of the American Kennel Club, United Kennel Club and the Australian Shepherd Club of America. For the 1989 show, Purina included the top show dogs of three breeds of the UKC and those of the ASCA. The invitations are sent directly to the owners of these dogs.

Ch. Pegden's Cactus Jack, a two-year-old Miniature Wirehaired Dachshund owned by Carl G. and Nancy Jo Fein of Tacoma, WA, and handler Mark Stephenson. Cactus Jack was chosen Best in Show at the third annual Purina Invitational Dog Show held May 2, 1988, in St. Louis. *Photo courtesy of Ralston Purina and Aaron Cushman and Associates.*

The show is held at Queeny Park in suburban St. Louis County, Missouri, which is also the home of The Dog Museum. Proceeds from the show benefit The Dog Museum and during the first three years, more than $57,000 was raised.

In 1989, a cash prize of $2,500 was given to the Best in Show dog, with a total of $18,000 in prizes awarded. The panel of judges included some of the best known and respected judges in the country. The seven groups consist of Herding, Hound, Non-Sporting, Sporting, Terrier, Toy, and Working breeds. Besides the Best in Show prize, the Reserve Best in Show dog won $1,500. The first through fourth place winners of each of the seven groups were also given cash awards. Each Best of Breed winner took home $50. The names of the Best in Show winners are inscribed on a large sterling silver loving cup housed at the Dog Museum.

The show judging progresses from Best of Breed to Group to Best in Show. The show runs for the full day and into the evening. Spectators may purchase a limited number of tickets for both day and evening events or for day events or evening events only.

The participants in the show are the best of the best in the dog show world. The show itself is a jewel, with the Best in Show winner really Top Dog of the Year.

Ch. Talludo Minstrel of Purston, or "Rags," a three-year-old Wirehaired Fox Terrier owned by Marilyn Laschinski and Janice Rue of Chicago, was Best in Show winner at the fourth annual Purina Invitational Dog Show 1989. Rags is pictured with handler Priscilla Wells of Ponca City, Oklahoma. *Photo courtesy of Ralston Purina and Aaron Cushman and Associates.*

NORTH AMERICAN FLYBALL ASSOCIATION

Another new sport, flyball, is gaining in popularity. Flyball is rather like baseball for dogs, but it is also similar to a relay race in track and field competition. Basically, two teams of dogs (four dogs on each team) jump four hurdles on the way to a box which contains tennis balls. The dogs trigger release of the balls by pushing a pedal, catch the balls in their mouths and turn around and return over the four hurdles to the starting line. This procedure is repeated until all dogs have run. The first team to finish is the winner of that heat. Heats are run until all teams have completed a run and the final winner is determined by a last heat consisting of the two fastest teams.

Flyball is a lot of fun for both dogs and their handlers, as well as for spectators. The competition draws large crowds of people rooting for the team they want to win. In 1985, the North American Flyball Association was formed. Tournaments are run under the rules of this association. Currently, there are three divisions for competing

Flyball is a great sport for dogs and spectators! Bearded Collie. *Photographed by Alice Bixler.*

teams: Championship Division for teams running under 24 seconds; Open for teams running in the 24-28 second range; and Novice for teams slower than 28 seconds. As their skills get better, the teams move up through these divisions. The NAFA offers the titles of Flyball Dog (FD), Flyball Dog Excellent (FDX), and Flyball Dog Champion (FDCh) on a point system.

The Canadian Kennel Club also recognizes flyball and these titles, when earned, may be used with the dog's name. The American Kennel Club and United Kennel Club do not recognize or sponsor flyball, so titles cannot be used with the dog's name, but your AKC or UKC registered dog can still earn the NAFA titles, as can dogs of mixed breeding.

Flyball is definitely a team sport. According to experts Deb and Marti McCann, puppies seven to ten weeks should be started on chasing, retrieving, and returning a tennis ball to the owners as quickly as possible. Also, basic obedience is absolutely essential, because the competing dogs are constrained only by the verbal command of their handlers. They *must* be trained to come when called, maintain a stay, and be steady in the midst of other dogs and handlers, and the noise of spectators. A Companion Dog degree in obedience competition isn't absolutely necessary, but it couldn't hurt!

If you have watched any type of relay competition in swimming or track and field, you know that speed is the main thing, but teamwork is essential as well. Even human beings sometimes make errors in relays. I'm sure you have seen a runner drop the baton when trying to pass it to the next runner, or a person lose a second because of a nervous pass. So, when dogs have to do the same type of thing, there are a lot of chances for mistakes. Very well-trained dogs are more likely to make a winning team.

The first North American Flyball Championship tournament was held in Toronto, Canada, on November 2-4, 1984. Ralston-Purina Co. of Canada sponsored the event, which was held in conjunction with the Metropolitan Kennel Club's bicentennial celebration show. Teams from all over the U.S. and Canada competed for the $5,000 in prizes.

In time, the field was narrowed to eight teams. These eight ran elimination heats for the best two out of three runs. The winning team was McCann vs. McCann, collecting a $1,000 prize. Money prizes went to second through fourth placements. Even the other four teams competing in the final run-offs received small cash prizes.

If you want to teach your dog flyball or are interested in forming a team, write to the North AMerican Flyball Association. (See Appendix C.) Rule books are available for $5.00. You can also get information on how to build a flyball box. Batter up!

DOG AGILITY

The sport of dog agility, conceived in England in 1977, requires a handler to direct his dog over a timed obstacle course. Scoring is determined by time with faults deducted for errors, similar to equestrian jumping events. John Varley, a member of the Crufts Dog Show entertainment committee, developed the agility test because it would have great spectator appeal. The first agility competition was held in England in 1978. In 1980 the Kennel Club of Great Britain gave official status to agility training.

Agility training is designed to build confidence and the equipment used requires a dog to be agile in many aspects. Speed is a big factor but also very important is the owner's handling skill. Both handler and dog run against the clock trying to make as few errors as possible. Teamwork is the key—the handler giving commands which the dog must understand immediately and execute. Slow reactions cost time. The dog must perform on a one-word command such as "up," "through," or "over."

USDAA

In 1986 Kenneth Tatsch established the United States Dog Agility Association (USDAA) to provide guidelines and a central organization for dog agility. The events combine elements from equestrian jumping events and the British military Canine Corps training program.

Agility is FUN for dog and owner!

A teeter board is usually one of the obstacles.

Since 1986 agility events have been presented as exhibitions and for awhile they were allowed as a non-regular obedience class at AKC shows, but this is no longer allowed. Actually, dog agility is an entirely separate sport. However, it does test handler control and the strength of the relationship between dog and handler.

Working and herding breeds are best at dog agility; toy and short-legged breeds are at a disadvantage. Dogs may be purebred or mixed breeds. Not allowed for competition are puppies under a year, bitches in season, deformed, injured or sick dogs, or overly aggressive dogs.

Memberships in USDAA are invited and an official rule book may be ordered (See Appendix). Agility clubs are forming over the country as more and more people become interested. Plans for making your own dog agility obstacles may be obtained through the USDAA. The organization also holds seminars and training workshops.

The Course

The test area must be a minimum of 8,000 square feet (80 ft. x 100 ft.) if all the obstacles are used, with not less than 15 feet between obstacles. The ideal size is 15,000 square feet (100 ft. x 150 ft.). Actually, when the course is all laid out with the obstacles in place, it looks a lot like a miniature golf course. There is a start and a finish line.

The Obstacles

There must be at least ten obstacles on the course. All the obstacles must conform to USDAA specifications and be safe. Obstacles include several types of jumps: spread bar (hurdle type), double bar/brush, single bar, high and broad jumps. There is a dog walk which requires each dog to be surefooted and assured on a scaffold plank. Poles spaced about 18 inches to 24 inches apart require the dog to weave in and out much like a ski racer competing in the slalom. Each dog must walk up and down a seesaw without fear, and must jump through a suspended hoop (or auto tire) with perfect timing.

Three types of tunnels may be used. The first is open with no curves or closures so the dogs can see the end. The closed tunnel starts with a rigid framework, but after two feet that ends; the rest is collapsible, cloth-like canvas. A dog has to find his way through the darkness to the other end. The third type of tunnel has a bend.

The cross-over/dog cross, with either two or four ramps a foot long fixed to the sides of a 4-foot-high table frame, is another obstacle. The dog must go up and down ramps specified by the judge.

The A-frame obstacle looks like the gable of a house. It may be made out of two doors hinged at their tops, adjustable for lowering and raising. Wooden strips are nailed at 8-inch intervals so the dogs will have something to grip as they climb. The dog must scale the A-frame and go down the other side. The height at the apex is 6 feet 3 inches.

The dogs are tested twice for being steady and under control: once on the table, which is about 3 feet square and 21 inches high for all dogs, and once on the pause box, which is a defined area of 4 feet x 4 feet within the course. The dogs must pause for five seconds either in a down, sit, or stand position. The position for the pause for each test is posted before the start and is the same for all dogs.

The Judge and Scoring

There is one judge and several stewards. Judges are required to have at least three years' experience in dog show or obedience trial competition and must be familiar with USDAA rules and regulations. The judge is responsible for measuring course distance, establishing standard course time and scoring the performance of each dog and handler.

If a dog and handler take more than the maximum course time (1½ x standard course time), the judge may disqualify and dismiss them from the ring. Scoring involves both time and deductions for committing errors. Penalty points or faults are assessed for various errors such as knocking down bars or planks on jumps; handler touching dog; not staying on seesaw until it touches the ground; not taking obstacles in proper sequence, and so on. The winner is the dog with the fastest time and fewest faults.

The Classes

Starters - for exhibitors and dogs which have never won an agility test.

Novice - for handlers and dogs which have not won twice in novice or open classes.

Intermediate - for handlers and dogs not eligible to compete in starters class.

Open - Starters, Novice and Seniors may compete.

Seniors - for handlers and dogs which have won twice in the novice or open classes.

Novelty Classes - description and scoring of these are included in the agility test schedule. They may include team, pairs, relay, gamblers, knockout, snooker or jumping.

A Sheltie competes in the 1988 Dog Agility Contest at Astro World.

Each winning handler receives a red, white and blue rosette with blue streamers bearing the USDAA logo. Smaller rosettes for additional placements may be awarded.

Pedigree Grand Prix of Dog Agility^{SM}

The USDAA has acquired a corporate supporter—*Pedigree*^{TM} brand dog food. In 1988 *Pedigree*^{TM} sponsored its first Grand Prix, and in 1989, the USDAA held its first national tournament at the Pedigree Grand Prix of Dog Agility^{SM}. Handlers and dogs qualify in regional competitions around the country. Winners go to the semi-finals and finals. At the Houston Astro Arena in early August of 1989, three days of fun and competition included a regional qualifying event, semi-finals, and finals competition plus a gamblers competition and a pairs relay.

There are no entry fees. *Pedigree*^{TM} dog food provides hotel accomodations and air fare for regional winners and prizes for national winners.

Competitors in the 1988 Dog Agility contest held at Astro World. Photographs compliments of U.S. Dog Agility Assocation.

PURINA   HI PRO DOG RUNS

One of the newer sports sponsored in the private sector is the Purina® Hi Pro Dog Runs. Purina® began its sponsorship in 1986 with a run in Houston, Texas adding one in Atlanta, Georgia, in 1987. In 1988 Hi Pro sponsored eleven runs across the country. Twenty runs are planned in 1989 in such cities as Houston, Chicago, Los Angeles, Indianapolis, and New York City.

Most of the runs consists of a one-mile walk/run and a two mile fun run. Safe conditions and veterinary aid are promoted. The purpose of the run is to have a lot of fun and win prizes such as dog bowls. Other activities may include pre-event silly pet tricks, costume contests, Spokesdog contest, oldest dog contest or a Frisbee® demonstration.

A record breaking crowd starts the Purina Hi Pro K-9 Fun Run. *Photo by E. Joseph Deering.*

Both dogs and owners are encouraged to run only if they are completely prepared. All dogs must have proof of rabies vaccination. No bitches in season are allowed to compete.

The dog runs are the idea of John Hobbs and his wife, Davia Gallulp (author of *Running With Man's Best Friend*, 1986, Alpine

Publications), who is the National Race director. The first run developed from seeing so many owner/dog pairs jogging around parks, and was held in Houston, Texas, in 1982.

According to Ralston Purina Company, more than half the breeds recognized by the AKC were represented in its Houston, 1988, run. The rarest breed present was the Otter Hound; the smallest were the Chihuahua and Pomeranian; and the largest were the Mastiff, Great Dane, and Great Pyreness. However, the most prevalent entrants are of mixed lineage. Dogs weighing over forty pounds also seem to be more popular for the runs. The 1988 Houston run made the *Guiness Book of World Records* with an entry of 1,795 dogs.

Proceeds of the runs benefit local dog shelters or humane societies. Scenic areas are chosen, and great fun is had by all. For run schedules, training tips, and information on how to get a Purina® Hi Pro Dog Run started in your area, write to the national director. (See Appendix C.)

22

ESPECIALLY FOR YOUNGSTERS

In both the United States and Canada, 4-H dog care and training projects, and Junior Showmanship classes in AKC/CKC shows, provide marvelous opportunities for young people to learn how to care for their dogs and handle them in obedience, junior handling, and even in the breed ring. They also become good handlers by learning responsibility, courtesy, general good manners, and good sportsmanship. Win or lose, youngsters who learn how to be really good sports are winners in the game of life.

4-H DOG PROJECTS

The child who participates in 4-H activities will learn by doing, with guidance from adult leaders. To find out about 4-H and how to get your child started, just call your County Extension office. Some 4-H clubs meet every week for a month or two and some meet once or twice a month all year long, depending on the group itself and what it wants to accomplish.

Any child who is nine years old (and will be ten before the year's end) up to nineteen years old (by the end of the year) may join a 4-H club. There are no dues unless the club wants to use them to offset the cost of its activities. Dues may not be used to prevent someone from joining 4-H.

A 4-H member receives the same type of training free in his club work that costs quite a bit in private classes at an obedience school. Besides that, he learns about the care of dogs, anatomy, pedigrees, building a crate and a doghouse, good sportsmanship, first aid, whelping and care of dam and puppies, and much, much more through the ongoing program year after year.

Many 4-H'ers in dog care and training projects become deeply involved and do an incredible amount of work. Out of love and caring for both dogs and other human beings, some have developed therapeutic programs for the elderly, visiting local nursing homes with their dogs for obedience demonstrations or petting and companionship; publishing newsletters in which they write about dog health, training and grooming; conducting dog care and training workshops; working with abused and emotionally disturbed children in dog training projects to help them build self-esteem; working as volunteers in small animal clinics; and training guide dog puppies for the blind.

What is 4-H? It is the youth education program of the Cooperative Extension Service of the State Land-Grant Universities and the U.S. Department of Agriculture. It is the largest extracurricular education program in this country, reaching twelve percent of the nine to nineteen age group. It involves an amazing 600,000 adults and teens as volunteer leaders. The Cooperative Extension Service was established by Congress in 1914 with the mission of "extending" the knowledge and scientific methods developed at land-grant institutions and by the USDA to people throughout the United States. They quickly

Dogs and kids—a natural combination. *Photo by Missy Green.*

Heeling practice at a 4-H dog
obedience club.

discovered that young people are most responsive and more eager learners than adults, hence the 4-H programs.

Since 1914, more than 40 million Americans have been involved in 4-H sometime during their lives. Many of our veterinarians, veterinary technicians and assistants, dog groomers, obedience trainers, breeders, exhibitors, and professional handlers in both dog shows and field trials first became interested in dogs through participation in 4-H clubs' dog projects.

For years I wondered what the four white H's, one in each leaf of the four-leaf clover, stood for. I finally asked—Head, Heart, Hands, and Health. 4-H members pledge:

> My head to clear thinking
> My heart to greater loyalty
> My hands to larger service
> My health to better living.

To become a 4-H club member, a child can live in the country, town, or city. Today's members are split—fifty-four percent from farms, rural communities and small towns and forty-six percent from cities over 10,000, but more members are from cities of over 50,000 population than from farms. So, 4-H is not just for rural youth, but for big city kids, too.

Enrollment dates for 4-H range from January 1 to May 1. During this time the county extension officer visits various schools in the county to recruit new members. If there is no local 4-H club, several interested young people with an adult or two to help them may start a new club. Your Extension Office will be able to tell you whether a dog care and training project is available.

Approximately 130,000 of the 4.6 million young people enrolled in 4-H participate in the dog care and training projects. To do this, of course, one needs a dog, but not necessarily a registered purebred dog. Quite often when a child shows he is really interested in the dog project, his parents buy him a purebred registered dog so that he can also participate in licensed AKC or CKC obedience trials or in AKC Junior Showmanship. There is a puppy placement program in which breeders donate registrable purebred puppies to deserving youngsters in 4-H. Sometimes, a breeder will offer on a co-ownership basis a retired show dog, and sometimes that dog is even a champion. (Write to Paul Nigro c/o *Dog World* magazine to find out more about this program. See Appendix.)

Besides the dog, a 4-H'er will need a choke collar and a six-foot training leash. Later on, he will need dumbbells, but expenses for equipment are quite minimal, especially when you consider the cost of a 4-H horse or livestock project. For Junior Showmanship, a show lead is needed. Also, grooming supplies are needed: brush, comb, beauty aids, etc. But the acquisition of dog and equipment is minimal when you consider that the whole family will enjoy the dog more because, through the 4-H'ers endeavors, the dog will become well-mannered and a real pleasure to have around.

Training classes run for ten weeks and culminate in competition at county and state fairs across the country in July and August. In my county (and in many others), the 4-H'ers meet and train in the building at the fairgrounds which also houses the County Extension Office. But meetings can be held in the leaders' or members' homes or garages or in any central place such as a school, church, or community room. The average club includes about ten to twenty members and two or three leaders.

The leader of the dog project decides on which phase to start with, but most 4-H clubs include both obedience and show training. The members' manuals reinforce the training received in meetings and actual classes. To obtain any of these manuals, contact Educational Aids, National 4-H Council (see Appendix). Which classes are offered are left up to the discretion of the instructor/leader and the desires of the group.

4-H members participate with both purebred and mixed-breed dogs.

"Training Your Dog for Family Living" is the basic course in the dog care and training project. It is designed to teach the 4-H member how to train his dog in the basics. In obedience training, the exercises meet requirements of 4-H and American Kennel Club obedience trials. In the Beginner class, the dogs must not have had training past the Beginner level. All exercises are performed on-lead and are scored on the basis of 160 points. A 4-H scorecard is used for all levels of the classes. The Graduate Beginner class has dogs that have not gone beyond this level. As is true of all the classes, the dogs learn to perform the Long Sit and Down, Stand for Examination, and Recall Off-Lead. Again, the basis of scoring is 160 points.

At the Novice level, the dogs must not have completed their Companion Dog (CD) degree. All exercises except the Heel On-Leash and Figure 8 are done off-lead. The scoring here is 200 points and the AKC scorecard is used.

The Brace class is for boys and girls who have two dogs of their own. The dogs are trained to work hooked together by a short coupler or "brace chain." Dogs of the same breed, size and color are preferred, but are not necessary. The Stand for Examination, Recall, Long Sit and Down are done off-lead. There is no level of training requirement, and the Graduate Beginner scorecard is used. There is also the Four Dog Team consisting of four dogs and four handlers. This does look rather difficult and takes a real spirit of teamwork for both dogs and kids. Part is off-lead and part on-lead and two judges are used. The Graduate Beginner scorecard again is used.

For the Graduate Novice Class, you go back to AKC scoring. Dogs that have a CD degree but not a CDX (Companion Dog Excellent) may be trained in this class. There is the Heel On-Leash, with all the rest off-lead with a three-minute Long Sit and five-minute Long Down (handler out of sight). Also in the Open Class, the dogs may have a CD but not a CDX, and scoring is by AKC rules. Exercises included are the Heel Free and Figure 8, Drop on Recall, Retrieve on the Flat, Retrieve over High Jump, Broad Jump, and the three-minute Long Sit and five-minute Long Down with the handler out of sight.

The Utility Class is for dogs that have a CDX but not the Utility (UD) degree. Judging is by AKC scoring and includes the Signal Exercise, Scent Discrimination, Directed Retrieve, Directed Jumping, and Moving Examination.

The Grooming and Handling Class teaches the children to properly groom their dogs and present them to their best advantage for observation by spectators. This is similar to Fitting and Showmanship in 4-H livestock projects. They learn how to gait the dogs in the ring, pose them to the best advantage, and how to follow the procedures of showing in the breed ring.

When July comes, the training classes have ended and the 4-H members get ready to show at the county fair. Most counties have a county fair board, but sometimes 4-H and the county fair board are one and the same. No entry fees are required of 4-H members. Only one dog may be trained in any given year and professionals are not allowed to compete; the dog must be trained by the 4-H member himself. Exhibitors must present veterinary certificates showing that the dogs' vaccinations are up-to-date, and the dog must belong to the exhibitors or their immediate family.

Obedience competition is offered at both county and state fairs at every level—first through the sixth year. Every division has a Champion and Reserve Champion—highest score and second highest—with placements from first through eighth, if the county has donors for that amount. In some areas, there may be only four placements. All the division winners advance to the final competition to determine the Grand Champion and Reserve Grand Champion of the fair. Ties are run off. Plaques and ribbons, funded by sponsors, are awarded the winners.

The 4-H members who have taken handling classes compete in showmanship. The classes for these are: Novice Showmanship, for any first year exhibitor; Junior Showmanship, for exhibitors under fourteen years old by January 1 of the current year, unless the 4-H'er won his Junior Class the year before (in that case, he must compete in Senior Showmanship regardless of age); and Senior Showmanship. Showmanship is scored in the following way:

General Appearance of Dog and Handler	40 points
Handling and Presentation	40 points
Gaiting of Dog	40 points
Attitude of Handler	20 points
Dog Anatomy	10 points
Maximum	150 points

There are five placements in each of the Showmanship classes, with plaques and ribbons awarded.

There is an additional 4-H program in which thousands of 4-H'ers participate—training guide dogs for the blind. Direct 4-H involvement in training and caring for guide dog puppies is limited to programs already in existence within the state, because the puppy suppliers and trainers must be located near the training centers of the guide dog organizations to facilitate supervision, training and eventual placement. If 4-H'ers are interested in raising a guide dog puppy, they must check with their County Extension Office to see if this is possible in their area. Pups from guide dog schools are paired with 4-H members who work with the dog for a year-and-a-half, teaching him basic obedience commands and seeing-eye skills. Other family pets are permitted, but the 4-H'er is allowed only to raise one guide dog puppy at a time. A pamphlet called "Dog Guides for the Blind" is available from the National 4-H Council.

Purina Awards

For over twenty-five years the National 4-H Council, with the support of Ralston Purina Company, has sponsored the 4-H Dog Care and Training Awards Program, stressing the importance of responsible pet ownership. From all the members participating in the dog care and training program, fifty receive state honors and the chance to attend the annual 4-H Congress held in Chicago at the end of November. Six of these 4-H'ers will win a $1,500 scholarship and all expenses paid to the Congress. They are recognized at an awards banquet for their outstanding achievements in the dog care and training project. Projects range from training dogs for the blind or therapy dogs for nursing homes or handicapped children, to research in canine hip dysplasia.

The awards program began in 1959 with 3,100 participants. To help put various aspects of the dog care and training program across, Purina provides technical and financial support in the development of the educational materials used, awards and prizes for club competitions, assistance in public relations, and the six yearly $1,000 scholarships.

AKC JUNIOR SHOWMANSHIP

Junior Showmanship is offered for youth from ten to seventeen years of age at most AKC licensed shows. Many 4-H club members who have taken the dog care and training programs and have a purebred dog registered with the AKC either in the name of the child or a family member go on to show their dogs in these classes. Junior Showmanship is judged solely on how well the junior handles and presents the dog, not on the dog's conformation. The classes are also called Junior Handling by many, or simply J.S. Some juniors also show their dogs in the breed rings and do so well that they end up with championships.

The regular Junior Showmanship classes are:

Novice—For boys and girls at least ten years old but under seventeen the day of the show and who have not won three first places in a Novice Class at a Licensed or Member Show.

1988 National Dog Care and Training winners with their Corporate Executive. Left to right: Zach F. Jones, Okla.; Ben Laseter, Ga.; Jennifer Leigh Kubesch, Texas; George P. Cook, director, professional programs, Ralston Purina Company, Purina Dog Foods Group; Debbie Tripp, Neb.; Clasina Segura, La.; and Tammy Lyn Lorch, Minn. *Photo courtesy of Ralston Purina Company.*

Open—For boys and girls ten to seventeen (as above) who have won three first place awards in the Novice Class.

The regular classes may be divided by age into *Junior* and *Senior* which must be specified in the premium list. The Junior class is for ages ten to thirteen, and the Senior for those thirteen to seventeen. Any or all classes may be divided by sex and this also must be specified in the premium list. So far, I have never seen classes divided this way.

At almost all shows where Junior Showmanship classes are offered, there are Novice Junior and Senior and Open Junior and Senior classes. Usually, a club offers a prize for Best Junior Handler and all the winners of the classes compete for this title. There are four placements in each class for which ribbons and sometimes prizes are awarded. The Best Junior Handler receives a rosette and a prize, such as a color photo of the win, plaque, trophy, or gift certificate.

Limited classes may be offered by a show-giving club, but if they are, the regular classes may not be offered. The club must specify in its premium lists what wins are prerequisite for entry in Limited classes, which are generally held in conjunction with a large and prestigious show such as at the Westminster Kennel Club in New York where no dogs may be entered for breed competition unless they are champions or have championship points. The club may specify a minimum of five or eight wins from Open classes. The wins must be in a specified twelve month period ending not more than three months prior to the show date. The entry is limited to junior handlers who live in a particular geographical area or who qualified at shows in that area.

Although these junior handlers are evaluated strictly on the way they handle and present their dogs, each dog must be well-groomed and trained. The juniors gait their dogs as in the breed ring, pose them, show the dog's teeth to the judge, and do all the things they would if they were actually showing in conformation. The judge goes over the dog, watches the gaiting and stacking (posing) of the dog, but he is reversing his role—watching the presentation and handling skills instead of trying to observe the dog. In short, the Junior Showmanship judge evaluates the handler; the conformation (breed) judge evaluates the dog.

Since this is true, juniors sometimes find that the type of dog shown in Junior Handling may influence the judging. The working and herding breeds are shown naturally and, if well-trained, will stack themselves with very little else required of their young handlers. The terrier and sporting breeds offer much more opportunity to show the judge what the junior can do. With these breeds the handler will have more work to do: placing the feet, holding up the tail, etc. No matter what the breed of dog, juniors learn the finer points of handling: proper appearance, good posture, smoothness and grace, working all sides of the dog, pointing out their dog's good points. They also learn that hard work, persistence, determination, and patience pay off.

Many junior handlers are the children of breeders and exhibitors; these children have an obvious advantage. However, there are also many whose parents never saw a show ring until their children became interested in handling their dogs, mostly through 4-H projects. If son or daughter has taken a sincere interest in the welfare and training of your AKC registered dog, you may want to look into both the 4-H program and Junior Showmanship. Your local kennel club is also a good way to get your child started.

All AKC show premium lists contain information on the Junior Showmanship competition and almost all show-giving clubs have junior classes at their shows. Entry fees usually run a little lower for Junior Showmanship participants, and if the dog to be shown in the Junior Showmanship class was already entered in a conformation or obedience class the J.S. entry fee may be even lower.

Dog World magazine has an excellent Junior Showmanship column. A pamphlet, "Regulations for Junior Showmanship," available from the American Kennel Club, gives full details on regulations and how classes are judged.

CANADIAN KENNEL CLUB JUNIOR HANDLING

CKC Junior Handling is very much like the Junior Showmanship of AKC. The handlers are judged on their attitude (courtesy and good sportsmanship), posing and gaiting the dog, and generally presenting him to the best advantage for the particular breed of dog. However, there are some differences. One of these is in the ages and name of the classes. The age for Novice class is eight to sixteen for handlers who have not won a first prize in Junior Handling classes at a Championship Show. For Junior Handler class the ages are eight to thirteen years inclusive, and for Senior Handler class, fourteen to sixteen years inclusive. The clubs also have the option of offering a Peewee class for children under eight years of age. The Best Junior Handler is chosen from the winners of these three classes just as at AKC shows. Entry fees are specified by the CKC to the kept at a minimal level (and they mean minimal).

Junior showmanship judging at an AKC show. *Photo courtesy of BJ McKinney.*

Another difference is that the junior handler is not required to own or co-own the dog or show one belonging to a member of his family. He may compete with *any* dog duly entered in the show provided he has the consent of the owner or agent to do so. He wears the armband already assigned to the dog while competing in the breed ring.

The four placements are the same in each class as the AKC, but there is a point system as the CKC has a Provincial Junior Handling Competition. The points are: first place, 6 points; second place, 4 points; third place, 3 points; and fourth place, 2 points. Ribbons and other prizes are awarded. These competitions are held once a year in Alberta and the Northwest Territories, British Columbia and the Yukon Territories, Manitoba, New Brunswick and Prince Edward Island, Nova Scotia and Newfoundland, Ontario, Quebec, and Saskatchewan.

Junior handlers may compete in only one provincial competition a year in the area where they live. Junior Handling wins for one year establish which juniors will compete in the provincial competitions held by August 31 of the following year. The ten junior handlers who compile the highest point ratings in their area are eligible to compete. These provincial competitions have a panel of two judges—one is responsible for ring procedure and the other observes. They must concur in their selection of the winner. A trophy and rosette are awarded to the winner, and prizes and ribbons may be offered to all participants. Also, a rosette and trophy are awarded to the junior handler who accumulates the highest number of points in Junior Handler competition at championship shows during the previous year. This award is called "Highest Aggregate, Junior Handling Competition."

Finally, a National Junior Handling Competition is held by December 31 of the same year as the provincial competitions. All winners of the provincial competitions are invited to compete, plus the junior who held the highest aggregate points in Canada for the previous year. The judging and prizes are the same as for the provincial competitions. (For more information on Junior Handling, write to the Canadian Kennel Club; see Appendix.)

ABOUT THE AUTHOR

A fifth-generation Texan from Houston, Ellie Milon now lives in Indiana. She majored in journalism at the University of Texas and with her husband, Gene, has bred and shown Shetland Sheepdogs since 1973. Her articles have appeared in *Dog World*, *The Shetland Sheepdog* and *The Sheltie Special* magazines. She is a prize-winning poet and also writes fiction.

Appendix A
BREEDS OF DOGS
American Kennel Club

The following breeds are recognized by and registered with AKC.

Sporting Group

Brittanys
Pointers
Pointers,
  German Shorthaired
  German Wirehaired
Retrievers,
  Chesapeake Bay
  Curly-Coated
  Flat-Coated
  Golden
  Labrador
Setters,
  English
  Gordon
  Irish
Spaniels,
  American Water
  Clumber
  Cocker
  English Cocker
  Field
  Irish Water
  Sussex
  Welsh Springer
Vizslas
Weimaraners
Wirehaired Pointed Griffons

Hound Group

Afghan Hounds
Basenjis
Basset Hounds
Beagles
Black & Tan Coonhounds
Bloodhounds
Borzois
Dachshunds
Foxhounds,
  American
  English
Greyhounds
Harriers
Ibizan Hounds
Irish Wolfhounds
Norwegian Elkhounds
Otter Hounds
Pharaoh Hounds
Rhodesian Ridgebacks
Salukis
Scottish Deerhounds
Whippets

Working Group

Akitas
Alaskan Malamutes
Bernese Mountain Dogs
Boxers
Bullmastiffs
Doberman Pinschers
Giant Schnauzers
Great Danes
Great Pyrenees
Komondorok
Kuvaszok
Mastiffs
Newfoundlands
Portuguese Water Dogs
Rottweilers
St. Bernards
Samoyeds
Siberian Huskies
Standard Schnauzers

Terrier Group

Airedale Terrier
American Staffordshire Terriers
Australian Terriers
Bedlington Terriers
Border Terriers
Bull Terriers
Cairn Terriers
Dandie Dinmont Terriers
Fox Terriers,
  Smooth
  Wire

Irish Terriers
Kerry Blue Terriers
Lakeland Terriers
Manchester Terriers
Norfolk Terriers
Norwich Terriers
Scottish Terriers
Sealyham Terriers
Skye Terriers
Soft-Coated Wheaten Terriers
Staffordshire Bull Terriers
Welsh Terriers
West Highland White Terriers

Toy Group

Affenpinschers
Brussels Griffons
Chihuahuas
English Toy Spaniels
Italian Greyhounds
Japanese Chin
Maltese
Manchester Terriers (Toy)
Miniature Pinschers
Papillons
Pekingese
Pomeranians
Poodles (Toy)
Pugs
Shih Tzu
Silky Terriers
Yorkshire Terriers

Non-Sporting Group

Bichon Frises
Boston Terriers
Bulldogs
Chow Chows
Dalmatians

Finnish Spitz
French Bulldogs
Keeshonden
Lhasa Apsos
Poodles,
   Miniature
   Standard
Schipperkes
Tibetan Spaniels
Tibetan Terriers

Herding Group

Australian Cattle Dogs
Bearded Collies
Belgian Malinois
Belgian Tervuren
Bouviers des Flandres
Briards
Collies
German Shepherd Dogs
Old English Sheep Dogs
Pulik
Shetland Sheepdogs
Welsh Corgis,
   Cardigan
   Pembroke

Miscellaneous

Australian Kelpies
Border Collies
Canaan Dog
Chinese Cresteds
Chinese Shar-Peis
Cavalier King Charles Spaniels
Finnish Spitz
Greater Swiss Mountain Dogs
Miniature Bull Terriers
Petit Basset Griffon Vendeen
Spinoni Italiani

Canadian Kennel Club

The Canadian Kennel Club recognizes the following breeds:

Sporting Group

Griffons,
  Wire-haired Pointing
Pointers,
  German Long-haired
  German Short-haired
  German Wire-haired
Pudelpointers
Retrievers,
  Chesapeake Bay
  Curly-Coated
  Flat-Coated
  Golden
  Labrador
  Nova Scotia Duck Tolling
Setters,
  English
  Gordon
  Irish
Spaniels,
  American Cocker
  American Water
  Brittany
  Clumber
  English Cocker
  Field
  French
  Irish Water
  Sussex
  Welsh Springer
Vizslas,
  Wire-haired
Weimaraners
Wirehaired Pointed Griffons

Sporting Dogs (Hounds)

Afghan Hounds
Basenjis
Beagles
Black & Tan Coonhounds
Bloodhounds
Borzois

Dachshunds,
  Miniature Long-haired
  Miniature Smooth
  Miniature Wire-haired
  Standard Long-haired
  Standard Smooth
  Standard Wire-haired
Deerhounds,
  Scottish
Drevers
Finnish Spitz
Foxhounds,
  American
  English
Greyhounds
Harriers
Ibizan Hounds
Irish Wolfhounds
Norwegian Elkhounds
Otterhounds
Petit Basset Griffon Vendeen
Pharaoh Hounds
Rhodesian Ridgebacks
Salukis
Whippets

Working Group

Akitas
Alaskan Malamutes
Bernese Mountain Dogs
Boxers
Bullmastiffs
Canadian Eskimo Dogs
Doberman Pinschers
Great Danes
Great Pyrenees
Karelian Bear Dogs
Komondorok
Kuvaszok
Mastiffs
Newfoundlands
Rottweilers
Samoyeds

Schnauzers,
  Giant
  Standard
Siberian Huskies
St. Bernards

Terrier Group

Airedale Terrier
American Staffordshire Terriers
Australian Terriers
Bedlington Terriers
Border Terriers
Bull Terriers
Cairn Terriers
Dandie Dinmont Terriers
Fox Terriers,
  Smooth
  Wire
Irish Terriers
Kerry Blue Terriers
Lakeland Terriers
Manchester Terriers
Miniature Schnauzers
Norfolk Terriers
Norwich Terriers
Scottish Terriers
Sealyham Terriers
Skye Terriers
Soft-Coated Wheaten Terriers
Staffordshire Bull Terriers
Staffordshire Terriers
Welsh Terriers
West Highland White Terriers

Toy Group

Affenpinschers
Brussels Griffons
Cavalier King Charles Spaniels
Chihuahuas,
  Long coat
  Short coat
English Toy Spaniels
Italian Greyhounds
Japanese Spaniels
Maltese
Mexican Hairless
Miniature Pinschers
Papillons
Pekingese
Pomeranians
Poodles (Toy)

Pugs
Silky Terriers
Toy Manchester Terriers
Toy Poodles
Yorkshire Terriers

Non-Sporting Group

Bichon Frises
Boston Terriers
Bulldogs
Chow Chows
Dalmatians
French Bulldogs
Keeshonden
Lhasa Apsos
Poodles,
  Miniature
  Standard
Schipperkes
Shih Tzus
Tibetan Spaniels
Tibetan Terriers

Herding Group

Australian Cattle Dogs
Bearded Collies
Belgian Sheepdogs
Bouviers des Flandres
Briards
Collies,
  Rough
  Smooth
German Shepherd Dogs
Old English Sheep Dogs
Pulik
Shetland Sheepdogs
Welsh Corgis,
  Cardigan
  Pembroke

Miscellaneous

Aida
Aires Mountain Dog
Anatolian Shepherd Dog
Appenzeli Mountain Dog
Ariegeois
Artesian Bassett
Artois Bassethound
Australian Kelpies
Austrian Hound

Austrian Short-Haired Pinscher
Balkan Hound
Barbet
Basset Bleu de Gascogne
Basset Fauve de Bretagne
Bavarian Mountain Hound
Belgian Griffon
Bergamasco
Berner Hound
Bichon Havanais
Billy
Black Forest Hound
Blue Picardy Spaniel
Bohemian Terrier
Bohemian Pointer (Rough Coat)
Bolognese
Border Collies
Bosnian Hound
Bouvier des Ardennes
Braque de l'Ariege
Braque du Bourbonnais
Braque Dupuy
Braque Saint-Germain
Briquet
Briquet Griffon Vendeen
Canaan Dog
Cao de Castro Laboriero
Catalan Sheepdog
Chien Francais (3 varieties)
Chinese Crested Dog,
  Hairless
  Powderpuff
Cirneco Dell Etna
Coton de Tulear
Croation Sheepdog
Dachsbracke
Drentse Patrijshond
Dunker
Dutch Shepherd Dog
Entlebucher Mountain Dog
Estrela Mountain Dog
Eurasier
Fila Brasileiro
Finnish Hound
Florentine Spitz
French Pointer,
  Gascogne
  Pyrenees
Gascon Saintongeois
German Jagdterrier
German Pinscher

German Spaniel
German Spitz (3 varieties)
Glen of Imaal Terrier
Grand Anglo-Francais (3 varieties)
Grand Griffon Vendeen
Great Blue Gascony
Great Swiss Mountain Dog
Greek Hound
Greenland Dog
Griffon Fauve de Bretagne
Griffon Nivernais
Halden Hound
Hamiltonstovare
Hanover Hound
Harlequin Pinscher
Hokkaido-Ken
Hovarwart
Hygen Hound
Iceland Dog
Istrian Hound,
  Smooth-haired
  Rough-haired
Italian Hound,
  Wire-haired
  Short-haired
Italian Pointer
Japanese Spitz
Japanese Terrier
Jura Hound
Karelian Bear Dog
Karst Sheepdog
Kishu
Kleiner Munsterlander Vorstehund
Kromfohrlander
Lancashire Heeler
Lapphund
Lapponian Herder
Large Munsterlander
Leonberger
Levesque
Lowchen
Lucernese Hound
Magyar Agar
Maremma Sheepdog
Miniature Bull Terriers
Mudi
Neopolitan Mastiff
Norbotten Spitz
Norwegian Buhund
Norwegian Lundehund
Old Danish Pointer

Perdiguero de Burgos
Perdiguero Portugues
Petit Brabancon
Petit Griffon Blue de Gascogne
Picardy Sheepdog (Berger Picard)
Picardy Spaniel (Epagneul Picard)
Podengo Portugues,
  Large
  Medium
  Small
Poitevin
Polish Hound
Pont-Audemere Spaniel
Porcelaine
Portuguese Water Dog
Posavac Hound
Pumi
Pyrenees Mastiff
Rafeiro do Alentejo
Rampur Hound
Sabueso Espanol
Saurlander Bassett
Schiller Hound
Shar-Pei
Sloughi
Slovensky Cuvac

Smalands Hound
Small Blue Gascony
Small Continental Spaniel
Small Norwegian Elkhound
Small Swiss Hound
Soft-Coated Griffon
Spanish Greyhound
Spanish Mastiff
Spinoni Italiani
Staby-Houn
Stichelhaar Hound
Stumpy-Tail Cattle Dog
Swedish Elkhound
Swedish Shepherd
Swiss Hound
Tahltan Bear Dogs
Tatra Sheepdog
Tibetan Mastiff
Tosa
Transylvanian Hound
Tyrolean Hound
Wetterhoun
Yugoslavian Mountain Hound
Yugoslavian Tricolour Hound
Yugoslavian Shepherd Dog

United Kennel Club

These breeds participate in United Kennel Club sponsored events.

Afghan Hound
Airedale Terrier
Akita
Alaskan Malamute
American Black & Tan Coonhound
American Eskimo
American Pit Bull Terrier
American Water Spaniel
Arctic Husky
Australian Kelpie
Australian Cattle Dog
Australian Terrier
Basenji
Basset Hound
Bearded Collie
Belgian Malinois
Belgian Sheepdog
Belgian Tervuren
Bernese Mountain Dog
Bloodhound
Bluetick Coonhound
Border Collie
Border Terrier
Borzoi
Boston Terrier
Bouvier des Flandres
Boxer
Boykin Spaniel
Briard
Brittany Spaniel
Brussels Griffon
Bull Terrier,
  Colored
  White
Cairn Terrier
Cavalier King Charles Spaniel
Chesapeake Bay Retriever
Chihuahua
Chinese Shar-Pei
Chow Chow
Cocker Spaniel
Curly-Coated Retriever

Dachshund,
  Longhaired
  Smooth
Dalmatian
Dandie Dinmont Terrier
Doberman Pinscher
English Beagle
English Cocker Spaniel
English Coonhound
English Pointer
English Setter
English Shepherd
English Springer Spaniel
Field Spaniel
Flat-Coated Retriever
Fox Terrier
German Shepherd
German Shorthaired Pointer
German Wirehaired Pointer
Golden Retriever
Great Dane
Great Pyrenees
Ibizan Hound
Irish Setter
Irish Terrier
Irish Water Spaniel
Irish Wolfhound
Keeshond
Kuvasz
Labrador Retriever
Lhasa Apso
Maltese
Miniature Pinscher
Newfoundland
Norfolk Terrier
Norwegian Elkhound
Norwich Terrier
Nova Scotia Duck Tolling Retriever
Papillon
Pekingese
Plott Hound
Pomeranian

Poodle,
  Miniature
  Standard
  Toy
Portuguese Water Dog
Pug
Puli
Redbone Coonhound
Rottweiler
Saint Bernard
Saluki
Samoyed
Silky Terrier
Schipperke
Scotch Collie
Scottish Deerhound
Schnauzer,
  Giant
  Miniature
  Standard

Shetland Sheepdog
Staffordshire Bull Terrier
Shih Tzu
Toy Fox Terrier
Treeing Walker Coonhound
Viszla
Weimaraner
Welsh Corgi,
  Cardigan
  Pembroke
Welsh Terrier
West Highland White Terrier
Whippet
Yorkshire Terrier

Appendix B
LICENSED SHOW SUPERINTENDENTS

American Kennel Club

William G. Antypas
Ms. M. Ann Baker
P.O. Box 7131
Pasadena, CA 91109

Willam A. Bird
52 Garfield Lane
Napa, CA 94558

Marjorie Brown
P.O. Box 494665
Redding, CA 96049

Norman E. Brown
P.O. Box 2566
Spokane, WA 99220

Thomas J. Crowe
P.O. Box 22107
Greensboro, NC 27420

Ace H. Mathews
Mrs. Nancy Mathews
P.O. Box 06150
Portland, OR 97206

Jack Onofrio
P.O. Box 25764
Oklahoma City, OK 73125

James A. Rau, Jr.
P.O. Box 6898
Reading, PA 19610

Jeannie B. Roberts
P.O. Box 4658
Federal Way, WA 98063

Kenneth A. Sleeper
P.O. Box 307
Garrett, IN 46738

Dorothy Sweet
2321 Blanco
San Antonio, TX 78212

Canadian Kennel Club

Ace Mathews Dog Shows
P.O. Box 06150
Portland, OR 97206

Al-Sec Associates
P.O. Box 2042
Calgary, Alberta,
Canada T2P 2M2

C&A Show Services
Vin Vista Drive, R.R. 3
Ingleside, Ontario,
Canada K0C 1M0

Canadian Dog Show Services
P.O. Box 226, Station "J"
Toronto, Ontario,
Canada M4J 4Y1

Canine Show Services
R.R. 2, Maple Avenue, W.
Brantford, Ontario,
Canada N3T 5L5

Ho-Har Show Services
W.A. Hobbs
341 Westwood Drive
Kitchener, Ontario,
Canada N2M 2L3

Pro-Cats
1080 Brock Road, Unit 3
Pickering, Ontario,
Canada V6B 3Y8

Mike Williams Dog Shows
Box 3639
Vancouver, BC,
Canada V6B 3Y8

Appendix C
CLUBS AND ORGANIZATIONS

For more information on activities under the auspices of your national breed club, write to the American Kennel Club or the Canadian Kennel Club for the address of the current secretary or person in charge of the activity you are interested in.

KENNEL CLUBS/REGISTRIES

American Kennel Club
51 Madison Avenue
New York, NY 10010

Canadian Kennel Club
89 Skyway Avenue
Etobicoke, Ontario M9W 6R4
CANADA

Field Dog Stud Book (FDSB)
542 S. Dearborn St.
Chicago, IL 60605

States Kennel Club
P.O. Box 389
Hattiesburg, MS 39403-0389

United Kennel Club
100 East Kilgore Road
Kalamazoo, MI 49001

COON HUNTING

National Kennel Club
c/o Melvin Hopper
1556 Cherrybrook Drive
Knoxville, TN 37912

Professional Kennel Club
RR 2, Box 292
Myrtle, MS 38650-9402

United Coon Hunters of America, Inc.
Route 4, Box 677
Paoli, IN 47454

HERDING

American Border Collie Association
Patty A. Rogers, Sec.-Treas.
Rt. 4, Box 255
Perkinston, MS 39573

American Herding Breed Association
Linda C. Rorem, Secretary
1548 Victoria Way
Pacifica, CA 94044

American Working Collie Association
c/o Linda C. Rorem
1548 Victoria Way
Pacifica, CA 94044

Australian Shepherd Club of America
c/o Michelle Berryessa, DVM
Stockdog Secretary
P.O. Box 519
Roy, WA 98580

Border Collie Club of America
c/o Ms. Janet E. Larson, Secretary
6 Pinecrest Lane
Durham, NH 03824

Border Collie Club of U.S.
Sunnybrook Farm
Whitepost, VA 22663

North American Sheep Dog Society
c/o Rossine Kirsh, Secretary
Route 3
McLeansboro, IL 62859

HOUNDS

National Beagle Club
Joseph B. Wiley, Secretary
Rover Road
Bedminster, NJ 07921

The United Houndsmen of America, Ltd.
Rd. #1 Box 257A
Kane, PA 16735

RETRIEVERS

Hunting Retriever Club
100 East Kilgore Road
Kalamazoo, MI 49001

North American Hunting Retriever Association
(NAHRA)
P.O. Box 154
Swanton, VT 05488

Professional Retriever Trainers Association
Jane Laman, Secretary
4670 Harbour Hills Drive
Manhattan, KS 66502

SCHUTZHUND

LV/DVG America
Sandi Nethercutt, Secretary
113 Vickie Drive
Del City, OK 73115

United Schutzhund Clubs of America
c/o Paul Meloy
3704 Lemay Ferry Road
St. Louis, MO 63125

SIGHTHOUNDS

American Sighthound Field Association
Vicky Clark, Editor
2234 Walnut Avenue
McKinnleyville, CA 95521

National Open Field Coursing Association
Registrar Susan Loop-Stanley
P.O. Box 68
Glenrock, WY 82637

WORKING TERRIERS

American Working Terrier Association
Frank Doig, Corresponding Secretary
P.O. Box QQ
East Quogue, NY 11942

Jack Russell Terrier Club of America
P.O. Box 365
Far Hills, NJ 07931

RUNNING

Purina Hi Pro Dog Runs
Davia Gallup, National Race Director
1711 Pineacre
Davenport, IA 52803

SLED DOGS

International Sled Dog Racing Association
c/o Donna Hawley
P.O. Box 446
Nordman, ID 83848

International Weight Pull Association
3455 Railroad Avenue
Post Falls, ID 83854

MISCELLANEOUS

American Boarding Kennels Association
4575 Galley Road - Suite 400 A
Colorado Springs, CO 80915

American Dog Owners Association, Inc.
1920 Route 1
Castleton, NY 12033

American Sighthound Field Association
Mr. Leigh A. Littleton - Corresponding Secretary
5717 South Maryland Avenue
Chicago, IL 60637

American Veterinary Medical Association
930 North Meacham Road
Schaumburg, IL 60196

Association of Obedience Clubs and Judges
Mrs. Mary Jean Knott, Secretary
ToMar, 4869 Avoca Avenue
Ellicott City, MD 21043

Dog Fanciers Club Inc.
Mrs. Billie McFadden
R.D. 2, Box 496
Flemington, NJ 08822

Gaines Obedience Program
250 North St.
White Plains, NY 10625

National Association of Dog Obedience Instructors
c/o Gwen Coon, Corresponding Secretary
2286 Steel Rd.
St. Johns, MI 48879

National 4-H Dog Project Director
National 4-H Council
7100 Connecticut Avenue
Chevy Chase, MD 20815

North American Flyball Association
Attn: Mike Randall
1342 Jeff St.
Ytsilanti, MI 48198

The National Committee for Dog Agility
c/o Bud Kramer
401 Bluemont Circle
Manhattan, KS 66052

United States Dog Agility Assn.
P.O. Box 850955
Richardson, TX 75085-0955

Appendix D
PUBLICATIONS

For names and addresses of breed-specific publications, contact your national or local breed club. The publications listed here are but a few of the many publications available on dog breeds and activities.

COON HUNTING

American Cooner
P.O. Box 211
Sesser, IL 62884

Coonhound Bloodlines
100 E. Kilgore Road
Kalamazoo, MI 49001-5598

GENERAL

Bloodlines (UKC)
100 E. Kilgore Rd.
Kalamazoo, MI 49001-5596

Dog Fancy Magazine
P.O. Box 53264
Boulder, CO 80322

Dogs in Canada
43 Railside Road
Don Mills, Ontario,
Canada M3A 3L9

Dog World
29 North Wacker Drive
Chicago, IL 60606

Pure-Bred Dogs/American Kennel Gazette
51 Madison Avenue
New York, NY 10010

HERDING

American Border Collie News
P.O. Box 596
King City, CA 93930

American Border Collie Newsletter
P.O. Box 148
King City, CA 93930

Border Collie News
Janet E. Larson
6 Pinecrest Lane
Durham, NH 03824